The Widowed Dancer

Growing Through Grief with Gratitude

Bryan Martin
(Sealionbryan)

Disclaimer

The following is a compilation of my personal experience growing through my grief. I share my story to help inspire and motivate others to continue moving forward after loss. This compilation should not be substituted for professional advice.

I am not a certified grief counselor or licensed therapist. This is not meant to diagnose, treat or cure anyone of grief and the emotions associated with it.

If someone reading these words does feel they need help, please reach out to a licensed professional to provide you with assistance.

Copyright © 2022   Bryan Martin (Sealionbryan)

All rights reserved. No part of this publication may be reproduced without the prior written permission of the copyright owner of this book, except as permitted by U.S. copyright law. For permissions contact: sealionbryan@gmail.com

Sealionbryan ™ is a trademark service mark under United States Patent and Trademark Office (USPTO)
Serial Number: 97430875
Sealionbryan, LLC

*"You can choose to stay in the storm,
or you can choose to be the break in the clouds."*

Bryan Martin
(Sealionbryan)

Table of Contents

Acknowledgments... 6

Preface – The Art of Honoring and Editing......................... 7

Introduction.. 8

On the Way to Being Widowed..................................... 9
    Grief While Growing Up
    Losing Dad and Doctor's Orders

The Diagnosis Days: Becoming a Caregiver..................... 15
    - A Season of Change
    - Searching Social Media for Support

The Care-Griever Years
    Year 1 A.C. (After Clayton) – The Fog Year................. 33
        - Saying Yes to Moving Forward
        - For Those Who Need These Words
    Year 2 A.C. – The Great Anger.............................. 69
    Year 3 A.C. – Pandemic and Passiveness................. 111
    Year 4 A.C. – Self-Generated Joy........................... 175
    Year 5 A.C. - Harvesting the Happy........................ 239

The Unconclusive Conclusion..................................... 269

Widowed Words of Wisdom.. 271

Resources and References... 279

Acknowledgments

In Loving Memory and Thank You

In loving memory of my late partner Clayton A. Bond and my father Wayne J. Martin. You both taught me so much in life and continue to do so as I walk along this combined grief journey. I share my emotions and experiences in the hope I inspire others to keep moving forward. I share about my love and loss so that you both will never be forgotten.

Thank you to my mother Karen who taught me how to be a selfless caregiver.

Thank you to my sister Stephanie who acted as our family anchor in the storms.

Thank you to my fiancé Devin who shows me unconditional love, support and understanding.

Thank you to my dear friend Jenny who saw potential in my writings and to the widowed community of Soaring Spirits International for all of their support for the widowed community and, especially, the widowed LGBTQIA community.

Thank you to my family, friends and followers – You all inspire me to continue to move forward and grow through grief with gratitude.

With all my love,

-Bryan (Sealionbryan)

Preface – The Art of Honoring not Editing

I want to start this journey with you in complete authenticity. My grief blog was written in the moment, exactly as I was feeling regardless of proper sentence structure. Grief is messy in all its spaces. Words and sentences pour onto these pages exactly as my mind and heart needed. For me to go back and change things to be grammatically correct only negates my true grief and growth. I will not dishonor my moments and memories for meticulous flow. My emotions hold more value than perfect English. Although some scholars may scoff at this declaration, I hold my truths as is - academically unapologetic.

This book is unconventionally laid out because my life is unconventional. There aren't defined "chapters" per se, but I have separated this book chronologically from my caregiver time through the "care griever" years which I have chosen to label as my years "AC" (After Clayton). Some weeks were novel and fresh widowed wounds while others reflect at blogs gone past. Sometimes there was a noticeable "then and now" while other times it felt more like a "then and again" as it's normal for grief experiences to repeat. The road through grief has many roundabouts and it takes seeing the same scenery repeated to fully understand where you were, where you are and where you're going. Many stay stuck speeding around the circle but the only way to reveal the exit is to slow down and obey the emotional signs.

You'll see paragraphs, Facebook excerpts, blog entries and pictures but somedays the words were hard, and the moment wasn't meant to be photographed. During Tin's (Clayton) illness, he didn't want any photos but, as the terminal truth of his life became more real, he wanted our moments turned into memories for me. These pages are not perfectly spaced because life isn't perfectly spaced.

Grief is natural. Grief is not an exact science. There is no way to fully define grief and the governing laws around it. Grief holds a magic that words cannot properly contain. Grief is an individual experience that takes on more forms than the stars. There is a common thread that ties all our grief together – the great awakening. Our lives are small and contained until loss creates an intense energy which explodes within causing bereavements "big bang". Our view expands exponentially, and we suddenly see many things around us we had never noticed before, or we had taken for granted. Grief, like the Universe, holds many scary mysteries but to view it through the great lens of gratitude reveals an endless expanse of breathtaking gifts.

Introduction

For over the past four years, I have been walking along a road I never knew existed on my map of life. June 29, 2017, my father Wayne passed away after a long battle with back pain that led to medication and alcohol addiction. Just 13 weeks later, my partner Clayton (Tin) ended up in the emergency room. He had been taking prescribed medications as directed. A simple ringworm infection from landscaping his mother's yard had gone systemic. Tin was diagnosed with terminal liver failure and given 8 months left to live. We had moved to a new area just a year before, so most of our friends were updated by my occasional Facebook posts. On April 16, 2018, Clayton passed away in his sleep. His life ended and my new widowed journey began. I continued to share my feelings of loss on social media.

My friend Jenny worked at Soaring Spirits International, an organization created for widowed support. Each day they had a specific blog writer who was willing to share their experiences in hopes those reading them would feel less alone. I agreed to be a writer and represent the LGBTQIA widowed community. This book is a compilation of social media posts and my weekly blog from the time Clayton became ill through his memorial service that was delayed for over four years due to unforeseen events including a pandemic.

Even though grief experiences are unique, my hope is that sharing my journey will help anyone else who finds they have been planted in a garden of grief. You never move on after losing a loved one, you can only grow through it. The important lesson I've learned is that you need to be the one who drives yourself up out of these saddened soils. Waiting will "grow you nowhere". The person you've lost can't come back and tend to you. You must grab the ground and start to push yourself upwards.

It has been four years and I have finally moved through all this widowed weight. I've unlocked the gift we so often forget we have – The power to generate joy. By accepting grief with gratitude, I have resurrected my abilities to create happiness, positivity and hopefully help others continue to move forward along this dance called life.

For those who need these words today, this widowed dancer's journey growing through grief with gratitude…

On the Way to Being Widowed

Grief While Growing Up
&
Losing Dad and Doctor's Orders

On the Way to Being Widowed - Grief While Growing Up

To say I had a fully joyful childhood would not be truthful. My parents did a wonderful job supporting my sister and I for all the things we wanted to do and become. Wayne, my father, and I just didn't have the same interests. He loved sports and building things. I was the science nerd with a secret. I knew at a very young age that I was gay and hiding it felt like survival mode. School was filled with bullies and there were days I prayed I'd have an asthma attack or be sick so I could just avoid it all. I preferred to spend time with adults because they seemed to just see me without judgement. I had a small group of close friends because trust is a valuable gift. I made it through high school always guarded, grieving and (sometimes) feeling guilty that I was gay. I wanted time to fast forward, but I didn't realize that wishing the days away would rush me towards regret. I didn't cherish the moments versus the minutes.

Later in life, I came out and both of my parents and entire family accepted me with open arms but for the first two decades I tried to hide. Until I knew I was ok being who I was, my dad and I bonded over scuba diving, video games, our love of music and dancing. I just wish I had been myself sooner so we could have had more time together with my guard down.

I didn't know that my career would take over my life putting family and friends on the backburner. I didn't know that the future holidays promised to my dad wouldn't arrive. I didn't know that telling my late partner Clayton I had to work longer would be me missing out on our very limited life together.

As I have grown through that time-lost guilt, I have realized I will never hold back celebrating me for who I am. That denies me joy and holds back who I am in my relationships. I am worth every smile the Universe blesses me with. It has taken the loss of two very important people in my life for me to embrace and love who I am –perfectly imperfect and capable of generating amazing energy. I've learned that within us all lies grief's greatest gift – gratitude.

On the Way to Being Widowed - Losing Dad and Doctor's Orders

Losing Dad

From a young age, my father had a work injury followed by multiple surgeries through out my childhood. He couldn't work and so I watched my mother act as caregiver before and after she went to work. Silently strong and unknowingly my shining example as caregiver who had to work full time. Our already limited list of common interests was held back from physical limitations. While other New England kids learned to ski, we stuck to sledding down our street. I understood and didn't mind. Sports was not my thing.

Both my parents fully supported my dream career to become a marine biologist and train dolphins. After high school, I attended Salem University, earned my degree and started my career in marine mammal training at the New England Aquarium in Boston, MA. I felt free and ready to fly. After 4 years, I moved to San Diego, CA to train sea lions and dolphins for the Navy Marine Mammal Program. The time difference, cost to travel and limited vacation kept me away from holidays at home for 10 years. Visits we limited and so was my foresight. I was so wrapped up in succeeding at my career that I missed major events both good and bad. My father's physical and mental state were declining. Depression and dependency taking its' toll on him, my mother and my sister. I held guilt I was far away and grief I couldn't help but what do you do when your career has limited options. Who am I if I don't do what I always said I was going to do? My worth was wrapped up in my work

In 2010, I took a position at the Georgia Aquarium in Atlanta, GA. Belugas and seals and otters – Oh my! I was in the most prominent new facility and closer to my family. This worked right? Wrong. I could barely afford to make ends meet. I barely had a social life in order to save money and taking time off was nearly impossible because we had so many projects and operational time constraints. All the while, my father continued to worsen, and my career choice locked me away. I settled for settling and bought a studio condo where I fell in love with Clayton.

By 2016, we needed to get out of the big city and be by the water. I was offered a supervisory position at Gulfarium Marine Adventure Park in Fort Walton Beach, Fl. and Clayton moved with me. Again, my limited career options were affecting those I loved but little did I know what the fates held for us in sunny Florida. Clayton's mother moved to the same town, and we were building our life as my dad was slowly losing his. Week after week he became weaker, and the family wanted him to just rest and be out of pain. It was just a matter of time. I went up to visit. He was frail and thin from not eating. I felt so much anger. Angry for what the medication had turned him into. Angry that my mother had to go through this. Angry at myself for not being around. I was angry and I saw no remorse from my father.

"Go to the corner store and grab me a pack of cigarettes." He handed me money.

I was enraged. I had never snapped at my father but every son, at some point, takes the control.

On the Way to Being Widowed - Losing Dad and Doctor's Orders

"No. I'm not adding to your problem.", I said.

"No? Did you just say no?", he replied getting close and looking me right in the eyes.

I knew that look. The look he'd give if I stepped out of line as a child. My mother in the background watching only fueled me and I fired back with a line he used to use on me:

"Did I stutter? I said no!"

I began to unleash all the hurt, anger and disappointment for how he had been acting. His eyes got bigger, and he stepped towards me. There we were face to face, but I didn't back down. I stood my ground for me. I stood fast for my mother. I didn't know what would come next until I saw the first tear fall from his eyes and he fell into my arms. He apologized and wished he wasn't the way he was. I couldn't fix him, but that moment brought us closer than we had ever emotionally been. What devastation medication and alcohol addiction can do turning an amazing man into a victim of the circumstances. That was a difficult moment, but I have gratitude for it because that was the last of my time with him…

June 29, 2017

Woken up on a weekday to a phone call. It was my mother telling me what we all knew was coming – My father had passed away in his sleep. Everything was a blur. I called work to tell them I was off to Boston. I booked the first flight out. Clayton would have to fly up in a few days. We jumped into his Jeep and headed to the airport. The sky released rain as if matching my emotions. The roads felt like they were flooded with my feelings. I only had 39 years with my dad and much of that was distant. All I wanted in that moment was another day closer but no matter how fast that plane flew, time would not turn back. I was not expecting it to speed up even faster. I didn't know that in 4 days, on the 4th of July, it would be the last anniversary that Clayton and I would have together…

On the Way to Being Widowed - Losing Dad and Doctor's Orders

Doctor's Orders

Clayton and I returned home from my father's funeral. Flooded feelings had receded and, because society gives you just 2 weeks of bereavement, I went back to work. I needed a schedule. I needed to dive back into work to keep from wallowing in my loss and the hurt I felt for my mother who was now widowed way too early in life. I remember feeling gratitude that I had Clayton; we were young and healthy. Well mostly healthy except for a ringworm spot on Clayton's leg from landscaping his mother's yard. Nothing unusual here in warm wet Florida but the way he got it was odd.

Just before my dad passed, Clayton was digging up flowerbeds and found buried black plastic. He reached for it and his hand broke through. He pulled it back to see his hand covered in a strange slime that he wiped on his leg and then washed off. Returning to the flowerbed revealed the plastic had been used to wrap the former homeowner's deceased dog. It was gross but we didn't think much about it

The summer passed quicky and so did the fungal infection. Going to an express medical clinic resulted in oral antifungals that were increased in dose, but bloodwork wasn't checked. I brought up my concerns, but Clayton didn't question "doctors orders". He started to feel tired, sick and bloated. He blamed bad food but there was much worse under the surface...

The Diagnosis Days

Becoming a Caregiver

A Season of Change
&
Searching Social Media for Support

The Diagnosis Days - Becoming a Caregiver

A Season of Change

September came and Clayton still was feeling off but, overall, still his headstrong and active self. I had a work trip to Mexico for the annual International Marine Mammal Trainer's conference. I was going to be presenting on our care experience with our newest penguin chick. Again, my excitement and energy for animal care stole my attention and time. While I enjoyed time with coworkers and collogues in a tropical location, Clayton's health was declining.

Hurricane Michael took form and passed by our resort in Cancun. A day later I flew around him home. Clayton picked me up at the airport and hunkered down at home waiting for Michael to hit. We were looking outward for threats not realizing the storm building within Clayton. He was feeling worse but wanted to wait to go to the doctor in case his mother needed us after the storm. I went to work the next day to help with cleanup and he stayed home. I hadn't heard from him much that day. I left work on time and found him on the couch a shade of yellow and very weak. I got him down three flights of stairs, into my car and to the emergency room.

Rushed in, hooked up to equipment and blood taken. The attending physician pulled me aside and said:

"I'm sorry but your friend has terminal acute liver failure. He has about 8 months."

"Oh, he is my partner. We are planning to get married." I replied

The doctor's response immediately sent me back to my childhood. His posture changed and his response poured salt into the new wound:

"I'm sorry about your friend."

He turned and walked away. Within moments of learning Clayton was going to die, our relationship was completely disregarded. With nothing else they could do, we left to start our new life – Terminal Patient and Care Giver.

The Diagnosis Days - Becoming a Caregiver

Searching Social Media For Support

It's at this time that the loneliness of our location set in. We hadn't lived in the area long enough to have a strong support system. People didn't understand how sick he was, so I began to share on Facebook to keep everyone updated but, mostly, to seek support for what I was witnessing. Again, these are taken exactly as I wrote them to honor the place and emotions that I was submerged in…

October 16, 2017

Update on Clayton Allen Bond
He's back in the hospital today. Serious liver issues. Keeping our fingers crossed and waiting on more tests... Just seems strange that of all tv shows to come on right now it's MASH. I haven't seen that show since I watched it with my Dad as a little kid. This is a tough year...

October 27, 2017

When you need a minute to stop thinking...there is always the ocean...♥️□□

The Diagnosis Days - Becoming a Caregiver

October 30, 2017

Update on Clayton Allen Bond for everyone...He is back home resting. He had 7 liters of fluid drained from his abdomen today. This is the third time in three weeks. He is fighting pancreatitis and liver failure. The doctors don't know much more until we can get him to a specialist. Primary care physicians here are either not accepting his insurance or taking new patients until March and we need a referral from a PCP to get Tin to a specialist. We are working on finding other options. Clayton is starting to eat more but still sleeps much of the day. He hasn't been energetic enough for many phone calls. Feel free to call or text but you might not hear from him right away. I'll keep everyone updated on his progress and feel free to call or text me. We've got lots of chicken soup, lifetime movies and hope ❤ ❤ ❤ ❤

November 1, 2017 – Changed my profile picture

Then changed it again.

The Diagnosis Days - Becoming a Caregiver

November 4, 2017

Update on Clayton Allen Bond Finally a doctor appointment in an hour. Hopefully we will have some answers and a productive care and recovery plan! ❤☐❤☐❤☐❤☐

Update on Clayton Allen Bond, Doctor appointment resulted in bad news. Getting a second opinion tomorrow…as of now we have been given 6 months ☐

Between the 4th and the 10th, I had made more trips to the beach. A few posts of "sea-renity" and my mom flew down to help.

November 10, 2017

Update on Clayton Allen Bond…He is home today. The newest outlook, they don't believe his liver will recover enough. They are saying he has 1-2 yrs at most unless he gets a transplant. So he goes on a list in 5 months and now it's a waiting game. I'm sorry to update this kind of information on Facebook but it's hard to keep up otherwise. Thank you to everyone who has shown amazing support! We will need it more than ever moving forward....

November 13, 2017 – My Last Birthday with Him

I got a surprise helicopter ride for my birthday!!!! Awesome!!!! I saw Gulfarium Marine Adventure Park from above!!! Thank you Clayton Allen Bond!!!!!!❤☐❤☐❤☐ Thank you Timberview Choppers!!!

The Diagnosis Days - Becoming a Caregiver

November 15th 2017

Just posting an image and trying to look for the good. At this point, Clayton didn't want any pictures taken of him, so I reluctantly obliged.

November 19, 2017

My Godparents came up to visit. Clayton joined us on the beach but drove himself. He was getting more adamant about his independence, but we could all see his struggle. We watched the sunset and than I helped him walk to his jeep. As he drove out of the parking lot, he was swerving a little and ran over the sidewalk onto the street. His depth perception and reflexes were failing, and it was a matter of time before he'd get into an accident or just have to give up driving. Luckily, he realized he was putting himself and others in danger and began to accept the fact that he could no longer trust himself to drive.

November 23, 2017

Our last Thanksgiving. All the fixings but not a big appetite. We didn't take pictures from this day. To see a man who used to pile food high on his plate not have the desire to eat much anymore hit us all hard. Were we going to get the 8 months the doctor predicted?

The Diagnosis Days - Becoming a Caregiver

November 27, 2017

It's about getting to pick out a Christmas tree together. One of my most treasured photos with my mom and Clayton choosing our last tree. Christmas was huge for him and, as far as I was concerned, he got to do everything and anything he wanted.

December 6, 2017

Update... Clayton Allen Bond continues to have weekly abdomen draining and testing. He is unbelievably strong and sassy in spirit! Blood values are increasing in a good direction, but his appetite and weight are strongly affected. Thanks to everyone for the support and concern!

The Diagnosis Days - Becoming a Caregiver

December 15, 2017

When you take a minute to look around.....

December 15, 2017

Clayton Allen Bond made Christmas cookies!!! It really was the little things that mattered to me now. It wasn't the cookies. It was that he had the energy and drive to live that day.

The Diagnosis Days - Becoming a Caregiver

12/25/2017 – Our Last Christmas

This is the first thing I see this morning when I wake up. Clearly someone is ready to open presents.

Little did Roan know he was going to be my day-to-day anchor in a few short months.

The Diagnosis Days - Becoming a Caregiver

December 31, 2017 - Our last New Year's Together

Happy New Years! Staying in with the boys. 27 degrees??

      Clayton stayed out of photos as much as he could, but I needed people to truly see what we were living. I told him that I needed the memories, so he started letting me take photos of him again. It was after this photo that everyone realized the seriousness and finality of what was happening. Now people were reaching out and planning to visit. Clayton's close family came to spend time knowing it would be their last chance. Others kept saying "We're planning on coming in the spring" or "We'll stop by this summer." Maybe they meant it or maybe they said it to feel better, either way I knew they weren't going to get to see him. It would be too late.

The Diagnosis Days - Becoming a Caregiver

January 17, 2018

Update on Clayton Allen Bond....Had to go to the ER last night due to abdominal swelling, bladder infection and pain. They admitted him knowing he needed a draining, collected the copayment and than told us there wasn't a doctor onsite to do the procedure. Gave him pain meds and sent us home at 1:30am. Now we are back and he is finally getting treatment. 8 liters of fluid...long day....

January 18, 2018

I simply posted a link to P!nk's "Barbies" song. All I wanted was to go back to a simpler time. What everyone didn't know is that I posted and than sat and sobbed on the beach listening to that beautifully sad song over and over. Social media hides the true depth of what we live. I finished crying and it felt like my tears had made the tide rise. I started walking back to my car and found this perfect sand dollar. To this day, this sand dollar is in my car as a reminder of the beauty found in the midst of a storm.

The rest of January was filled with work, more family visits and friends tagging Tin in old memories. His Facebook page still lives on as a memorial.

The Diagnosis Days - Becoming a Caregiver

February was a blur and March came in like a lion and went out like one as well. March 24th was my Father's birthday, the first without him. I decided to take a trip to Orlando to celebrate my best friend Christina's birthday on the 25th. My dad adored her and would want me to celebrate. With Clayton set, I went away to decompress. It only took a few drinks and an off-color comment about God punishing me that the floodgates opened and I lost control. I cried and cried on the bathroom floor surrounded by partygoers. I couldn't hold it in anymore. It was the first time I knew that praying for him to live longer was now selfish. As a caregiver, you struggle with the emotional balance of wanting to support their life as best you can but not being greedy you get to keep them longer than the Universe intends. There is caregiver guilt in both directions. You want to save them, but you also want them to have peace. It's a complex set of contradictory emotions that has taken me years to work through. I still go back to those moments and ask if I did everything I could.

April 3, 2018 - I reposted a photo from 2015:

Not knowing the future, I can honestly say I have many candid pictures of moments I never take for granted ❤☐❤☐ Hang on Tin! Mayo Clinic in only 14 days

Later that day I had to bring him back to the hospital. The doctor came into the room and rudely accused him of drinking.

The Diagnosis Days - Becoming a Caregiver

April 3, 2018 (continued)

Update on Clayton Allen Bond, he continues to grow weaker and has difficulty eating. We are at the ER now. Ammonia levels are high and we are waiting for further tests...❤☐❤☐❤☐

Second update...blood values way out of range and could be serious. He has been admitted for the night ❤☐❤☐❤☐❤☐

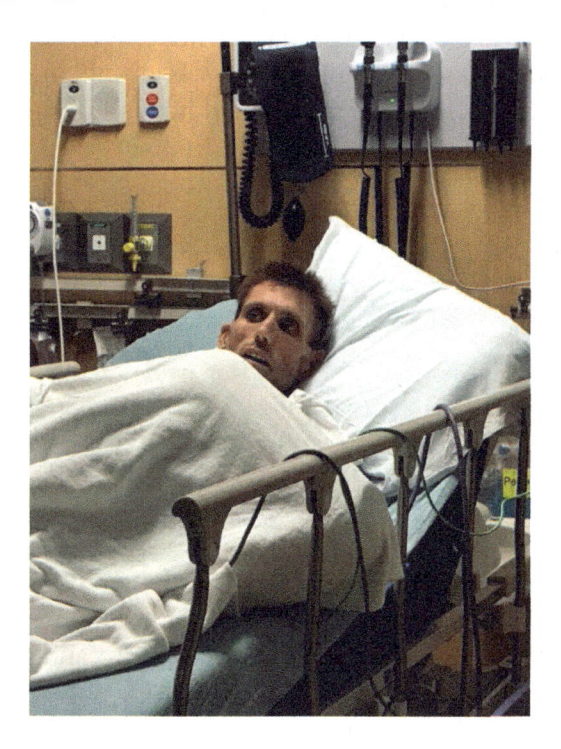

It's hard to revisit these images. I know that it will be shocking or some to see, but I can't tell our story without full transparency in what Tin looked like. It broke my heart to know he was dying but it shattered my heart to pieces seeing what he physically, emotionally and mentally was enduring. Watching someone slowly fade away is a unique trauma.

April 4, 2018

Thank you everyone for the continued support for Clayton Allen Bond. After last night's hospital admission, Tin has been moved to the ICU unit. They are having trouble getting his blood levels to stabilize. Based on his current condition, the hospital has told us that his condition would not allow him to travel to the Mayo Clinic and his condition is too poor for the Mayo Clinic assessment. We are unsure of the near future but he will be surrounded by friends and family in the upcoming days. ❤☐❤☐❤☐

The Diagnosis Days - Becoming a Caregiver

April 7, 2018

[Clayton Allen Bond](#) was released from the hospital on Thursday. Today we had to bring him back to the ER. We have called family and close friends and at this time I am very sad to say that Clayton is no longer a candidate for the Mayo Clinic. His health has declined past recovery. We are setting up Hospice care to make him as comfortable as possible in the upcoming days. I want to thank everyone for their continued support and prayers as we go through this time. People have been asking what we need. We need family and friends. Some have asked if they can visit soon and I want anyone who wants to visit to ask me and I will talk to Tin. It may be a few days until we understand how all of this will be organized. It is hard to keep up with texting and phone calls but I will do my best.

Thank you all.

I love you Clayton ❤️ ❤️ ❤️

April 10, 2018

Clayton's dear friend Christina set up a GoFund Me to help cover bills and rent. People showed up and donated so things could be a little easier around us and I could focus on my time with him. I'm eternally grateful for the generosity, heart and time I was given.

"Hi all. You asked how you could help our wonderful, crazy, wild, and funny friend Clayton Bond... well here you go. Thank you for all the support. Please feel free to share away."

The Diagnosis Days - Becoming a Caregiver

April 14, 2018 – A Fantastic Gift

Never underestimate and never understate the power of an act of pure prismatic kindness. As Clayton Allen Bond and I continue on our journey, we have been recipients of messages and gifts of care and compassion. We are so thankful for each and every single one. We do want to take a moment to pay a special thank you to an amazing family for their support. Some of you may know that we know a confectionary wizard who won Food Network #kidsbakingchampionship Saying that Clayton is obsessed with Foodnetwork is an understatement. This week, Clayton's food drive has decreased until he was gifted two homemade confections made late the night before. Clayton lit up and immediately began eating desserts made by a baking champion. The surprise on Clayton's face and the pure joy of eating those cakes gave our family an extra wonderful memory we will cherish forever. Most people do not know that Clayton and I had briefly mentioned getting married after we settled down in our new beach town. Time and fate have taken that opportunity from us but, as far as I am concerned, we had our "wedding cake" made by a Food Network baking Star and we cannot thank him and his family enough for that moment of pure love. Thank you so much!! ❤☐❤☐❤☐

The Diagnosis Days - Becoming a Caregiver

      My post for the 14th was of a night earlier in the week. On this actual day, Clayton wanted to go to the Gulfarium. He had very little energy. We went at the very end of the day after the park was closed. All he really wanted was to see his favorite penguin, Becky. We spent some time with her and than went across the street to grab dinner. At the end of dinner, I helped Clayton to the bathroom where he said he wanted to go to our home. I was tired. I knew it would be a tough three flight climb up the stairs and that he would want to stay the night. I wanted to say yes but all his medications and supplies were at his mother's house. We could organize it all in the morning and bring him home the next day. He began to yell. "I want to go to my home." I was exhausted. I wanted to sleep and him going to our place would be such a battle. I promised and promised I'd bring him over the next day, and he agreed. Had I only known…

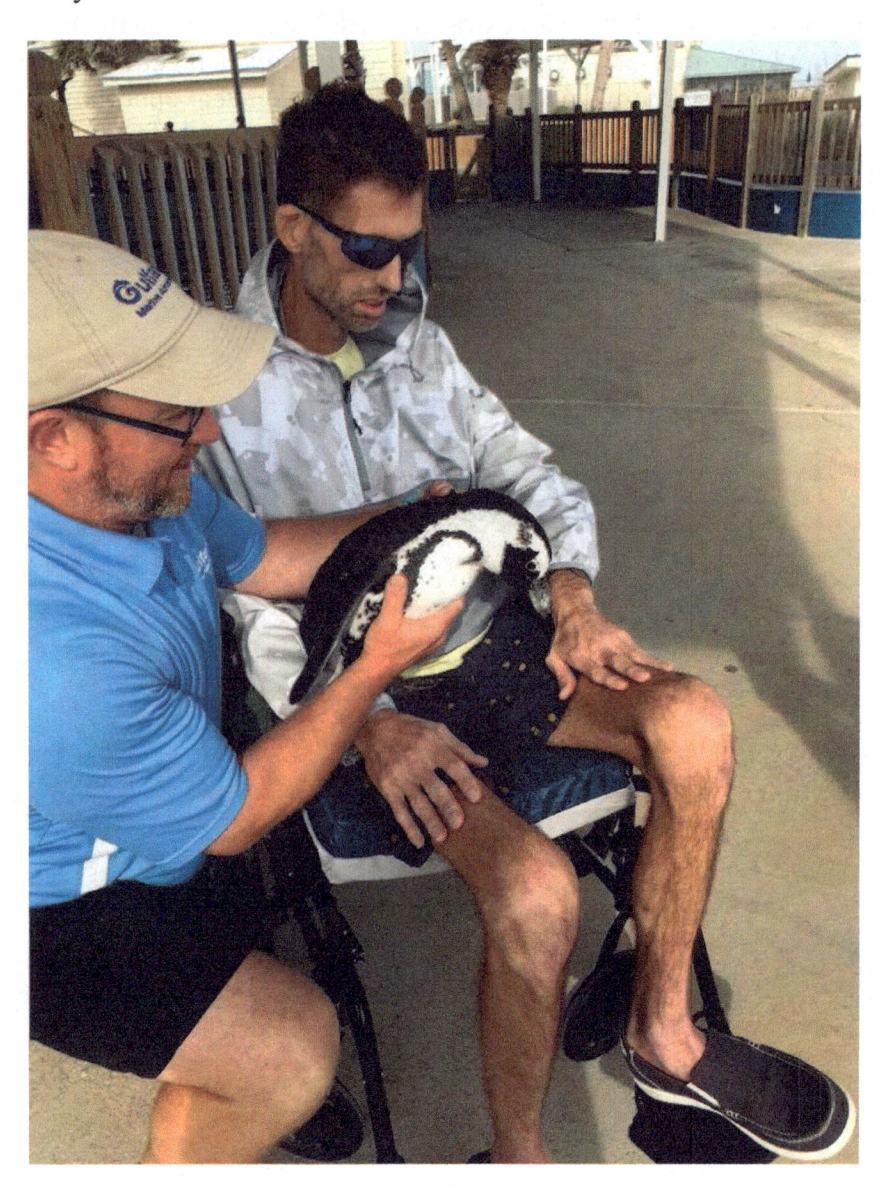

The Diagnosis Days: Becoming a Caregiver

April 15, 2018

He didn't feel up to going out. He didn't have the energy to get out of bed. We sat together for a few hours, and I had a sense that time was running out quickly. I reminded him that today was my sister's birthday just in hopes he would hold on one more day. He was getting tired and falling asleep. Family left the room and our friend Katy said good night to him. Alone, I looked into his eyes and saw that he was weakening. His eyes were glazing. He was sleepy. I kissed him on the forehead and said, "I love you".

He smiled a little and nodded. "I love you" he whispered.

"I'll see you tomorrow."

Katy and I got in the car and we both began to cry. The end was near. I collected myself and drove us to my apartment. There I cried to my mom knowing he was going to be gone soon.

April 16, 2018

At 3am I woke up crying. I felt him. Roan and our cat Stalone were both on the bed pressed against me. They knew. He had held on and waited until after my sister's birthday – his last gift…

I fell back to sleep and woke up to a phone call. Much like when my mother called me about my father 10 months earlier, Clayton's mother was on the other line and through tears she said:

"He's gone. Clay's gone."

Although I sensed it in the early morning hours, at that moment on the end of her sentence, I was officially widowed…

The Care-Griever Years:
Year 1 A.C. (After Clayton)
The Fog Year

Saying Yes to Moving Forward
&
For Those Who Need These Words

The Care-Griever Years: Year 1 A.C. - Saying Yes to Moving Forward

Before I continue with the rest of the day of my widowing, I want to point out that Year 1 for me was "The Fog Year". I felt like I was in a dream, nothing felt real. I had difficulties understanding who I was, where I was and had trouble remembering basic things all because of the trauma. Year 2 would be a far different experience…

April 16, 2018 (continued)

I needed to split this day from Caregiver to Care-Griever to really demonstrate that my life changed in an instant. As soon as I heard the words that Tin was gone, my whole life changed.

I sobbed for quite a while after I hung up the phone. I shook. I gasped for air. I let it all out. A storm of emotions ranging from deep sadness, despair, loneliness, fear, anger and relief, relief for him that he wasn't suffering anymore. The storm surge kept recycling from whipping widowed winds and the guilt that set in during the storm's calm center. I asked allowed:

"Did I really do everything I could?"

I didn't realize that was just the energy the storm needed to repeat it's ravage and I sobbed again.

Burning eyes and a heavy heart, my mother and I went over to Judy's house. There he was laying right where I last saw him. Eyes open but no Clayton to be found within. I kissed him on the forehead and said goodbye to his "person" one last time. The funeral home took his body and I composed myself to start calling friends and family before I shared on social media. I saw a notification on my phone only to find that Clayton's mother's cousin had, without consent, messaged Tin's ex-boyfriend to inform him who, in turn, posted on Facebook before his family knew. Enraged, I messaged him to take it down and told his cousin exactly how I felt. Up to this point we had not gotten along but at her arrival in the final days, she tried to push me aside and declare she knew what was best for him. I reminded her that a caregiver doesn't show up in the final hour for the fame.

Calyton's mother Judy, her cousin, my mother and I went to the funeral home shortly after. He was to be cremated and his cousin (she who shall not be named) began to impose her views on every urn she saw selecting vessels Clayton would kick and break before being buried in one. I suggested a beautiful urn with sea birds and his cousin immediately disagreed and began to manipulate Judy by suggesting how Clayton wouldn't like it and that she knew he'd prefer one that she had pointed out earlier. Finally, to my relief, Judy snapped and declared:

"Enough! This is Bryan and My decision. I agree with Bryan about the sea birds. Clay loved the ocean and that's that."

The Care-Griever Years: Year 1 A.C. - Saying Yes to Moving Forward

His cousin shot me a glare and, in that moment, I soaked up my victory with a grin and an eyebrow raise. Death brings out the worst in family and she wasn't going to disrespect and overshadow his honor with her greed.

April 16, 2018 - Facebook Announcement

It comes with great sadness to tell everyone that Clayton Allen Bond passed away in his sleep last night. He spent his last days surrounded by family and friends. This has been a very difficult year as I have lost both of the most important men in my life, my father Wayne and my greatest love Clayton.
We cannot thank everyone enough for your support so far and the support we will need in the upcoming weeks. I know I have a lot to process. Now how do I explain to Roan that his dad is gone...

I love you Tin ❤☐❤☐❤☐

  My biggest fear was that everyone else would eventually forget about him and our memories would start to fade…

The Care-Griever Years: Year 1 A.C. - Saying Yes to Moving Forward

It had been over a month into widowhood. I went back to work after the "two weeks allowed for bereavement". Parents get more time with a newborn. That's a whole other jab for the grieving.

"You've spent years and years with this person, but you need to get over it in 2 weeks" says "Society"

But I digress…

My friend Jenny (who was also widowed a couple years earlier from my friend Cole) reached out to let me know she was there and understood. It took some time and we finally got on the phone. Jenny shared her sympathy and understanding. To be on the phone speaking to someone that just "gets it" felt like a huge relief. Jenny had left the animal care world after Cole passed. In her search for support, she found Soaring Spirits International (SSI), a nonprofit widowed support community founded by executive director Michele Neff Hernandez. Jenny explained the vast resources SSI had and that there were blog writers for each day. Jenny continued to share and mentioned that my writing style, recent experience and being in the widowed minority within the LGBTQIA community gave me a unique voice that could help others. I hesitated not knowing if I wanted a weekly responsibility. Jenny suggested to speak to Michele without any pressure.

About a week later, I spoke with Michele. I listened to her experience. I listened to the work she was dedicated to and that building a strong community of support never ends. As I listened, I felt all the loss and emptiness surrounding me. Talking and writing my feelings have always been my way of working through things. Why deny myself (or others) from my own healthy emotional expressions? So, I said yes to being the representative LGBTQIA blog writer. The commitment was 1 year. I thought to myself:

"Only a year? I can do that. By then, I won't be grieving anymore."

Well, we all know now that is certainly not how grief works. So started my weekly habit pouring my heart out. For the first 2 years, my blogs were just shared with the widowed community until the pandemic hit and I recognized the global grief. I had no idea what impact sharing my blogs on social media would be. All I wanted was to help others feel less alone.

For those who need these words, this week's widowed blog…

The Care-Griever Years: Year 1 A.C. - For Those Who Need These Words

June 16, 2018 - Navigating My New Normal

It's been 7 short weeks since I lost my Partner of 4 yrs. – Clayton, or as my family calls him "Tin". Right now I am sitting, ironically, at the Atlanta airport on a layover to go home to Boston for my cousin's wedding. Tin and I met in Atlanta and left the city to move to the beach, get married and make a life. Everyone has been saying "Great! You get to see your family!" "You need a break!" "Have a great vacation!" They are right that I do need a break, but as I type these words I am deeply terrified. This visit will be a hurricane of emotional tests and trials.

Last year I lost my father at the end of this very month. I haven't been home since. Shortly after, Tin was diagnosed with terminal liver failure. My mother was the only family member who could come down when Tin passed so I am about to walk into a tidal wave of in-person condolences that normally happen much sooner for others. Not having seen anyone else, the weak scars of seven weeks healing will undoubtedly be torn open. I feel like Dante beginning his journey through the Inferno. This plane is a ride on the boat crossing the river of the damned. I see the other side and along the banks are demons whispering dreaded questions that people ask to show support only to be used by my demons as worded weapons. Dante's Inferno is my favorite book. I guess knowing that Dante eventually leaves Inferno provides me with a bit of hope that someday I too may reach Paradiso.

I had to consciously choose to go up three days before the wedding so I could get the "I'm so very sorrys" over before the wedding but there will be people I won't get to see before hand. I'm preparing myself for the words "How are you?" "Are you angry, because it's ok to be angry?" "Have you moved on?" The only answer I have:

I am utterly heartbroken and there is no other way to explain it.

I am happy for my cousin while concurrently having to accept that Tin and I can no longer reach that goal together. How do I deal with such conflicting emotions? I feel like I'm bipolar but I know I'm not. I'm just being thrust into an emotional experience that is a combination of a million to one. Why do I have to be the one?

Things might be a little easier if I had the opportunity to go through a funeral service for Tin. As fate would have it, Tin's mother had a stroke after his passing. Everything is on pause. Like the loss wasn't enough and the Universe felt it necessary to punish me more by delaying some closure. Than again, this may just be a lesson I'm supposed to learn. I can't believe I control my own destiny and also that everything happens for a reason. I'll go with the latter to save me some tiny bit of grief. Until everything is sorted out, Tin sits and waits in a beautiful blue vessel the color of the ocean with seagulls rising to meet the clouds. I cannot take care of him and I cannot be responsible to care for his mother. Here is where the demons of my guilt hide.

The Care-Griever Years: Year 1 A.C. - For Those Who Need These Words

I've now started my connecting flight up in the clouds crossing this airy river towards I don't know what. Will I be able to handle it all? Will I be able to fight the demons off? Part of me thinks that holding the demons at bay is survival. However, there is a small voice inside me telling me the demons are not to be feared but faced. Experience them to take away their power so I can be granted safe passage. Perhaps I should name that little voice Virgil….

It's Saturday and while you read this blog I am getting ready for the wedding without Tin here to fix my tie and hold my hand as I step onto this new shore….

The Care-Griever Years: Year 1 A.C. - For Those Who Need These Words

June 23, 201 - An Unexpected Return Home

Well I made it. I made it through the first wedding since Tin passed only two months ago and it was followed by the next day being the first Father's Day without my father. There were times I couldn't hold back the tears and times I couldn't catch my breath. I felt like a stranded fish. How ironic to be a crying stranded fish that needs salt water to breathe but the water is blurring you vision instead of spilling over your gills. I made it through the night with the fun songs, the heartbreaking songs that meant joy to all the others in the room, the condolences from family that haven't seen me since Tin passed and catching myself rubbing my own palm and realizing I was just hoping to feel Tin take my hand. It's not just losing the person it's losing all the plans you had with that person and watching other people be rewarded with what you have lost.

The plane ride home was going well until I fell asleep. Dreams of the plane crashing, my apartment being robbed while I was gone and "Oh my God is my dog safe?". What would I do if Roan was gone? I need to get home and the panic sets in. I move forward and jolted awake startling the guy in the seat next to me realizing I was locked 10,000 ft. from the answers to cure my panic. Of course everything was fine and Roan was tail wag crazy but as I returned home so did the stomachaches and dark clouds I had been carrying before my trip. It was an unexpected return home to realize how lonely and depressed I was. Skip it and go to bed. Work in the morning.

Now I find myself typing because of another's return home. Tin's ashes have been staying over his mother's house until we could take him up to the family farm to be buried on his birthday July 15th. Another date I'm scared to meet which is rushing towards me. Tin's mother Judy had a stroke and has been in the hospital. Today I got the call that she is being flown up to live near Chicago. She won't get to go to her home before she goes. Everything she has will be left behind for her niece to handle as her health shows her fate. By chance I asked (assuming) that Tin's cousin had taken Tin's ashes up with her on her recent visit. She hadn't. My stomach turned and my heart dropped…Tin has been in his mother's house in the dark all alone waiting for someone to return for him. The brick wall of guilt and wave of sadness is something I can't describe. I left work and went to rescue him. He had wanted to come home one last time before passing but the three flights of stairs were too much and the reality too hard for us to endure that final climb. I picked up Tin's ashes and I held him in my arms. I realized this was going to be his last visit. This was my last time helping him up those stairs. He lighter and my heart heavier on his unexpected return home.

The Care-Griever Years: Year 1 A.C. - For Those Who Need These Words

June 30, 2018 - The Wax and the Wayne

Another week past and overall things have been even keel. However the dreaded dates pile one on top of another. July 15th is Tin's first birthday. July 4th is Tin's and my anniversary and today, June 29th, 2018 is the first anniversary of my father Wayne's passing.

I know this writing is not based mainly on my lost partner Tin but it has a strong and strange effect on my healing. My father passed away 3 months before Tin was diagnosed with terminal liver failure. My father had over 13 back surgeries, was addicted to pain medication and became an alcoholic to try to manage what the pills could not do. We all thought he would pass away from liver failure. He had heart failure the same as his father Thomas whom I got my middle name from. The irony is that Tin, who did not drink nearly as much as my father, passed away from acute liver failure. I have recently been diagnosed with high blood pressure so now I fear the fate of my father and grandfather. All the while, a glass of red wine is good for the heart but bad for the liver. So life feels like a walking contradiction. I have new fears that never occurred to me until the past year. As I write this there is a commercial for a heart attack medication on the television and I can't help but wonder if it is a "sign".

I know that I have better health than both of the men that left my life but perhaps that is another complexity of being a gay man. You lose your father, you lose your partner and you could have the same ending. It's easy to support family and friends that have breast cancer but that is an evil disease that effects women much more often and a man has a harder time relating to that disease. My mother has beat breast cancer and I am so thankful. A dear friend beat cervical cancer and I can provide all the support possible but I can't relate. She could do the same but not relate if someone had prostate cancer. I'm rambling but this is what goes on in my head. Either way my fears have intensely heightened.

Back to today, back to the title of this blog entry. Obviously it is a play on the waxing and waning of things and how this ties into the loss of my partner. All day I found myself going back and forth grieving Tin and grieving my father. One triggered the other and it, at times, was relentless. It brought stress, anger, tears, fear and the worst was guilt. Why guilt? Here is an emotional mind-screw…I couldn't focus on giving Tin and my Dad my undivided attention. I felt like if I was thinking of one than I was ignoring the other. I'm not sure how to do this but it is 8:00 PM at night and somehow I have the ability to put it all aside and write down these feelings. I'm sure when I'm done I'll feel a bit relieved to let it all out and than the guilt that I took more time away from them focusing on the both of them. Losing one major loved one is hard enough but to lose two so close together is a whole other level of hurt and confusion…. I miss you both terribly….

The Care-Griever Years: Year 1 A.C. - For Those Who Need These Words

July 7, 2018 - History Repeats Itself All Too Often Too Soon

Since losing Tin, I look to each new week as a new horizon that will bring brighter days. This is my fourth post and I thought, maybe by now, my blog would have small sparks of settlement in the chaos. I guess it is good to hope but bad to assume. A very fine line that I often fail to recognize these days. I'll keep the faith that those brighter days are to come but it is difficult with the unexpected challenges that continue to appear. I feel as though I have never heard of anyone else going through all of the milestone days associated with a loss along with the strange scenarios I have recently found myself cornered in. Yes cornered is a great description of how I feel and this week has been one of the most unmanageable yet.

Those who haven't lost a partner can't understand the extent of the loneliness. No one to wake up to. No one texting through the day to see how you are. No one to plan dinner with. No one to fold laundry with. No one in the room at the end of the night to wish you sweet dreams and provide a sense of safety through the night. Worst of all – No one to enjoy those special dates with. The lack of a person makes them almost unbearable.

This week was one of those weeks. Fourth of July would be our 4th anniversary and the days leading up to it were full of discomfort, no appetite and depression. I feel like a ghost sometimes just floating around except I actually want to be invisible sometimes. My plan on our anniversary was to be invisible, stay home, order Tin's favorite food and ignore that the pops and bangs around the neighborhood were others celebrating their independence while I only feel pain and a new emptiness from mine. Of course the creativity of the Universe decided otherwise. Tin's cousin was in town to start going through his mother's house and it just so happens that 4th of July was the better night to go to dinner. We went out and I had fun but I felt guilty I wasn't home reserving this night as our night. The next day would be tough to go to his mother's house and start sorting. Tin's cousin asked me to bring his ashes over so she could transport them up to Chicago for burial. This would be the last time he would leave our home. I buckled him in the passenger seat, said my goodbyes and carried him into his mother's home. After a couple of hours of tears and confusion, his cousin asked if I would take Tin back to my apartment because she did not think she could carry him on a plane. I had gone through our anniversary and having to say goodbye again only to bring him back home. So I buckled him in on the passenger side, drove home, parked and carried Tin in one hand while walking Roan on leash. There we were, the three of us climbing the stairs together again not knowing when Tin would leave us again permanently….

The Care-Griever Years: Year 1 A.C. - For Those Who Need These Words

July 14, 2018 - Sympathy Pains

I'm sitting in the waiting room at the doctor's office. About a week ago I started having stomach pain and strong exhaustion. I, uncharacteristically, do not have an appetite and I have lost 10 lbs in less than two weeks. At first I thought it was something I ate. A few days passed and I thought it was probably just a stomach bug. After a week it eased up and I had a few days of "normal" and the odd pain and discomfort has returned.

At any other point in life, I wouldn't think too much about my digestion being off. That happens to everyone, right? However, the loss of Tin makes me unique compared to many other people. I just watched my partner's health rapidly decline and he lost his life. What's worse - To lose someone suddenly or to watch it slowly happen? You can argue both sides and both sides have their own traumatic effects in one's mind creating a vessel full of emotions. Like a pot of boiling water, if you keep watching it never boils but as soon as you let your guard down and look away those tiny little bubbles join forces, take over the pot and spill your head and heart onto the fire.

For me, watching Tin fade and go through liver failure all in 8 short months has been difficult and this week I noticed a silent and deep wound, my new fear - Will I suffer the same fate? Why would I think this could happen and why be so afraid? Because I now have the knowledge of how this disease could slowly take me. Irrational? Yes. That doesn't stop the wound because it is etched into my mind that Tin's illness was unexpected and began with stomach discomfort and exhaustion.

I have talked myself off the ledge of panic. I have texted and talked to people to calm me down. I understand that the chance of me having terminal liver failure is very low. I eat well, exercise and I definitely watch what alcohol I drink but the fear keeps getting the best of me. There is a very good chance that my body is finally bringing the stress to the surface to release the built up tension. So the best that I can do is live healthfully, be proactive and wait for the blood test results to see what the Universe has in store for me next. I'm guardedly optimistic that I've been through enough and this is my time to live my best days.

There is but one other psychological twist to these aches I have been having. As Tin's disease progressed, there were moments and days that I wish I could have taken that pain for him and that I could endure some of his suffering to remove the burden. Now that my caregiver guard is down and the adrenaline has subsided, is it possible that my emotions are fully flowing and all of these physical ailments are my feelings manifested as latent sympathy pains…

The Care-Griever Years: Year 1 A.C. - For Those Who Need These Words

July 21, 2018 - The Loudest Sound is Sometimes No Sound at All

So if you read my last blog, I was pretty stressed last week waiting for blood results and I'm happy to say everything is fine so I guess my stomach issues were really emotionally based. I do want to take a moment to thank everyone who has read my blog and the kind comments. I haven't commented which has struck me by surprise since I am typically a talker.

Knowing that I had a blog entry to write, I thought about the kind of week I had dealing with Tin's first birthday. It had been week after week of tough first days and this week was finally quiet. My mind is suddenly quiet. Today I realized, in my efforts to make it through the days, I am running from one task to another. I had told myself that I had to deal with my loss and not avoid it with a full schedule. Funny how you elude your own rules without realizing you are disobeying yourself. The heart wants what it wants.

Back to why I haven't responded to comments on my blog. I feel like my blog entries communicate what I feel exactly when I write them. Once it's published, I have to accept my truth. I feel like adding more comments change the raw truth in the post. Almost like commenting would be some strange version of backtracking. I'm sure as I continue to process losing Tin I will find it easier to engage in comments but right now it feels strange. I do love the comments so please continue. This is such a great group!

I'm realizing a new side of myself. Humor, talking and staying busy are not my only coping mechanisms. I can go quiet. I was a bit terrified to be caught in the silence but right now typing this post I actually feel relaxed. I've been so worried about stopping in fear of my new lonely normal. Ironically this deafening quiet is accompanied by an unfamiliar sense of calm.

I guess the loudest sound is sometimes no sound of all…

July 28, 2018 - The White Rabbit

Alarm goes off and it hurts to get out of bed. I was asleep by 10 pm last night and it's 5am now. That's 7 hours! 7!! Why am I exhausted? Up I go and into the bathroom. Brush my teeth, get dressed, take meds, get yelled at for food by the cat, walk the dog, pack my lunch, rush to eat breakfast, gym for 1 hour, catch up on texts, emails and Facebook on the elliptical machine…Breathe…

Work at 8am! Work is so busy there isn't a break, meeting, questions, meeting, annoyed guest, annoyed staff so no lunch, meeting, sudden change in the day's plan and I'm supposed to be out by 4:30pm yet it's 5:15pm, off to the grocery store, check the mail, get greeted by the dog, get yelled at for food by the cat, put the groceries on the counter, take the dog on a walk and catch up on texts, emails and Facebook…Breathe…

The Care-Griever Years: Year 1 A.C. - For Those Who Need These Words

Back in the house, phones going crazy because everyone else is off of work and asking for things, make the dog dinner, take a shower, probably laundry but the laundry from 2 days ago is still in the washing machine so re-wash and realize there is still clothes in the dryer so you add them to the pile on the living room chair….Breathe…

So what's next? Put on the tv so you can hear what disasters are occurring in other people's lives…Breathe ---Ahhhhhh!!!! I haven't eaten since like 7 am!

Look in the fridge. Look in the pantry. Back to the fridge. Maybe the freezer? Kind of not hungry but might as well. Pasta and meatballs? Too many carbs. Meatloaf? No that takes too long. Soup? What are you nuts, it's Summer. Ok fruit? Too many carbs! Alright then so a salad with chicken and Olive Garden Dressing! Yum! Wait so the pasta and fruit are both no but the high calorie salad dressing makes the cut? But now I'm hungry and I do love that dressing. It's fine I need to eat. Ugh the salad bag went bad. I'm done. Dinner is cereal! No milk! AHHHHHHHH! Greek yogurt will have to do. Sit down to eat and the phone rings, washer buzzes, Facebook messages ding. You mute your phone and pick up the remote….Breathe --- Ahhhhhhh the cable isn't working. The connection needs to be reset! Why right NOW?!?!

Lost my appetite so clean the dishes or it's more to do tomorrow. Switch the laundry to the wash. How is it 9pm? Cable is working again. Sit on the couch and check your phone. Dog is whining because of something. I don't know. Oh wait you haven't spent time with him. Put the phone down. Cuddle with the dog…..Breathe….

Phone goes off and the dog exhales in disgust…..

"Sorry Buddy"

Text message is your Mom that you forgot to call

"Sorry Mom, I'll call tomorrow"

Text message from a coworker that you need to get more done for work

Umm remember when I didn't get lunch and stayed late today but…

"Sorry I'll get to it tomorrow"

Dog huffs

    "Sorry Buddy"

The Care-Griever Years: Year 1 A.C. - For Those Who Need These Words

Dryer Dings

"Damn it"

It's 10 pm and tomorrow starts early so forget the dry clothes I'll get to them tomorrow…

Shut off the lights, dog sulks to bed, cry a little because it's your fault and you don't know what to do because all of a sudden you have to do everything all by yourself and all the people that ran to your side have suddenly disappeared than returned like nothing happened and are demanding your time but where is the time going? Text ding. Ugggghhhh!!!! What time is it? What??? 11pm! I'll be exhausted. I have to go to sleep! I'm late! I'm late! Down the rabbit hole to sleep. It's dark and quite for a minute…Breathe in. Breath out…

"Off with his head!"

The alarm goes off and this rabbit jumps back onto the hamster wheel….I don't know why that pocket watch is running faster and faster but my Cheshire Cat disappeared. I don't want to drink anything. I don't want to eat anything. The Queen of Hearts has stolen my own heart. A caterpillar is blowing smoke in my face and all my friends have come back to my new "table for one" acting crazy yet somehow I'm the one who feels like the damn Mad Hatter.

I'm not crazy! They all don't understand that life without you is incredibly lonely yet so busy that my life is a blur….I miss you so much Tin…

Breathe Bryan. Breathe….

August 4, 2018 - The Forgotten

Seconds filled with thoughts turn to minutes and the minutes to hours. It's only been 3 months so there isn't going to be a whole day that I won't be affected by losing you. In all honesty, I will never go a day without missing you. So why does it feel like everyone else has forgotten you?

When you left, I was surrounded by family and friends. They were watching my every move and analyzing my every word. I was instantly under a microscope being dissected in hopes they would find a cure. There is no cure for life without you. There is only numbing and bandages until the break in my heart heals enough to beat stronger again but the scar will always remain.

"Do you feel you are getting over it?"

It? It? What is IT? Losing my person? Being left suddenly alone? Being made responsible for all of the bills? Having to empty closets? Having to watch objects in my life be taken and

The Care-Griever Years: Year 1 A.C. - For Those Who Need These Words

sent away to others because instead of signing a marriage license we had to rush a Will? What exactly is the "it" you are referring to?

"Do you feel you are getting over losing Clayton?"

Ahhhh, so Clayton was the "it". Clayton – a human being. Clayton – your friend. Clayton - my other half. Clayton – my dog's other dad. Clayton – my nephews' "Uncle Tin". Clayton – my love. It's been 3 months and you now refer to him as "it".

Most of those people that gallantly came to check on me at my lowest have gone silent. I feel forgotten. I feel like Clayton has been forgotten.

This must be what they mean when they say "out of sight, out of mind". I'm still here and I still think of Clayton every day but we have been forgotten….

August 11, 2018 - The Spice of Life

It's amazing how simple things can etch a memory deep into your heart. Music, sights, sounds and smells. Food and cooking has always brought back memories of family holidays and campfire stories. Tin loved food. That's basically the understatement of the year. He would take anything we had in the kitchen and in an hour there would be a beautiful meal on the table and every pot and pan in the sink. Tin was also an avid gardener so it's only natural that he loved fresh herbs.

When we first met, I went over to his apartment and sat on the balcony. It was like a rainforest in the middle of Atlanta. Palms growing as tall as the ceiling would let them and flowers in every corner. A thunderstorm was approaching and we sat and talked watching the beautiful sky change and fill the air with electric excitement. The rain began to fall. A breeze accompanied the drops and sprayed them into the rainforest. I remember distinctly starting to get the summer rain smell as I listened to Clayton and the rain share their stories. I took in a deep breath and was captivated by a new note in the song of the storm. The breeze and the rain had rustled past a small bush nearby and brought to me an amazing aromatic blend of summer rain and Thai basil. It became a favorite of ours and we often spoke of that day whenever we cooked with Thai basil. That day we were etched.

When Clayton became sick last October, he could no longer garden. He could no longer do much of anything except to cook and eat. His hunger drive and specific food desires at random times grew stronger by the day. He began to show anger if he couldn't have what he wanted when he wanted it. To some it appeared childish but to us we knew that food was the last thing Tin had control over as he moved towards his final meals. To give him back some of his gardening, for Christmas I bought him an indoor gardening kit with Thai Basil seeds. I had him open it last as the big surprise. He was excited and wanted some time to read everything and get his garden growing. Deep down it was my way to show him that he still had the ability to hold life.

The Care-Griever Years: Year 1 A.C. - For Those Who Need These Words

That garden never had the chance to grow. I never had one last time for Tin and I to smell that sweet smell together. His illness took his life before he had a chance to create another's. I hesitated for days and then I set up the garden. He would be there with me somehow. As the week went by the seeds grew and my sadness shrunk. There were a handful of herbs and the Thai Basil. After a month the Thai Basil had become so big that it suffocated the others and was left to stand solo – a natural gift and a painful reminder that I too was alone.

So why am I sitting here writing about the past as this blog is to share my present? Well without the past you wouldn't understand how my week went. For the past few weeks I have had to trim the basil back. Within days it grew and reached beyond it's artificial sun as if it was headed to Heaven. Part of me wanted to let it grow in hopes that I could climb it and find Tin at the top. I trimmed it this past weekend and by Tuesday it was overgrown again. I distinctly remember saying out loud to my dog Roan that I'd have to trim it when I get home.

I got a surprise call later that day from Tin's cousin Stacey. She asked if I remembered the strange conversation Tin had with his mother in the hospital about how I was going to be alone. Of course I remembered. I was right next to them filling out his Will. It was a discussion between a mother and her dying son so I kept to myself. Stacey began to explain that Tin had asked his mom to give me what she would have given him and that was an inheritance that would pay off all of my debt, cover the rent I now had on my own and extra to have a cushion. I have never felt such opposing extreme emotions in my entire life. I was shocked, relieved, excited, angry, embarrassed and deeply saddened. My life was going to be much easier. My life was going to be financially more stable. Nothing is worth losing Tin.

When I got home I greeted Roan and took him on a walk as usual. When we came back in I started getting our dinner ready and I noticed a handful of dry leaves on the counter. I looked up and the beautiful full Thai basil I expected to see from the morning had withered, dried and dropped its leaves. I had watered it just that morning. My last living piece of Tin was gone…

So I know this is a long blog that spans the course of our relationship but this is my now. I am sitting here with Roan looking at our lost Thai Basil and it occurred to me that our favorite spice in life flourished until the day that Tin's final dying wish was fulfilled. The house feels oddly empty and, like that Basil plant, I now stand alone. A fresh start? A new normal? A new recipe…

August 18, 2018 - A Wolf in Family Clothing

Over the river and through the woods, Tin's mother's cousin had come down to see him before he passed and to help his mother handle a mother's worst nightmare losing a child. "She" watched him grow, watched him thrive and now held him as he faded away. I can't imagine and it seems unholy although if Jesus' mother had to go through it than who am I to judge the workings of the Universe. Either way, it hurt to be losing him and it hurt to watch her lose him.

The Care-Griever Years: Year 1 A.C. - For Those Who Need These Words

I had heard wonderful things and Tin was so excited "she" would finally come down and meet me. We had been together for 4 years and I looked forward to meeting her. After a long day at work, I picked up my mother at my apartment and we went to meet the visiting family. Tin had a procedure that day. I still feel guilty that I had to work and I couldn't go with him. When we got to the house I said hello and then checked on Tin and his new medical directions. While reading, she stated that she was in town and that she was with him all day today and that she was handling his medications now. I was torn. Up until now I had made sure his medications were correct. Her tone implied that I lost my rank because she was family and I had to work. On the other hand I felt relieved that I could spend time with him and let someone else deal with the chemistry. Seeing that she wanted to come in and take over, I let it go. Shortly after she felt Tin needed pain meds without him asking. I thought that was strange and I said he tended to not like them because he felt too tired. She scoffed at me and started pulling pills that were not the pills he was supposed to get. I got up and stepped in reading his new doctor's orders and pointed out that his new medical directions had adjusted and stopped some of the meds she was getting. Her response in front of everyone was that I asked ridiculous questions and that she was there now to handle it. In one statement she dismissed everything I had done as well as the importance of our relationship. I was just the partner. She had no idea she had opened a door I boarded tightly shut. I unleashed 10 months of anger pointing out that she did not get to sweep in for the final hour and claim heroism. She put her hand in my face and told me to go home. My mother started crying and said she couldn't stay and so we left.

Tin called me shortly after and I was still crying and heart broken. "She" had taken away what little time I could have with him. I told Tin how sad it was to care for him this whole time, to know I would lose him and how horrible it was to be dismissed. I told him that his favorite cousin couldn't possibly care if she treated me that way.

I found out later that Tin had cried for hours after our phone call. At times I feel guilt, at times I feel sad and at times I feel incredible rage at "She's" selfishness. Tin said something to her because from the next day on "She" was disgustingly sweet to me. I left it at that and after he passed she carried on with her life. A drive to see her family, a back injury along the drive home and forced to call her estranged brother to come get her in Atlanta from Chicago.

Flash forward to this week. Clayton's mom had suffered a stroke shortly after he passed and can no longer live without assistance. His family moved her up to Chicago to be closer. Tin's cousin is the power of attorney and "She" had asked for Tin's mom to give her $3,000 to cover her medical bills. Why? "She" claims that her back issue was because she drove down to see Tin so she was hoping for compensation because of her kind heart. Yeah, you read that right and you should feel as disgusted as I am. Well it gets even better than that my friends. In my last blog I spoke about the inheritance that I was told I am getting. "She" had found out about it. She decided to call me at 7am on my day off because she happened to go visit Tin's mother. I saw her name and went back to sleep. When I woke up I forced myself to listen to the message. "She" so kindly told me that Tin's mom was doing well and that she was getting her own cell phone and would love to hear from me. (Mind you I speak to Tin's

The Care-Griever Years: Year 1 A.C. - For Those Who Need These Words

cousin a few times a week and I am up to date on his mom but work and timing are sometimes off). Well dear "She" forgot to actually hang up. She didn't realize that for the next 2 minutes I heard her mumble to Tin's mom "No need to care now." She was badmouthing me to Tin's mom, conveniently after she had found out about my inheritance. Needless to say she called Tin's cousin and asked for more money after that. His cousin didn't answer…I'm just glad that Tin wasn't witness when the wolf in family clothing had been exposed…

August 25, 2018 - The Already and the Only

There are minutes, hours, days that seem to fly by while seconds seem to drag on forever. It has only and already been 4 months since Tin has passed - only and already.

For those that don't lose their "person", it is hard to explain that time's guidelines begin to bend in ways we never knew. Good days go fast. Bad days go slow. Yet the next week reverses and bad days go fast and good days go slow. Either way I'm keeping busy but the one thing I can't run from is the building feeling of being lonely. I'm filling my days but not with new things and social events…I have to do everything around the house and I've also added 2 other side jobs to cover the cost of being alone. I'm busy but when I look at my day:

Weekdays - Wake up, walk Roan, gym, work, walk Roan, check work stuff for job 2 and 3, bed, repeat.

Weekends - get up, walk Roan, clean, run errands, walk Roan, check work stuff for job 2 and 3, bed, repeat.

Tin and I were only here for 1 year before he became ill. We didn't have time to get settled and make a circle of friends. I already feel the emptiness and loneliness of not having family and friends in the area and I can't see where I might have time to build a new life. I'm only one man and I'm already alone…

Two days before Tin passed away he wanted to go back to our home to see everything one last time. It was very late and I was burnt out. I promised him I would bring him up early the next day so he could have the whole day to look at everything and just enjoy the calm of our home. Tin felt too tired the next day and couldn't come over. Early the next morning he passed away. He only wanted to go home one last time and I already regret that I didn't take him the night he asked. I'm so so very sorry Tin. I didn't know how fast that last day would pass… If only…

September 1, 2018 - Determination vs. Distraction

In all honesty, this week has been pretty good. I mean I have had my sad moments and the little things that remind me of Tin have shown up here and there. What I'm noticing though is that my reactions are changing. What used to immediately bring up tears and sorrow now

The Care-Griever Years: Year 1 A.C. - For Those Who Need These Words

brings up tears and a little smile sometimes a chuckle. I've noticed this week that I am talking more about Tin in regular conversations without feeling strangely disconnected from the room. Is it that I'm getting used to my new normal? Is this part of the process? Of course, I ask myself if this is a normal reaction 4 months after losing someone? Does this make sense because I had known last October to prepare for life without Tin? Then I tell myself that it's ok to settle down and coast a little. I still will have to work through more firsts: My birthday (Never thought my 40th would have so much significance), Thanksgiving, Christmas, New Year's, Valentine's Day and the first anniversary of the day he passed….

There are days where I am so busy that I haven't dwelled or stressed. That's good but I also don't want to distract myself to avoid the process that I still am just at the start of experiencing. I have new healthy goals and I'm very determined to reach them. I guess this week's blog is more of a question for all of you:

How do you know you are balancing determination and distraction?

September 8, 2018 - The Phoenix and the Dragon

It comes in waves, those flames: the flames of fear and the flames of future, the flames of anguish and the flames of anger. You do your best to fight the fire but it is erupting from within you. As if you haven't fought enough, you are constantly fighting with your inner beast but you never know whom. Is it your inner phoenix or is it your inner dragon? Phoenix is a rebirth out of the ashes but develop too quickly and your heart's new house will burn down. The dragon brings strength to walk the path but beware your breath as you may strike fear in the ones you meet along the way. One must tread lightly around stirring giants. In their glory, both are majestic and rule with kindness and wisdom but at their worst they can destroy entire villages. Young beast master, do not try to wake them until you are ready to control them or you will lose control of yourself…

"I'll never be able to move on" - The sparks fly

"It will get easier" - The pressure builds

"Have you moved on?" - The fire is stoked

It's not under our control what feeds the beast and which beast we are nourishing. It breathes when it wants, it feeds when it wants and it sleeps when it wants - Caution to those that wake either of the sleeping beasts. Caution to all who wake both…

It's been a long time since I have had a night out with others. There have been dinners, a mellow movie night but not one of those "Let's grill! Neighbors are coming over and we can party"…I just had one of those nights. It felt like a relief but little did I know that the start of the relief was a release of the phoenix and the dragon.

The Care-Griever Years: Year 1 A.C. - For Those Who Need These Words

The phoenix has long been a symbol of rebirth and strength. How enchanting and desirable in a time like this…the dragon, although just a stereotype, is defensive and aggressive. Both are just trying to survive. Perhaps they are one in the same placed in different challenges. One must take time to master the valor found in both. Yin and Yang as the Phoenix is rebirth and the dragon is mastered wisdom from life's experiences.

Since Tin passed, I have focused on rejuvenating and revitalizing my life, in the honor of the phoenix. I try to be strong and make well-guided decisions in the honor of the dragon. This week I let my guard down and both beasts emerged untethered and leveled everyone in the room.

I relaxed and drank some whiskey and water while others took shots and tossed back drinks. I was the most in control. I was finally laughing out loud uninhibited and it felt like the world's weight fell off my shoulders. My stories created excitement and my jokes placed us all in high spirits. I didn't realize how high I had flown. The phoenix awakens. Positive energy surrounded the group for hours. I finally felt safe enough to share that I was gay and my partner passed in April…we hit serious talk. Everyone was supportive and the phoenix grew. I felt warm. I felt the sadness but I also felt the support. This was the start of a new chapter in life…

As the night fizzled, others left the gathering to wrap up the night. There were three of us left and that should have been an indication that something was going to pivot. Sitting around the patio was straight Chris (a big muscle guy confident in who he was and cool with us "gays"), my gay friend Chris and I. It was nice to have two Chris's from each side…..Yeah, it means a lot when a straight guy doesn't care who we are romantic with and still want to love us as friends. Sometimes that means more.

Well straight Chris had a fair amount to drink and began acting strange. I asked if he was ok and his response was "No". It was straight guy sad moment so I rolled with it but what came out of his mouth turned the heartfelt phoenix and wise tempered dragon into a full firestorm. Animals that no one in the room had ever known existed…

Chris was acting panicked and sad so I reached out. His sadness was not from the loss of another but a loss of himself. Chris began to tell me how hard it was to be with someone but still go back to his ex for fun. All I saw was red. Without an ounce of thought the Phoenix tore at Chris for his unfaithfulness and dishonesty as the phoenix thrives on loyalty and dependability.

"How dare you betray her trust?" I was in Chris's face screeching like a falcon ready to sink in my talons but just then the inner storm changed the direction of the flames.

"Release the dragon" said the storm and so my voice grew lower and my eyes searched to find a lost soul somewhere behind Chris's eyes. The dragon came forth to speak not wisdom for guidance but wisdom to invoke a fire of fear.

The Care-Griever Years: Year 1 A.C. - For Those Who Need These Words

"How dare you sit in that chair and ask for sympathy because you are unhappy with the person you are with? How dare you after I gained the courage to tell a new friend that my deepest loss happened 5 months ago and here you are taking her for granted."

The 220lb muscle man sunk in his chair and looked down at the ground. The dragon had him right where he wanted him for one last quick lick of the flames…

"How would you feel if she died tomorrow tough guy? Would that make you regret what your doing? Would that break your heart?"

He nodded.

"Then maybe you should think about the fact that you could lose her at any moment and never ever take time with her for granted."

I slammed my empty glass down, stated goodnight and went into my friend's house to put the whimpering beasts back to sleep with my tears, the wound on my heart torn a little bit deeper.

Rest now young beast tamer. Tomorrow is another day…

September 15, 2018 - Half the Road of the First Year – Just Let it Flow

Tomorrow marks 6 months since Tin has passed. How am I already here? How does time move so slowly and so quickly at the same time? Honestly it is Life's biggest blessing and curse. As I look back at these 6 months, I see a new road behind me that I have paved on my own. Of course there have been others to help me through the thick brush but I had to be the one to cut through the weeds. Every once in awhile I see something amazing and I catch myself talking to Tin. Sometimes it feels good and sometimes it causes an upset. Either way I never expected to be where I am today only 6 months after my greatest loss.

I'm writing this as I sit in a hotel room near Niagara Falls. I've never been here and the site of the Falls is awe inspiring to say the least. Gallons upon gallons of water pouring and churning is a beautiful and perfect comparison for the way these past months have been. I'm in Niagara because out of nowhere I was asked to come up to the Aquarium to consult. A huge deal in my industry and a huge check I wasn't expecting. The stress flow slows and the success flow increases. It's been an amazing visit but that's not all. Earlier this week I was promoted to Director of Animal Management at my full time position. Another huge huge success in a very small and competitive industry. With one Facebook update, my stature grew tenfold and I'm already being asked advice from others. Acknowledgement and a raise. The stress flow slows and the satisfaction flow increases. Couldn't be better but it doesn't stop there. I work a third "job" selling all natural products that I truly stand by. Anyone who has started a business knows it can be difficult, hard work and long hours. I put that time in three months ago and in 90 days my team's success is multiplying. Last night I was updated

The Care-Griever Years: Year 1 A.C. - For Those Who Need These Words

that my business grew 25% this month and it is only mid-month. I honestly don't know what to think except incredible gratitude.

I feel like I'm in a fairy tale and I'm so happy for all I'm now being giving but never doubt for one minute that I have forgotten my long lost Prince Charming. I truly believe he is with me and guiding me through the woods towards all these great things. There is no other explanation…

I love you Tin and I miss you every single day…

September 22, 2018 - The Song in Your Heart

Sometimes a song is a gentle reminder and sometimes a song is a stick of dynamite…

I woke up feeling more relaxed than usual today. I went to the gym before work and felt centered and ready for the workday. I have a 5 minute drive to work which usually happens in a blink of an eye until Adele comes over the radio. Tin absolutely loved Adele. She was his girl! Anytime Adele came on the radio the volume went to max and he belted out whatever he thought the lyrics were. I have heard her song since his passing. They bring me some sadness and other memories. Today felt different. My heart sunk as she began to sing and I began to break down. My right arm was on the arm rest and I felt someone hold my hand and squeeze. The feeling passed when I looked down at my hand but I didn't feel alone in the car. Tears came full force and I had to change the station – Work was 3 minutes away and I couldn't show up as the manager for the day with red eyes and a broken heart on my sleeve.

I pushed through the day staying busy and keeping a river of notes from bubbling up and forming more emotion evoking harmonies. I was efficient and effective for my day job and immediately went to a vendor event next for my second job. We drank wine and socialized. They began to play music and the first song out wasn't Adele, it was "Sugar Pie Honeybunch" by the Four Tops - My late father's song for my sister. I had let my guard down and the notes pulled another chord of my heart. Fast paced questions about products generated immediate distraction and I sailed through the stormy song without alerting to anyone I was in possible emotional peril. The coast had cleared and a neighbor stopped by to ask how I was doing since Tin had passed. More chords struck and I couldn't hide looking at the floor and putting my hands in my pockets. I jumped onto another topic but the choir of "I'm sorry for your loss" echoed again and again in the background.

With the event over I had to pack up quickly and run home to my dog Roan. He had been home by himself a little longer than normal. As always, I'm greeted at the door by my best friend who covers me in doggy kisses and piles of fur. It's my favorite time of the day. Late, dark and quiet we wondered around the apartment complex as I messaged my sister how the night went. I got home, made us dinner and finally ate at 9pm. I took a breath and, sank into the couch and dropped my defenses. The feeling of being alone suddenly left and Roan

The Care-Griever Years: Year 1 A.C. - For Those Who Need These Words

looked up in the room. A wave of sadness came over me and a song from my past came up from the chords of my heart and I lost all control. I can't get the song out of my heart and I can't keep the dam under control today. Tin I miss you so very much. I repeated the song "Ghost" by the Indigo Girls from their Rites of Passage album again and again until I fell asleep.

September 30, 2018 - Catastrophic Compensation

I've tried to write more about the good things in life recently but every week brings a new strange situation that results in processing new thoughts and difficult emotions. What does one think when they are given inheritance?

So many people are gifted property and money as their older family and friends pass away. It's understood that each new generation gets a little lift from the ones before. Passing away at an old age allows for the ones left behind to process the loss as it comes closer. That death, albeit hard, is expected. Therein lies the trap for those of us whom have lost someone out of phase. Sudden loss or early loss due to illness steals our one chance to collect the time and memories of a life long lived. So when life starts to settle after the loss, the remaining possessions are passed around - Inheritance. Inherently designed to help after loss as a loving gift, inheritance takes on another form for those of us with an early loss.

Yesterday I received an inheritance check from Tin's mom. I knew it was coming. I knew the amount. I knew it was Tin's last wish to help me continue on by myself without worrying how I'd pay for the basics in life without him. Seeing that envelope caused relief and a sickening feeling in my stomach. It makes sense why I would feel relief but why the sinking feeling? That check feels like the Universe trying to compensate for what it took from me. As if it would be ok for someone to come into your home, take items and leave a check while you're out at the grocery store. You come back and feel violated yet there is a trade on the table that is supposed to make it all ok. It feels cheap. It does make my life easier but it, in no way, does not begin to compensate for taking Tin.

So I have no choice but to cash the check and pay my debt all while feeling like I'm accepting the payoff that Death has sent for its debt. Cashing the check does not clear the Universe of its egregious act against me but I have no choice when the ultimate Judge makes the final ruling…

October 7, 2018 - "Oh My God! I'm So Sorry! I Just Heard"

Time goes on and life begins to settle. You think you are past the hardest conversations until you get a message from out of the blue…

"Oh My God! I'm So Sorry! I Just Heard"

The Care-Griever Years: Year 1 A.C. - For Those Who Need These Words

These words come in a text message, a social media tag, in an email and, rarely, in a phone call. Mine came just a few minutes ago through Facebook. It's one of those messages you don't ever expect from someone you really never thought you'd hear from again and you dread reading it. To be honest I did really look at my phone and say to myself "What in Gay Hell?" That's a movie quote from Too Wong Foo. Tin loved that movie and I use that quote more often these days. It usually gets a good laugh.

As if we are really friends with everyone we call "Facebook Friends", there is a sharper edge to the knife when the person that reaches out is someone that never really thought much about others unless they needed something. They gush over just how wonderful your person was and how sad. I have little patience nowadays as I figure out what to do with my new unwanted freedom. I need to fill my abundant time alone with things that allow me to feel and process but not trigger the feelings like I'm back reliving "D" day. I need to focus on the essential things in life and their importance in rebuilding my foundation.

I know that there are those people who honestly do care and didn't know because life pulls us together and apart. That message I would have been saddened by but not annoyed..

"How are you?"

How the Hell do you think I am? Seriously, why is this a question? Can we please all get together and write a comedy of all the things that make us roll our eyes, cringe, want to lay on the ground and, most importantly, want to just smack someone upside the head? Can we? All you bloggers are obviously writers so let's start assigning Chapters! LOL! I have to joke and laugh because, if I didn't, I would cry.

How am I? How am I? In all honesty, I can't tell you because I haven't had enough time to learn who I am…

October 20, 2018 - Damned Either Way

So I missed a week. I didn't have a blog post for last week and I felt bad like I had let a bunch of people down in some way. I mean, I know it is a voluntary thing but I don't like missing deadlines and I don't like making an excuse. I create pressure that doesn't exist. The sink is full of dishes. The carpet hasn't been vacuumed. I almost ran out of gas in my car because I can't focus on what "a day in the life of" should be.

UGGGHHHHHH!! I hate that phrase! "Don't make an excuse". I have been taught my whole life that I can't make excuses for things but when is it not an excuse and it's a legitimate reason? Who gets to decide? It always seems like it is the person that has everything going right in their life. I have this voice inside me that keeps telling me that talking about Tin is now just an excuse to not do things. Meanwhile, I will admit that I am hesitating to look at a bookcase of objects in the next room because it hurts.

The Care-Griever Years: Year 1 A.C. - For Those Who Need These Words

So when is hurting not an excuse but an acceptable emotion? When is it considered acceptable emotion without other motives? Why does there feel like there is a social timeline for when a heart is done being broken? My heart will never be fixed. It may heal but there will always be a scar and I guess that scar is the reminder that losing Tin is a battle that most people don't have to suffer. Losing your person is never an excuse. Losing your person is heartbreaking…

October 27, 201 - To Urn or Not to Urn?

We still haven't been able to put Clayton to rest. His mother's stroke has resulted in her having to move near relatives and figure out a new life. Until then, Clayton sits in a (beautiful) Urn in our apartment. At first it was unsettling, having to look at a container that holds the dust of the person you want to hold the most. You want to keep it and put them to rest all at the same time for, what feels like, competing selfish reasons but that is another layer of the loss.

I don't have many friends in the small beach town where I live. When we moved here, my job took a lot of time and Clayton's job had us with different days off. There wasn't time to meet people before we lost time. Now that Clayton is gone, I have a lot of empty space and time. This past week I invited 41 people that I knew in the area to come over for wine and some social time. I set up my house and got all the fun drinks and food for a mellow social evening. The house was cleaned and I was ready to go but then Clayton caught my eye. His Urn is in the living room where everyone would be and everyone knows that he is here. I didn't know what to do. Too urn or not to urn? That was an awful question and a terrible feeling. Do I keep Clayton's Urn where it is because he was (and is) a huge part of my life or do I put his urn in the bedroom to keep things from being awkward? Either way I felt incredible guilt.

Well 4 people showed up and did not stay long. Others that said they would come either messaged last minute or didn't at all. As soon as the "party" started it had ended and everything was empty including the spot in the living room where Clayton had been every day. I was truly alone and the saddest part is that I would rather have kept his urn where it was and not have a party than to have an unsuccessful party without him in the room.

The loneliness wave has been one of the hardest so far…

November 3, 2018 - Unexpected Messages

It's been a long day. I worked, came home, took the dog out, prepping dinner and the dishes of the past few nights are sitting in the sink reminding me that no one else will help me. It's a regular reminder as I try to find a balance to this new unwanted bachelor life. It's November already and Clayton has been gone for almost 6 months. I'm not doing better, I'm just getting better at acting. I just don't know I my new abilities are going to be strong enough to get me through the next most difficult tasks before me - My 40th birthday, Thanksgiving, Christmas

The Care-Griever Years: Year 1 A.C. - For Those Who Need These Words

and starting a New Year alone. I'm already unbelievably overwhelmed and I feel like the loss is starting all over again. The intensity might even be stronger than when he passed. There is no immediate shock and adrenaline like there was in April. Again I feel myself back to the beginning of Dante Alighieri's Inferno

"When I had journeyed half of our life's way,

I found myself within a shadowed forest,

For I had lost the path that dos not stray"

Much like Dante, this season is a dark forest and before me stands a lion, a leopard and a she-wolf. My birthday. The holidays. The birth of a new year. They block my way to the great mountain and there will be Hell before there is Heaven. I knew the path would not be easy. In Dante's struggle to move forward he was visited by a shade. This shade was sent by Dante's deceased love Beatrice to bring words to Dante and aid his path.

I started cleaning those dishes wishing I could rinse the loneliness down the drain with the leftovers. My phone lit up with a message.

"Ugh. Now what?"

I opened the message send from a ghost of past, a friend of Tin's. He had gone to a medium to connect with his mother that passed but had a message for me. Tin had come through clearly with knowledge that only Tin would know. Tin acknowledged the ones that cared for him. Tell them he is ok. Talk about a dog he loves. The phone shade didn't know we had a dog. Tin adored Roan.

These woods are so dark but there is a faint familiar voice telling me to keep searching for the way. There's more than one way to climb a mountain…

The Care-Griever Years: Year 1 A.C. - For Those Who Need These Words

November 10, 2018 - Bizarre Birthday

I'm sitting at the airport this morning headed to spend the weekend with my best friend from junior high. It's my 40th birthday weekend and I'm all over the place in my head. Today's blog is more of a list of competing emotions rather than a discussion or story…Sometimes bullet points get "the point" across better. See what I did there? ;-)

Ok here goes:

- Turning 40! Excited and how the Hell did I get this old?
- Yay! Friends and fun!
- Yay a break from work!
- Oh God this is my first birthday without Clayton. Can I hold it together?
- What's next? Holidays? Oh God I won't have him for holidays!
- Do I want to even decorate? Too sad but he would want me to.
- Seriously 40? I did not envision my life would be so shaken up at 40. Ugh
- Ok deep breath! Birthday weekend!! I'm grateful for what I have but I'm also excited for presents :)

- Birthday cake! Oh damn with 40 candles! Good thing I brought my inhaler! LOL!
- I can't have cake. My metabolism stopped at 35 and my height stopped at 5'6". Too much cake and I'm going to be a hobbit by 41.
- Clayton would have laughed at that. I miss him. He always dropped me off and picked me up at airports. I loved seeing him there right when I got home. He won't be in a few days. He won't be for my next trip or any trip after. It's kind of hard to be at home and to leave home.
- Ok back to the fact that I'm turning 40! Deep breath!

Can't stop any of these events from coming so I might as well start enjoying every minute! Happy Birthday Bryan. You are doing good! One day at a time…

November 17, 2018 - Newborn Fears

I caught myself today. I caught myself leaving for work, locking the door and checking the handle – 7 times. I pulled and pushed on the handle to make sure it was definitely locked. Then I pushed on the door itself. "It's locked'" I said to myself. I walked down the hall to the stairs and paused. I felt sick to my stomach. I turned around and went back to check the door again…

I didn't sleep well last night. My dreams were all over the place, in and out of new scenes mixed into others that seemed hauntingly familiar. People I knew in my life were all gone and all the new people I met were untrustworthy, up to something, lurking in the shadows. I ran around this new world struggling to find an anchor. Then I saw my dog Roan. He was

The Care-Griever Years: Year 1 A.C. - For Those Who Need These Words

running toward me and was knocked into the street and run over. I woke up screaming and in tears. I felt that everything was out of control and the fear grew stronger.

I lost my security when I lost Tin. I check door locks all day. I'm scared to leave home because something might happen. I'm scared to come home because something might have happened. It may seem irrational to many but the fear is very real for me. Very very real…

December 8, 2018 - A Turning Point Kind of a Question

I'm not sure if it is just a part of the process, self-preservation or something supernatural but I caught myself of guard the other day. You see, I was quite surprised when an acquaintance walked by me at work and in front of everyone he grabbed my shoulder and asked me how I was. It might not seem much to some but everyone at work registered something was different. He acted like we knew each other very well and we only said hi in passing. The moment passed and everyone asked if we were friends outside work and were we seeing each other. They were shocked to hear me say no and the speculation began.

"Oh my God. Do you think he's gay? I think he likes you! He's really cute!"

Well yes he is a handsome guy but really? I mean no I don't think. No. Whatever. I can't even begin to think about anyone wanting to start anything with me. Too much baggage from the start. Even if he did like me he'd run knowing the grief I carry. Besides, I'm not ready. It is a flattering thought though…

My coworkers spent the rest of the day analyzing that interaction and the number of smiles and glances that apparently were sent from the handsome man. I rolled my eyes and said to myself "Even if I was ready, what's the point in getting excited only to get disappointed?" I sucker punched myself with that statement. My throat closed and my eyes watered. I bit my tongue, took a deep breath and moved on with my day.

When I got home my mind wandered back to the idea that some day, some one could fill the void. Not replace Tin but be my companion and then it happened -

Out loud as if Tin was in the room I asked:

"What do you think Tin? Would you approve? He seems like a nice guy."

I caught myself by surprise when I realized I expected an answer. There was no answer but, than again, maybe there was….

The Care-Griever Years: Year 1 A.C. - For Those Who Need These Words

December 15, 2018 - The Grocery Store

This week I felt like writing about how the arrival of the holidays has already been extremely difficult for me. These are the first holidays without Clayton. Those Facebook "memories" that pop up in my news feed are like a sharp knife from a friend. Nothing is safe from the reminders. I don't know if I can even decorate this year but decorating is not what my words are for this week. It is the place that no one would ever think could be a heart-wrenching trigger. A place everyone goes that is designed to help you live but, as a widow, it is a place that can take more of you away…The Grocery Store.

I walked through the store early last week grabbing regular groceries and saw the turkeys on sale. Thanksgiving was days away. I had the holiday off but I don't have friends here because Clayton was sick soon after we moved here. I'm friendly with my staff but I can't hang out with them on a regular basis because others would fear favoritism – Career FOMO. (Side note - Snowflakes are making my life way harder than it should be. If they can't handle that Starbuck's ran out of pumpkin spiced everything than I pray for them when real life hits…) I digress. So here I am in the grocery store grabbing a turkey. Thanksgiving is my favorite holiday so I started thinking about the different sides I would make and then there it was – A box of those crispy onion things that go on that green bean casserole stuff (Not my tradition – Sorry, not sorry). I froze.

"Clayton loves green bean casserole. Wait, Clayton loved green bean casserole."

My heart sank. Tunnel vision. Deep sadness. Anxiety. Panic. Dizzy. I had to get out. This wasn't the first time I had to just leave a cart and walk out but I had to buy dog food so I rushed up to the front to checkout.

"Hi. Having a good night?" The cashier asked.

Oh God! I thought to myself. Don't ask. Please I can't.

"Yup! Just in a rush."

I made it out the door. I put the groceries in the car. I returned the cart. I sat in the car. I lost it. I couldn't control myself. A good 10 minutes of intense hurt and sadness. I pulled myself together. Drove home. Fed the dog and went to bed. For a holiday known to make people feel full, I have never felt so empty this Thanksgiving…

Fast forward to today. I stopped at the store to grab dinner. Everything was fine until I heard the Christmas music playing. I bit my tongue to fight back the tears. Everywhere I looked were foods Clayton loved, foods that brought back memories, foods I have been avoiding because they remind me of him. I had to get out! This time I felt the sadness, tears as I drove but I narrowly escaped the meltdown. I had gotten out before the full effects hit. I was lucky

The Care-Griever Years: Year 1 A.C. - For Those Who Need These Words

tonight but I don't know what's going to happen the next time I have to go back into a place I need in order to live that constantly reminds me that Clayton has died…

December 22, 2018 - A Haunting Hallmark Holiday

Tis' the season for all the things that remind us of what we have and what we have lost. This year, for me, there has been more loss and it's much harder to shake that feeling as those around me put up lights, throw holiday parties and decorate. I can't put up a Christmas tree. I can't decorate. I wrapped one present and I just can't. So I don't and I tell myself that there is nothing wrong with skipping the traditions this year. With everything added up, I've earned a hall pass to the holiday blizzard we all experience every year. However, there is one thing I can't control….The mail.

It's obviously not a competition but Clayton and I are even for the number of Holiday Cards we have received. Of course his are random retailers and old accounts wishing "Happy Holidays" to someone who has passed away but, none the less, he is getting holiday wishes. Yet he's actually in first place because all of his friends that used to send us Christmas Cards have skipped me over. The year I could use more wishes for a happy holiday is ironically the year I have received the least. Maybe they don't want to send me something because it might upset me? Maybe when he passed away I fell out of thought. My all time greatest fear – Out of sight is out of mind.

I wish nothing more than to have Clayton back. In many ways he is still with me but the holiday reminders are haunting…

December 28, 2018 - Stranger in the Room

I've made it through our anniversary, his birthday, Halloween, my birthday, Thanksgiving and now Christmas. Each one felt empty in ways I couldn't explain. You truly don't realize how much a person is part of you until that part is suddenly gone. I made a point for me to be back home with my family for Christmas. My career has made me miss many holidays with family but I couldn't miss this one. I'd feel too lonely, or so I thought…

Don't get me wrong, my trip home was wonderful!

They threw me a belated surprise birthday party. I was so excited to see so many people I care about and I caught myself reaching back to grab Tin's hand in excitement and he wasn't there. I started to cry and played it off as happy tears but that empty air left me gasping….

A fun brunch to celebrate a successful business my sister and I joined this year. We all talked about how much we love the products and how we just want everyone to be involved to feel like we do but in the moment I didn't want anyone to feel the way I did. Everyone was joking how their person was involved or not involved and there were plenty of jokes but I didn't have any…

The Care-Griever Years: Year 1 A.C. - For Those Who Need These Words

Christmas Eve full of food Tin would have loved. Tin loved being with my family because it is a large, loud and loving band of Bostonians. The attention was on the kids and the surprise visit by Santa (my Uncle dressed up every year). It was a comfortable reminder of my childhood but than he asked those young kids "What would you like for Christmas?" and I felt sick. There's no magic red bag big enough and no team of reindeer strong enough to get Tin back under my tree Santa…

Christmas Day and I got to see my nephews wake up (one snuck down the stairs early lol) and open their presents from Santa. The full stockings were placed by the chimney with care. So were the half eaten cookies and carrots I created the night before. The other side of the family took the day. Kids running around, new toys everywhere, more good food than one ever needs, families, parents, couples and than just me…

In rooms full of friends and family, I was a stranger in a familiar crowd. My next three big firsts are a bit different: New Years with no plans, Valentine's with no one and the first anniversary of Tin's passing. Crowd or no crowd, I'm now the familiar stranger in the room…

January 12, 2019 - Losing the Holiday Weight

The holidays were rough. My first without Tin and there were days I just could barely keep it together. Christmas is over and I spent New Year's alone for the first time in years with no one to plan a new year of adventures with. It's been a struggle and I have 3 more months before I hit the anniversary of his passing. I felt like I was carrying a thousand pounds through the holidays. I get holiday weight but that was not what I was ever expecting.

Now I've had a couple of weeks post-holiday and it hit me today that I have had sad moments but not anything like the strength and weight 3 weeks ago. I'm very busy with two jobs to stay afloat so maybe that's it. My goal for the new year was to loose some weight I had gained while caring for Tin. Sitting here and thinking about how I feel in this moment I feel better, less burdened by my feelings like I have lost some of that holiday weight. I have been keeping so busy, running around to stop and think that maybe I haven't let myself stop and talk to myself. Sure I could lose a few pounds but I'm realizing that's not the weight I need to focus on losing…

January 20, 2019 - Social Media Surprises

When Tin passed away, my social media was flooded with posts and photos showing just how much he was loved and how much support I had to lean on taking my first steps on this new beach. Each day had been continued support helping me step forward and weather the waves.

Over time, the posts and check-ins faded and I found myself a bit bipolar about it. On one hand I wasn't being flooded and reminded every day of the hardest loss of my life but on the

The Care-Griever Years: Year 1 A.C. - For Those Who Need These Words

other hand it felt like people forgot I wasn't ok yet. Worst of all, it felt like they all already forgot about Tin. I know they haven't and that the wave of salt water blurs your eyes as your trying to tread water over the abyss but it's very easy to feel alone without your person to anchor you through the storms.

So I've gotten used to making dinner for myself and cleaning the dishes alone. I've gotten used to cleaning laundry and folding it alone. I've started getting used to going to bed alone but waking up alone still has a rougher feel. That is where social media can make or break you. I woke up and my Facebook memory (that they suggested I remember) is one of my favorite memories of Tin and I celebrating his birthday. It was the first birthday we celebrated together and seeing that unexpectedly was a sharp blow to the chest. Before I knew it I was uncontrollably sobbing and I was right back to day one without him.

There are so many wonderful things about social media. Staying connected with people helps keep us afloat when storms hit. However there is always a gamble I will get a "friendly" reminder that I've suffered a life altering loss followed immediately by posts from friends who have the one thing in life I can never get back – Tin…

January 26, 2019 - Home is Where the Heart Is

It's taken me months and months to bring up the courage to go to dinner with a friend. Sounds crazy but she was Clayton's favorite coworker and he is all we have in common. I knew it hit her hard when he passed and I knew she would want to talk about it. I guess that is just another layer of widowhood that others don't understand – We want to see you but the memories you trigger are to strong for us to handle right now.

I finally said yes and we went to a local restaurant. It was wonderful to see her! We caught up and laughed, we talked about Tin and how much we missed him. It was scary at first but I realize hearing her remember him was a gift. It's so easy to think that, for others, out of sight is out of mind…

The evening was wonderful and we talked about many different things. My career and second job (which I need to cover my widowed bills) are both very successful. She asked if I was planning to move home near my family but, overall, things are good here so I'm staying. It wasn't the memories of Tin that crushed me. It wasn't being at a restaurant that he and I went to often. It was a question that I never thought of and certainly didn't expect the impact when asked.

"Wow! You are doing so well you should move and buy a place!"

The moths of mourning fluttered in my stomach and up in my throat. Move? Buy my own place? Leave our home? I hadn't thought of any of those ideas. I felt sick but I kept it together until we went our separate ways. I cried heading home and when I got home I

The Care-Griever Years: Year 1 A.C. - For Those Who Need These Words

looked around for any changes. It took me a bit to settle and when I did I asked myself why that idea of moving was so hard. Here is my answer…

Tin designed the layout of our apartment. Tin surprised me by painting the rooms when I was at work. Tin hung all the photos himself. If I take it down he won't be here to help me put it back up. He put so much of his heart into our home. If I move than I lose more of Tin…..

February 3, 2019 - Sticks and Stones - Sticks and stones…They were wrong, words do hurt….

Today I went to pay bills and my computer needed to be restarted. It had erased a password to sign in and pay the water bill. I knew I had it written down somewhere but, of course, my life has been tuned upside-down for the past 10 months and things are not organized like they should be. Whatever. So I started rustling through paperwork in the office I rarely use. I opened a folder and started tearing up. A page of Tin's scribbled notes I forgot I had but couldn't bring myself to throw away. There was nothing on the paper I needed. Notes he made for himself when we first moved here and he was looking for a job.

His handwriting was very distinct. Tin's passion was architectural design. He was incredible drawing straight lines with no ruler and his writing reflected that talent. Some of our friends joked referring to it as "serial killer handwriting".

Well it used to be a joke but now that writing does kill me to see. Who knew that the alphabet, 26 letters, rearranged in a specific way with a specific style could invoke immediate pain and sorrow? I just wanted to pay the water bill. Why does everything have to be so hard….

February 19, 2019 - A Hallmark Heartbreak Kind of Holiday

My birthday was hard. Thanksgiving was hard. Christmas and New Years were both hard. Yet it is the "Hallmark Holiday" that seems to burn more than build the wave of sadness.

Every Valentine's Day growing up, I wrote out cards and put them in classmates construction paper mailboxes but only for the girls. Life is different now and kids can like whomever they like but I had to give Valentine's to Allison when I really wanted to give it to Andy. Either way, all I wanted growing up was to find that one Valentine.

This is the first sweetheart holiday without Tin. I'm 2 months away from the anniversary of his death. Am I the only person that wants to walk into the grocery store, dump all the Valentine cards on the floor, throw boxes of chocolates and stomp on every flower in sight? I couldn't give Andy a Valentine in high school and now I can't give Tin one now. I feel like I'm a heartbroken teenager all over again…

The Care-Griever Years: Year 1 A.C. - For Those Who Need These Words

February 16, 2019 - A Piercing Perspective

How many of us had dreamed of being super heroes when we were younger? Pulled between imagining magic powers and wishing we were older so we could do whatever we want and "oh how perfect life would be". It's true when they say to be careful what you wish for…

Well growing older and being an adult has turned out to be much different than what we expected with the exception of a gift. A super power if you will. One we never expected and some of us may not realize we own. We must only use this power for the greater good but that can be to lift others from the darkness as well as shock those who need to see the light. Hands down and unexpected, our gift is the experience of our loss…Saying that hurts but it is true…

You and I know it exists, our super power. Like all super heroes, it haunts us until it helps us. I'll admit that I have used it for good and I have used it to win a battle. We have the gift of experience. Sometimes I have helped by using my superpower to show others that there is a future after loss. Sometimes I have used my superpower to strike guilt and fear into those that take life for granted. I have never liked saying things that make others uncomfortable but I feel it is part of my journey to share my "loss gift" to make the world a bit more appreciative. We can share what we have gone through by inspiring others, who have not lost, to cherish what they still keep. I wish I had a superhero back when I had Tin. I would have worked less, complained less and enjoyed my time with him much more. Don't hide your superpower my friends because Humanity needs us…

February 23, 2019 - The Sting of Spring

As the first anniversary of Tin's passing ebbs closer, I find myself at the gate to the last season of the firsts.

I've made it through the summer days at the beach, cookouts and fireworks. I've made it through the changing leaves, crisp fall air and a Thanksgiving I wasn't very thankful to experience. I've made it through everyone else being happy through the holidays, singing carols, holding hands by the fire and kissing on New Year's.

Spring is a double-edged sword. I want to get through it but once I'm through it the first year is passed and that makes it more real. The sting of spring is sharp as everyone else emerges from their gentle hibernation. Their grass is greener. Their breezes are warmer. Their blooming flowers smell sweeter.

In the season of rebirth and renewal, I carry on my journey not refreshed from a winter slumber but worn down from a year of emotional erosion. If we are considered a block of stone and our life experience carves our statue than grief is a widow's weathering wind…

The Care-Griever Years: Year 1 A.C. - For Those Who Need These Words

March 2, 2019 - Wanted: Aspiring Assistant Manager

Eleven months and from the outside I have everything together but on the inside I still am an unorganized man just trying to make it day by day. There are dishes in the sink since Tuesday. I haven't vacuumed in a week and my dog hasn't had nearly enough of my attention.

The rush of responsibility in the week leaves little time to think and I'm so worn out by the weekend that I hardly have the energy to do more tasks. So the dishes pile up, the carpet gathers time and man's best friend stays loyal in the wind.

I have realized that being a widow is a fulltime job and, for now, grief is my manager - On call at any point in the day to stop and respond. Just like any job, I'll work hard. I'll answer the calls but I'll use those calls to gain experience. With experience and time, the old manager will move on and I will take its place and begin to manage myself how I choose but never forgetting my humble beginnings. For now I have to accept that Grief is my new mentor…

March 23, 2019 - When Their Truth Hits

I've had very few visitors since Tin passed away. I don't know if the reason is avoidance, being unsure of how I'll be with guests or just that life goes on and we become too busy for the little things. Approaching the first anniversary of Tin's passing, as the warmer month's and spring break approaches, I'm starting to get the calls to stop in for a weekend.

I just finished the first visit from a friend that came to see Tin and I every year. He skipped last year knowing how sick Tin was and that our time together was short. It wasn't my friend's arrival seeing me for the first time that triggered him fully into understanding my new truth. Not until the third day at brunch, unlocked and escorted by mimosas, did my truth finally become my friend's truth. He began to talk about Tin out of nowhere. No easy merge onto the highway of conversation – an instant and unexpected left turn of thoughts and feelings poured out of his mouth. He was scared to see me but worried about me all the time. He was happy to visit but sad to be in the apartment decorated by Tin. He felt a new emptiness beyond what he was expecting and I couldn't hold back the tears. I held back the sobbing but I couldn't control the tears.

I knew that moment was coming and I had trained and trained for it. To hold myself together when others had to finally face my truth. Train all I may, I can't train myself to be strong for others when their truth hits. Like an avalanche of feelings, their new truth breaks away the new walls I've built to define my new truth.

As I bare the burden, that boulder of grief, ever pushing uphill, I cannot see what's coming my way. I get stronger with each push but there are times I must rest. There are times I stumble. There are times I slip. There are times that the landslide brings me down…

The Care-Griever Years: Year 1 A.C. - For Those Who Need These Words

March 30, 2019 - The Changing of the Guards

I did it. Maybe I didn't outwardly realize I was doing it but I did it. I ignored the rising flood.

For the past week I have made myself more and more busy. I have extended myself to help others beyond the norm. I have taken on more responsibility. It all seemed fine and balanced. Late to bed and early to rise with something pressing to think about from dusk to dawn. I kept placing sandbags up against the rising waters and ignored any emotional leaks. Eh they'll go away. Well I was right. The leaks went away because the wall broke at the changing of the guards.

I ran around all week holding in the building anxiety that Clayton's first anniversary is less than three weeks away. I fooled myself, saying that it is the day that is sad and not the lead up. Well it's the lead up.

My Friday night and I finally had nothing to do. No second job, no cleaning, easy dinner. I ate and put the dishes in the kitchen sink. I'd get to them later. Time to relax. As I sank into the couch my heart sank into my stomach. I wasn't busy. There was no guard on duty. I had nothing to distract me and I was alone. The damn broke and so did I.

The Care-Griever Years:
Year 2 A.C.
The Great Anger

Year 2 A.C. – The Great Anger

Year 2 A.C. and I've said it time and time again – Year 2 is painfully crystal clear. I couldn't write a blog this year on the Saturday approaching his death date. The grief was too overwhelming when I finally accepted, he really wasn't coming back…

April 20, 2019 - Please Sign and Date

Well the past two weeks I have been absent from blog writing. The first anniversary of Tin's passing was quickly approaching and I honestly was scared. Scared to think about it. Scared to talk about it. Scared that when the day came, it would make it more true. For the first few months, holidays, birthdays I felt like it was a short enough time span to still be a dream yet the passing of the first anniversary meant it really wasn't a dream. It wasn't a nighttime nightmare. It was reality...

When your person leaves this world you will always remember the day. I have no choice but to remember and be reminded. Tin passed away on the anniversary of when we moved to our new life on the beach. This would be the start of our fourth year in our apartment but the first time I signed our lease alone.

I knew the renewal was coming. The amazing Apartment Complex Staff are extremely supportive and respectful of my loss. I set the renewal date to be just a few days before so I wouldn't have to take care of it on April 16th. How fitting that tax day, April 15th, and the most emotionally taxing day would be one following the other. April showers better bring May flowers.

With documents in hand, I arrived at my appointment in an upbeat mood. I have been very fortunate to have a full time job I love and, after Tin passed, fell into a part-time gig that provides me with support and excitement. All of my financial obligations and then some were managed. I was not worried about keeping our apartment on my own for another year. I could breathe.

I grabbed a seat and I grabbed a pen. The office assistance pulled my file and said

"I had a hard time putting this together myself so I understand if you need to do this another day."

I cleared my throat and said:

"Nope! I'd rather get this done now."

Or so I thought….

As we went page by page filling in simple items I turned to the last one

"Just please sign and date at the bottom." She said reluctantly.

Year 2 A.C. – The Great Anger

I breezed down the page without reading because it was now the fourth time signing and there at the bottom was two blank lines. It was the first time signing by myself. My eyes welled up and I gasped. She reiterated that "we can do this another time" but I knew I had to get it over with. So I signed and left the office.

As the fates would have it, we moved to our dream location on April 16th. The same day two years later Clayton moved from this life. The same day three years later, I have to sign by myself. As long as I stay in our apartment, I will always have to write my signature down to stay renewing things on the day he died. It's as if I've come to a forced annual binding agreement with the Universe stating I agree to the terms at hand…

"Please sign and date"

May 4, 2019 - Small Screen Surprises

I had my sister and a friend in town this past week and it was wonderful. We had a great time relaxing and just enjoying each others' company. All of us are working a side business together with a big company and doing very well. The company had recently reached out to me and asked me to host a local event. What an honor and what an amazing time. Tin would have loved all of it.

When they left I jumped into cleaning the house and getting back into the swing of things. I finally put away the vacuum cleaner and sat down to relax. With my first deep breath I took in the surrounding quiet and I began to sob. It has become so difficult for me to slow down. It has become so difficult for me to take a time out. It has become so difficult when visitors leave because the quiet is so very lonely. The damn breaks every time and the build up sorrow spills out uncontrollably. There is nothing I can do but go with the flow of tears.

Once the tide had subsided, I shook it off and took another deep breath to seal the damn back up ready to hold back until the next cracks give way. I'm learning that I don't take care of myself or give myself enough grace but I'm trying. Seems kind of selfish to be upset when I'm the one alive and Tin had to know every day he was going to die but I am allowed to hurt. I caved in and shut the world off for the night. I turned on my trusty diffuser and filled I with all the oils known for emotional support. I was going to pick a light-hearted fantasy movie.

Bridge to Terabithia. Hmm. I heard about the book and the fantasyland visited by a boy and girl. Sounded perfect! The storyline was a feel good coming of age that I needed with one lesson I did not anticipate. The young boy decided one day to go to a museum instead of hang out with his friend. She went to their secret magical land on her own. You needed to use a rope swing to get through the magical gate and that rope failed for the first time sending her into rain swelled river waters to drown. Upon his return he learned his person was gone and

Year 2 A.C. – The Great Anger

the waves of guilt hit him for going to the museum without her. We traveled with him through shock, denial, sadness and anger. I felt just like him. I felt the waters behind my damn rising faster than ever. I thought I had it under control and made it to the next scene.

In a classroom full of bullies and the "mean" teacher" this young widow was a ghost in the crowd. Behind him came a voice that tormented him for his friend's passing and that hurt young man stood up and used all of his heartbreak to hit the boy behind him. The mean teacher reacted by yelling at the young widow and telling him to go in the hallway. I expected her to reprimand him for hitting someone but instead she took a deep slow breath, the same breath I had taken earlier and she began to speak so beautifully to him about how she understood his heartache because she had lost her person. She too was a widow and he was suddenly not alone anymore. I couldn't control the flood waters...

Thank You Soaring Spirits for being there for me, a terrified and heartbroken little boy who no longer feels alone after losing my person…

May 11, 2019 - What Lies Within

It's an interesting thing how people around you say they understand and they will be there for you. However when you have a tough day and they respond by saying:

"I thought you said you were ok and moving on."

"I was ok that day but there are no rules to what's going on in my heart and my head."

In all honesty I don't know how to say what it feels like when you let someone in a little and they back away instead of standing by you. The best I can do is tell you to listen to P!NK's song "Attic".

May 18, 2019 – Defiantly Defined

So this blog is a bit different than I usually write. This week I've been obsessed with terminology. Have you ever stopped for a minute and thought about words? Where did they come from? How they got their meaning and if they fit? Well it hit me this week that I HATE the terms widow and widower. I think the definitions are ridiculous and need to be changed. Let's look them over, shall we?

*According to https://www.merriam-webster.com/ (Bolded in this blog entry below)

Widow

1. **a woman who has lost her spouse by death and has not remarried.**

Year 2 A.C. – The Great Anger

Ok so than you are no longer a widow if you remarry. Your loss is magically gone. Congratulations! What in gay hell is that?

Classy Example: a woman whose spouse is often away participating in a specified sport or activity. "a golf widow"

Maybe if her spouse was an idiot and golfed in a thunderstorm! Honestly with this!

> 2. **a last word or short last line of a paragraph falling at the top of a page or column and considered undesirable.**

Ah yes…considered undesirable. Short like not whole. A broken sentence just like how us widowed people are broken right? This is ridiculous.

> 1. **become a widow or widower; lose one's spouse through death.**

"he was recently widowed"

"Become" like someone asks "what do you want to be when you grow up?" and your answer is gleefully "A Widow"

Of course we have to always separate men and women. So guys, here is our dictionary fate….

Widower

> 1. **a man who has lost his spouse by death and has not remarried.**

I always understood most words that were nouns and ended in "er" showed action by the thing. So basically widower means "one who widows" like we caused it ourselves. Great! Add blame to the mix. Thanks dick-tionary!

Widow's Peak

The term stems from the belief that hair growing to a point on the forehead – suggestive of the peak of a widow's hood – is an omen of early widowhood.[6] The use of peak in relation to hair dates from 1833.[7] The expression widow's peak dates from 1849.[7] The use of peak may refer to the beak or bill of a headdress, particularly the distinctive hood with a pointed piece in front – a biquoquet[8] – which widows wore as a hood of mourning dating from 1530.[7] Another explanation for the origin of the phrase suggests that it may be related to the mourning caps worn as early as the 16th century. A mourning cap or 'Mary Stuart Cap' is a cap which features a very distinctive

Year 2 A.C. – The Great Anger

triangular fold of cloth in the middle of the forehead, creating an artificial widow's peak. The use of peak referring to a point in the cloth covering the forehead dates to at least 1509 when it appears in <u>Alexander Barclay</u>'s *The Shyp of Folys***:**

Well that's a bad hair day. This omen is false because I never had a widow's peak. My hair all just basically fell out in my 20s. Where was my warning of early widowhood? So that myth is clearly debunked.

Widow's Walk

A widow's walk, also known as a widow's watch or roofwalk, is a railed <u>rooftop</u> platform often with a small enclosed cupola frequently found on 19th-century North American coastal houses. The name is said to come from the <u>wives</u> of <u>mariners</u>, who would watch for their spouses' return, often in vain as the ocean took the lives of the mariners, leaving the women <u>widows</u>.[1] In other coastal communities, the platforms were called Captain's Walk, as they topped the homes of the more successful captains; supposedly, ship owners and captains would use them to search the horizon for ships due in port.

So should people avoid purchasing homes with widow's walks? A girl can't even enjoy a view without people judging. So dramatic.

Than there's this gem:

Widowmaker

- **<u>Widowmaker (forestry)</u>, any loose overhead debris such as limbs or tree tops that may fall at any time**

Forestry? OMG! Why stop there? Great White Sharks didn't make the list? Golf in a thunderstorm would fall into this category correct or does it have to be lumber based?

- **<u>Widow maker (medicine)</u>, a nickname used to describe a highly stenotic left main coronary artery or proximal left anterior descending (LAD) coronary artery of the heart**

Just the coronary artery – Not cancer. Not HIV. Not liver failure…

Here's where definitions take a disturbing turn:

Black widow spider

The prevalence of <u>sexual cannibalism</u>, a behaviour in which the female eats the male after mating, has inspired the <u>common name</u> "widow spiders".[8] This behaviour may

Year 2 A.C. – The Great Anger

promote the survival odds of the offspring;[9] however, females of some species only rarely show this behaviour, and much of the documented evidence for sexual cannibalism has been observed in laboratory cages where the males could not escape. Male black widow spiders tend to select their mates by determining if the female has eaten already to avoid being eaten themselves. They are able to tell if the female has fed by sensing chemicals in the web.[10][11]

Now that is a widower spider as far as I'm concerned!

Ok so this blog isn't full of deep emotions and philosophical contemplations. Sometimes I just have to point out stupidity…

June 1, 2019 - The Scariest Part of Surgery

This blog will be short because I had a Lasik procedure this week and my eyes get tired quickly.

I've never been one to be comfortable with eye stuff. I hate eye drops and the thought of contact lenses makes me cringe but I was so fed up with glasses that I decided to go through with the surgery and get it over with. As the day got closer, I got more nervous. Afraid of the unknown and afraid things would go wrong and I'd lose my vision. I was scared.

I worked the first half of the day to keep my mind focused on something. Everyone kept telling me that I would be fine ad so many people had been through the procedure successfully. I knew all of that but there was something else bothering me that I just couldn't figure out. That is until I got into the car with my friend who was driving me. She asked if I was ready as I reached to close the car door and I started to shake. I started to panic. I started to cry.

She said - "It'll be ok. You'll be ok."

I said – "But if I'm not ok than Clayton isn't here to help me."

There it was. There was the root of my fear that I couldn't unearth until that moment. Yes I was scared to have surgery but I was more scared to have to recover or handle complications without Clayton. Widowhood is many expected things but it's the unexpected ones that make our journey sometimes so terrifyingly unique.

I made it through surgery fine. The doctors say I went from 20/40 to 20/20 in 24 hours and it will continue to improve. Today was a tough day of blurry vision and soreness. I find it an odd coincidence that as I write these words I cannot help but cry yet the tears are bringing my eyes relief and my vision is crystal clear…

Year 2 A.C. – The Great Anger

June 8, 2019 - Complicated Companions

Perspective is in the eye of the beholder. Everyone gets tunnel vision but what I have learned is that our loss is actually a painful gift. I know that sounds strange to view the loss of our person as a gift but that's the only perspective that keeps me going. That there is a reason I finally found Clayton and he was taken away from me. I can share what the loss is so others appreciate what they have, however, people quickly forget the trial and tribulations of others.

It's so difficult to hear couples complain about each other or aspects of their lives.

"Jenny/ Jonny just keeps nagging for us to get a bigger house."

Oh I'm so sorry that is your biggest problem. I'm so sorry that the person you are with wants to continue your journey together and you guys are doing so well that you can upgrade to a 4 bed 3 bath with a yard, pool, hot tub and room to park the boat. Yeah that must suck. Glad I don't have to deal with that difficulty…

Here is where I want to actually dive into the difficulties of being a widowed LGBTQ person. I'm not saying it is harder for us. Not by any stretch but I will say we have some different challenges. I think? With Clayton being sick and having just moved here, I don't have many friends. I am cautious hanging out with people from work because I am their director. I don't ever want anyone to feel there is favoritism. So I don't go out much and don't meet people much. Now for the "gay" thing…

I live on the panhandle of Florida. This is not the most progressive area. There are times I am concerned about the community's perspectives. There are a handful of military bases and it's a tourist town. The gay dating world is not an easy playing field. Around here, people are closeted, bi-curious, just want a friend with benefits or are traveling through and looking for a hookup. I don't judge any of them for the way they want to live their lives but I know that eventually I want to find someone I can share my life with. It's already a struggle to find the "right guy" but it's even harder where there are so few that also want the "right guy" and a guy who is a widow comes with baggage…

June 15, 2019 - Return to Sender

So you are having a great day. Your future is brightening. The birthday of your passed person is on the horizon so you book two trips to help you through the day and allow yourself to get away and enjoy life.

You don't want to be alone and think of the 43 candles he won't be blowing out with you this year. You don't have to stress about finding the right birthday present but you also don't get to see his face when his eyes light up as he pulls away the wrapping paper. You want to acknowledge the deep emptiness of the day but you know he would want you to go out and

Year 2 A.C. – The Great Anger

celebrate. He will be there with you. You may not see him but you will feel his presence and know he is there celebrating with you. Your excitement builds with something to look forward too. Finally you have the big boat before the storm hits. You've begun to prepare.

A text message comes through while you're thinking of the fun adventures to come and you open that little message which shatters the hull of your vessel. The family has finally decided to have a service for him on his birthday in less than a month with no warning and they hope you can be there. Your heart sinks and you are suddenly drowning. Rogue wave!

You explain that you already planned two trips and you can't back out of them. You planned trips to help your grief because they didn't tell you their plans to have a service for your person. YOUR PERSON! Not their person! Your person! They say they will talk about it and see if there is another day. Graciously you understand if his mother is set on that day but his ashes are with you. You can't drive him up to his family before this all happens. If they move forward with his birthday for his burial than the last time you'll hold him will be when you drop him off at the funeral home to be wrapped in padding, boxed up with labels and shipped.

Deep in your heart you wished that the labels read "Return to Sender" and in a week there would be a special delivery - He would magically walk through your front door…

June 29, 2019 - Sometimes the Scary Thing Brings the Most Support – Sharing

So I'll finally share with you that when Clayton passed away I was terrified of the insecurity and my financial stability. I had no idea what to do and the thought of getting a third job (because grief is my second job) was overwhelming.

At the time, my sister had started using essential oils and had just started sharing them with her friends and was able to earn a little money on the side. In her desire to help after Clayton's death, she sent me some of their products and I began resting better. It also gave me something I could focus on and learn about. So my sister, being amazing, said "Let's do this business together. You can do as little or as much as you want."

I was hesitant for all the reasons someone could have been but I was at rock bottom and this was the only rope being thrown down to me. I said yes, grabbed the rope and started to climb. That was a little over a year ago. I have worked hard at my own pace and that hard work has paid off financially enough for me to cover the bills. Not millions of dollars but no grandiose dream was ever promised to me. No rug has been pulled out from under me and everything has been straightforward and legitimate. No I'm not going to name the company, this isn't a sales pitch. This is part of my journey through widowhood and if I didn't share then I wouldn't be honest. And since the importance of sharing is the point of this week's post…

Year 2 A.C. – The Great Anger

Since Clayton had passed, I held many things in. Let's be honest, I held and hid many things while I cared for him. I didn't want him to see me upset and I buried those feelings. I didn't share with many because I had to be strong but, since his passing, the need for the emotional dam doesn't exist and the dam is starting to crumble. If I don't share, that dam will break and so will I. As hard as it is, I need to share my story because that is my Why. Why I can go on.

You see – the team I'm involved in has resulted in something amazing that I never expected out of deciding to join my sister in this business – A support system. All of the people that I collaborate with want everyone to succeed whether or not it benefits them directly. For the past year, I have been growing within the company and meeting more and more people. These people owe me nothing, yet have given me everything with their caring and support. I had found a positive purpose and a huge group of people supporting me in my journey. A few of them knew my "Why" for starting to grow a business but many had not heard it. They instead know me as the comic relief and the guy who can come up with motivational quotes and cheer people on.

So what does this have to do with my journey as a widowed person? I realize now, I have a bigger purpose and I can help others. I knew this blog was helping others just as much as it helped me to write my feelings, but I never expected what was to come next from sharing my Why with others on my team.

Someone had posted a question in the oils group about how oils can support our emotions because they wanted to help a widowed friend. I was tagged in it and the gates opened. Now they knew. I began to get comments and messages. People who had recently added me as a friend on Facebook began looking further back than they had before and began commenting on the posts from when Clayton was ill, when Clayton passed, and posts on how I was moving forward. Since FB has an algorithm that puts active posts to the top of people's pages, my whole journey was replaying for all of my friends. New friends joined old friends to come running to my aid. I felt strange. Do I back off because this is overwhelming? Do I embrace it? Backing down wasn't going to get me anywhere so I embraced it and began to tell my oily friends about my story and how I had gotten to this point.

Flash forward to this past month and I was being asked for advice on how to help with grieving and how people could help others that were grieving (you know how you all of a sudden become the "widow whisperer"?). My journey was bringing awareness and support for others. Another dear oily widowed friend and I started a Facebook group for those in our oily teams who could understand the widowed journey and come together in support. More people were being helped because we shared.

Flash forward again to this past week and I was asked to go live in a Facebook group of over 4,000 people and tell them my Why. As I told my story the comments and reactions exploded in love, support and relief. That video had touched hundreds of people who felt down and who were struggling for their own reasons. I began to get messages thanking me for sharing, thanking me for being open and thanking me for being inspirational. All I did was share but

Year 2 A.C. – The Great Anger

that is all I had to do to reach others who were feeling down. It has been 4 days, the video has over 2,000 views and has been shared around social media. Never in my life did I ever think that my story of my deepest loss would have this kind of impact all because I shared.

So what is the moral of this blog? You are who you are because of what you have been through and someone somewhere may need you to share your story of courage so that they can feel the ground under their feet and start taking steps toward their new future. You never know how strong you are until you have to be, until strong is your only choice. There is strength in numbers so share…

July 6, 2019 - Understanding "Freedom"

The Fourth of July - All things summer right? It's cookouts, pool, family, sunscreen and fireworks. All the freedoms you get living in the good ole USA. It's funny how the word freedom is used. By definition, freedom means you are not enslaved or forced to act or be a certain way. You are not trapped. Of course, for the USA freedom means all of those things to show our independence. Interesting, that word freedom, because it is purely based on one's perception of the situation.

The fourth of July does not necessarily mean freedom for me. The fourth of July is my anniversary with Clayton. It made sense when we picked it. That was the night we officially picked each other and we saw fireworks. Fireworks now mean an entirely different thing to me.

Fireworks make me sad.

I might be the only person in the world to ever write that sentence. Maybe?

Perception is a fickle beast because what is freedom to one means loss to another. You see, the two are one in the same depending upon your viewpoint. Some want to be single while so many of us long for our loss. Both are inherently freedom yet viewed entirely different. I never wanted to be free of Clayton. I never wanted to be free from his hold on me. I never wanted to be free from his voice, his smile or his laugh. This type of freedom isn't a celebration at all. It is quite the opposite. Although I am free to do whatever I choose, I am a prisoner of my loss. The emotional punishment may lighten and the chains may loosen over time but I will never be free from his hold on my heart. I'm shackled forever to his memory so I can never truly be free and I don't want to be. I will always love him.

As difficult as this journey has been, I wouldn't erase the time I had with Clayton to pardon myself from the pain. On one hand, I have had a great loss but on the other I have a great gain. It's entirely based on which side of the coin lands upright each morning and how I choose to read the outcome. I control the direction I aim my perception. I've lost Clayton but I have learned I am a strong and caring person. In my loss, I gained more respect and appreciation for who I am as a person for the way I have and still rise to the challenge of my

Year 2 A.C. – The Great Anger

new forced freedom. It's strange to read that word freedom in this context but I gain control and power over it because I decide the definition.

For whatever reason, I am still on this journey without him. I still have a purpose and reason for being the one that stayed behind. Perhaps this is a journey I'm enslaved too so, in time, I fully understand who I am. The only way I can achieve whatever I am meant to achieve is to accept one leap of faith - All that has happened to me makes me who I am and the more I know me the more I hope to understand and know true freedom…

July 20, 2019 - Castle Made of Sand

Monday mornings are typically tough getting back into the grind but when your person's birthday consumes that first day of a new week's energy you can barely make it through the day let alone the week. This is the second birthday without him. These milestones seem to be flying by faster and faster but the space Tin filled seems to be just as big as the day he passed. It sometimes feels like I am drowning in the waves of emptiness. There is no other way to describe it.

Once again the sweet sting of social media hits with Facebook reminding the world that Clayton's birthday is July 15th. Everyone just saw my post to him on our 4th of July anniversary so when the "Send Clayton a Birthday Message" pops up 11 days later on everyone's feed they feel a little more of what is my daily normal reminders. One after another after another I'm reminded every day.

There isn't much time between the anniversary of Tin's death, the anniversary of my father's death, Tin and my anniversary marked yearly with a huge national reminder accompanied with fireworks and than his birthday. Forget a Monday being exhausting, when everyone is stretching and emerging for spring and the start of summer, I just want to hibernate. April through July is emotionally draining and just like that the summer is half gone and I have little time to build the walls up before the stormy waves of another my birthday, Thanksgiving and Christmas without him arrive unforgivingly.

I can see the tide rising already. Summer starts to peak and vacationers begin to complain about having to go back to their lives. Kids dread going back to school and parents start to long for more quiet at home. I know they don't get it but all I have is quiet at home. I wish they wouldn't wish for a temporary version of what I am permanently living. I guess that is the dark gift we have all been given – pure appreciation for each and every second. I feel like the universe threw his hourglass at me and I missed catching him. Now I'm left cut deep by glass shards and looking down at all our sandy spilled memories. So many people take for granted that they get another chance to flip their hourglass and watch the sand flow while I can only use those scattered grains to try and rebuild my castle made of sand.

Year 2 A.C. – The Great Anger

August 10, 2019 - Some Thing Old, Something New, Something Borrowed and I'm Blue

Last weekend I was at a close friends wedding. I loved the people, the venue and the time away from my regular hectic schedule. On a beautiful hill at a colonial inn in rural New Hampshire, we all gathered under three towering maple trees to watch two friends join together.

I was in the wedding party. We had rehearsed the walk through the perfectly manicure grass to the shady cathedral. I was really proud of myself for honoring my feelings of grief but maintaining composure. I was being true to myself and I was ok at a wedding. I overheard my friend saying that a group of pictures by the reception were of those people he had lost and wanted to remember. I knew that he was going to have a photo of Tin on that table and I was honored. No matter what, I knew Tin was going to be there with us. I walked over to see what photo he had chosen from the 4 years he had know Tin. Would it be one of Tin's goofy looks? Would it be Tin and our dog Roan? I was secure and confident I could look at whatever photo he had chosen, I could cherish that moment again and I could go on with our celebration. Good job Bryan. Good job.

The wedding was about to start and I made my way over to line up and there it was. My friend had chosen the first time he had ever met Tin and took a photo. I fully understood why he chose that photo but he did not understand what that photo would mean for me. You see, he had chosen a photo from that first meeting that had Tin and I in it and there I was on the table of "we wish you were here" except for the fact that I was there. There is no other way to symbolize the part of me that died when Tin died than choosing that photo. The emotions hit hard and strong but I kept it together (for the most part.) People in the wedding party saw the photo and, knowing the story, consoled me as we stood and waited to walk down that grassy isle. I appreciate the care but what they didn't understand was what that photo would mean for the rest of the night. I mean how could they get it? Unless you're a widow than you can't really think like one of us…

I was the only living person in all of those photos. I was the living person that was going to hold the weight of that table. The sorrow. The pity. It came out in looks, comments and "I'm so sorry" hugs. I appreciated the support but it wasn't my day. I wanted that love to all be directed to my friends. I didn't want to be that guy at the wedding. The widow. The lonely. The opposite of celebration. So I stood strong and danced for joy at the reception. I do admit I left the reception once when they called all the people in love to the dance floor. I could tolerate being there with the song but I'd stick out like a sore thumb as the lonely gay widow sitting by himself but who am I kidding? No matter how hard I try, I am that guy…

August 17, 2019 - A Reset of the Mindset

So the feelings are the same, just as intense but not as often and demanding. I miss Clayton every day but the immediate sting when the thoughts rush forward is milder with time. My eyes still water each day but there are more days of laughter than tears. The dust has settled

Year 2 A.C. – The Great Anger

and now I'm feeling unsettled. A year ago I feared I would have to move out of the apartment that Tin and I shared. People don't realize that when you become a widow most often times your finances flip. Your household income drops but all the same responsibilities are there. We, the widowed, are billed for our loss. As if life isn't taxing already.

In my state of self-preservation, I began a second job that has turned into a gift, a labor of love and a passion for helping others. My finances have stabilized and allowed me to find my footing in the shifting sands. There is no immediate threat to my daily survival. I have been able to take time to absorb my new normal and choose my new direction. I'm finding that my goals in life are beginning to change. The things that I held up in importance and as signs of a successful life are changing. I am growing.

So now I have caught myself looking at homes for sale online. I can't afford that yet and I'm traveling a good amount for work and fun the rest of the year. It's kind of cool actually, I have never been able to travel much but when Tin passed away I put faith in the Universe and the Law of Attraction. I started a dream board and almost everything on it has come to fruition including travel to some pretty amazing places. A year ago I couldn't stomach the thought of taking down the photos Tin hung around our home and, very suddenly, I now feel a shift in energy and mindset. I don't feel like I belong in the place I am in right now. There is a calling to move on to the next space in my journey. Like a gentle breeze it whispers in my ear. It's not strong enough to cause a sudden change but a slow consistent push can cause a tree to grow in any direction…

August 24, 2019 - The Weight of a Living Legacy

Shortly after losing Tin I was honored being asked to write in this space. I quickly felt the weight of grief ease as the words hit the paper. An amazing thing began to happen, others started to respond to my writing that they felt connected again and that lifted my grief a bit more. As I continued moving forward, I had started to use essential oils for support and the community surrounded me with support and asked me to share my story with others. No matter how many times I share my story it never gets easier, just different. However, I keep telling my story because each time I see my words create a space of safety for others even if it's for just a moment where they don't feel alone.

Recently I shared my story in a Facebook group. Shortly after, the President of the essential oils company contacted me and offered for me to fly up to the corporate office to share my story with the executive directors. I'm leaving for the meeting in two days. I have no problems sharing the story I have now told over 100 times. I have no issue speaking in front of large groups yet I am feeling this new weight on my shoulders. It's noticeable and felt very confusing to me. Where has the unsure tension come from? I am not in the least bit intimidated by the people I'm speaking with on Tuesday.

Last night, a group of oils leaders and I made history by creating and launching the first ever LGBTQ+ essential oils Facebook support group. It launched and within 12 hours had almost

Year 2 A.C. – The Great Anger

600 members. We created a space that so many had hoped for but no one had stepped up to the plate. My phone has been ringing and dinging nonstop all morning. As I took in all of the messages of celebration and support I can't help but wish Tin was here to be a part of the new rev-oil-ution. I began to think about what I would add to my story for the executive team and the weighted feeling increased as I realized it's nature. Every time I speak about Tin, I am bringing him back into this world and introducing them to man I love and miss terribly. My words are more than providing a space for other to feel understood. My words are breathing him back to life. Now I'm about to get up in front of a billion dollar company and introduce them to Tin.

The weight I now am feeling is from wanting to do my best to breathe all the life I can into Tin's legacy. He apologized to me near the end of his time because he was leaving us. I know he felt guilt. If only he could have known than that he would have such a profound positive impact on so many other people. I truly believe he is here and the driving force for all that is opening up to me and I feel proud to carry the weight of his living legacy.

September 14, 2019 - The Grief Summit

I haven't written in a couple of weeks. I could say I've been busy but really it is because I didn't feel inspired to write. Writing for me is very specific. I have to feel I need to write to portray an aspect of my life that might help another. I don't want to just write anything to have something written. There is an emptiness to that method. There was another reason hanging in the shadows and distracting me from being in the moment. I was gearing up for a professional conference that I was going to present at. Was it the presentation? No and yes. The last time I saw all of these people was 2 years ago when Tin was texting me he thought he had the flu. I wish he had gone to the doctor right than but he waited for me to get home. There is unnecessary guilt here, regardless if it is warranted, it is here. Had I only been home, had I only picked a career that didn't take away valuable time from him. Had I only solved it sooner than he would be here and I wouldn't be headed to a grief summit.

I knew it was coming. I knew I would see friends and old coworkers that wanted to express their condolences. I knew there would be people who hadn't heard and would ask how he was and than I'd have to tell them of my loss, which would cause them to feel guilt for asking and I would have guilt for sharing. This was going to be a mountain of emotional experiences. It all came to fruition. Each day was peppered with conversations about how I was holding up. How did I do it? How could I always be so positive? My response was a bit shocking but it was the truth…

"The outside doesn't always match the inside."

That caused a variety of responses from silence to people asking me if I needed to seek help and if I was "having bad thoughts". No. No I am not thinking of joining Tin, The Universe

Year 2 A.C. – The Great Anger

will decide that it is time but your grief goes to such a deep level when someone brings that touchy topic up. Sometimes I feel like a court jester juggling all of these emotions. I guess now I understand the tears of a clown.

I made it through the check-ins but what I didn't make it through was a simple joke, a side comment meant to jest the jester. It was a comment that would have me laugh at any other time. A simple joke about me being 40 and time was fading to find a husband sent me over the edge. The entire weight of the trip was unbearable. I immediately walked outside, sat on the cement stairs and began to sob. Friends came to my aid realizing that the inside couldn't be held at bay by the outside. It's a game of Jekyll and Hyde. As hard as you try, the beast demands attention and freedom.

Once the storm was out of my system, I put my brave face back on and carried on as though the breakdown was just a dream. With the conference over, I piled my stuff in my car and got in the driver's seat. I took a deep breath and began to sob. This was the first conference I would be heading back to an empty home…

September 21, 2019 - Ostracized Honesty

It's time I dive into a topic that is always at the heart of gay men dating – HIV/AIDS. Growing up I watched as the disease came forth, took lives and drove the world to treat the LGBTQ+ community worse than ever. There was fear of being accused and harmed and there was (and still is) fear of contracting the disease. From my biology background, I see medications and treatments have advanced to amazing supportive levels for those affected. A new preventative medication PREP has reached the mainstream and decreases the chance of contracting the virus to almost zero but nothing is ever 100%.

In my new widowed world, I take my health seriously. As someone who does not have HIV, I spoke to my doctor about this new medication to assure I would have as much education as possible so I could feel I was protecting myself. Living in the panhandle of Florida has been a challenge with acceptance and my doctor refused to discuss my options. His response: "It really wouldn't matter". So then, in his eyes, my health doesn't matter and so than I don't matter. Just another gay man he'd apparently like to see go away. How comforting as I move through this new life without Tin. My honesty got me less help. That makes it hard to try and reach out again to any doctor. It's enough for me to question if I should leave the area entirely. I could just get it online but most of my life is now just on a screen showing an socially perfect world. I just wanted someone to talk too…

Recently there was a nice guy that showed up in one of my Facebook groups - Gay, handsome, good personality and HIV positive. My friends in the group began messaging (not calling because that's too hard) telling me we would be such a great couple! We would be so happy! They were so sure until I shared my honesty – No matter how wonderful someone is I can't be with someone who has HIV/AIDS. I watched Tin fade away over 8 months from acute liver failure. I can't go through that again. Yes they may live to be 100yrs old but what

Year 2 A.C. – The Great Anger

if they succumb sooner? I can't look into someone's eyes again and watch my dreams to be together and married pass away. My heart, my mind and my body can't handle that. On the flip side, I don't want to risk contracting the disease only to have my family watch me if the virus beats the medicine.

The uniqueness of being a widow in the LGBTQ+ community comes with so many different challenges but this is the hardest. Finding someone is difficult enough in the Florida panhandle but adding another layer of limiting factors slims the chances. I met a man the other day that I would consider dating. He wanted to go out and he readily informed me in a message:

"Oh and by the way I'm positive but undetectable so everything is fine. You can't contract it if we decide to become romantically involved."

"Oh that adds some complications for me", I messaged back.

"Seriously? You know you can't get it and it's fine. Take PREP. Honestly get educated!"

My heart sank, the words stung and all I could do was reply in truth:

"Honestly, I know all of that but I lost my partner to a terminal illness last year. I took care of him while his illness erased our dreams. I can't go through that again. I'm sorry but I hope you understand."

I haven't heard back since. No sympathy for my loss. No words of understanding. Perhaps it struck a chord in him that he might put someone else into the position of caring for him if the illness took over. Perhaps it was too much for him to process. I imagine that is a great fear in those with HIV/AIDS. Either way it was another moment of ostracized honesty. How is it that I can be misunderstood, treated poorly and dismissed for carrying the widowed disease? An emotional "virus" that has no cure but causes others to retract away in anger or fear? Hard to not feel like I'm covered in "broken".

So than there is the other side of the coin where now I have dated a guy that immediately became too attached. He did not drink alcohol because he had a big problem with it in college but that wasn't an issue for me at the start. However, he wanted to spend all our time together from the beginning. He wanted our dogs to get along from the start. He wanted to basically get married from the start. I couldn't breathe and felt something was very off. Why would I be opposed to being showered in affection? This seemed so strange to me but I had to break it off. In our conversations afterwards it occurred to me that he latched on not because he liked me but because he knew I lost Tin. He knew I was a committed and dedicated partner so if he got me than I could always take care of him and not leave if something went wrong. His addiction for alcohol turned into other addictions that could make him feel safer. He was in it for himself and his own long-term welfare not mine. My loss was being used for someone else's gain. Human behavior is often unsettling.

Year 2 A.C. – The Great Anger

There is one word that always comes to me when people ask what I want since losing Tin. My answer is simple but surprising to most – Safety. I just want safety. To feel safe, stable and hopefully find someone who can travel this road with me. I turn 41 in a couple of months. Age is increasingly on my mind since time has taken so much from me so quickly. Honestly, solitude is safe but very lonely…

September 28, 2019 - The Wings of the Widowed

I can easily say that I do not reach out to Tin's mother and family as much as I should. I want to speak with them but it's hard for me and I feel like I am the immediate reminder, that I trigger all of the grief for them. These widowed weights on my shoulders press down hard at times. It's a double-edged burden. I want to speak with them but I don't want to upset them. So conversations don't happen as often as they maybe should.

I don't know what's harder. Calling? Not calling? Calling and no one answers? Or that no one calls me? I think the hardest is that last one. Once Tin was gone there wasn't really a connection left. They move about their lives with their loss at a distance and I wake up to his pictures, his clothes and his empty side of the bed. The more days that go by the more the family fades. I know they think of me but when someone doesn't tell you than you start to feel the truth that being out of sight is certainly being out of mind. It's frustrating and fearful to feel you're forgotten when your not the one who has passed on.

As the widowed, we know all to well that, overtime, it feels like people have forgotten about our lost love. What they also don't realize is that this feels like we have passed away a little our selves. Now we walk the Earth as souls still with a worldly presence to many but invisible to those who used to see us clearly every day. It's hard not to feel like a phone call from me conjures up an anxious apparition causing them to spook and me to fade back into the safety of the shadows.

In Dante's Divine Comedy there is Inferno, Purgatorio and Paridiso. All those that dwell there are referred to as shades and they make their way through this misty eternal world until they receive their judgment and pass through the gates. I have been through Inferno and I now float in Purgatorio trying to heal from the fires. I fear being sent back through another fiery wave of life so I catch myself always looking behind me while trying to be hopeful for my ascendance. A lost faded shade, I press on.

As I move towards Paridiso, I've realized that the weight behind my shoulders is actually the physical manifestation of my evolution. I can feel the slight beatings start as I grow my widowed wings. Earned for the battles fought, they lift me ever so slightly out of bed, off to work and onto the next step of my journey but when they don't give me rise I am drained by the weight of these great widowed wings. Some days it takes all of my effort to stand and stretch them but when I have the strength to spread them out they provide a safe space for those shades that are not ready to rise yet. I know one day that these frail feathers will be

Year 2 A.C. – The Great Anger

long, wide and strong as long as I keep trusting them. In time they will lift me from the shadows and those stilled shades watching will see that all is possible and they will stand…

October 5, 2019 - Diagnosis Date

We all know the dreaded dates. The anniversary of their death, birthdays, togetherness anniversaries, holidays but there's one more on my list that adds another dark mark on my year - His diagnosis date.

Tin just felt off like he had the flu or something. No strange symptoms. No sudden pains. Just an off feeling. He did complain that he felt bloated but he just thought it might be a stomach bug and just like that, the next day, he had barely any energy and yellowing skin.

That sight is forever trapped in my memories, haunting my recollections of the past. To come home from a regular good work day excited to see him only to find him gravely ill. Unfortunately now I can say I have seen "gravely".

Down three flights of stairs and put him into the car. The hospital was packed, blood was taken and tests were run. My 20 years in animal care gave me a sinking feeling. I had an idea of what was to come.

"Acute terminal liver failure " was all I heard and than the sounds of the room muffled. He was given 8 months to live but he only held on for seven. That was 2 years ago this week and it's more clear and more present than a conversation I had yesterday.

"Bryan, don't you remember what we talked about yesterday?"

"No. I'm sorry. My widowed wisdom hasn't left me any room for new memories..."

October 26, 2019 - Traveler's Remorse

Two weeks traveling abroad in the Brazilian Amazon! How amazing! So exciting! I have never traveled out of the country besides Cancun, Mexico so this was a huge step outside my comfort zone. I haven't had an actual vacation since Tin passed so this would be a break for me to soak up the experience and take the much earned downtime to recharge.

I slept more than I have in two years. I ate more than I have in two years yet now I feel more lost than I have in two years. My trip away didn't help me move forward. I've fallen.I've relapsed big time and I don't have much strength to pull myself up. The flight home built anxiety. Walking into this empty apartment brought clarity. I'm worn down. I'm tired. I'm lost in a familiar places, in familiar crowds. Just lost.

Year 2 A.C. – The Great Anger

Feeling depressed, I went against my better judgment and joined friends at a party tonight. All I could see were the couples that surrounded me making holiday plans, wedding plans, baby plans. I have no plans…I was so excited for my trip but now I realize that it was an escape from an empty life that was patiently waiting for me upon return. No one to pick me up from the airport. No one to grab takeout with. No one to cuddle and share my adventures. Tin is gone and I'm heartbroken.

I don't know what is worse, staying home and missing life or traveling to avoid the fact that life is missing…

November 2, 2019 - Second Season of Spirits

Holidays are hard for me now since Tin and my father are gone. They passed away 10 months apart and it is very clear that so much has gone on that I can't process some situations better than I thought I would. Round 2 of the holidays coming and I'm worse than last year. I guess it makes sense. That whole first year is a blur trying to manage what was going on inside with what had to go on outside and nothing meeting in the middle. I swear it was just the start of the summer and now Halloween has passed and I feel the heavy.

Everyone celebrating pumpkin spice everything, excited about costumes and I can barely fake a smile. Group themed work costumes dumped onto me so, you know, I have too. We have kids' Halloween events at work and I'm a go-to-guy for announcements and costume contest hosting. Surrounded by the Fall festivities, I'm full of Autumn anxiety and everyone is assuming I'm ok.

While everyone was dressed at the start, I waited. I technically didn't need to be in costume early. I had a coworker ask why I wasn't dressed yet in a jokingly judgmental tone. It wasn't the direct question I wanted at the start of this seasonal oppression but it was close enough. I was honest. Clayton and I loved Halloween and now I hate it. Maybe one day I'll enjoy it but not now. He was obviously taken aback but I didn't stop explaining how hard it is to see families with happy dads and kids, couples' costumes, hearing people planning parties you don't want to go to and pretending to be ok. I'm not ok. I'm sad in this season of spirits and it's just beginning.

I got dressed, did my job and got out of costume right away. You'd think that I'd like to pretend to be someone else for a little while but the return from the fantasy hurts worse than staying in my truth. I don't want to be someone else. I just want people to remember who I am, that I am widowed and they should ask how I'm doing. I've always feared that if I'm out of sight than I am out of mind. It's partially true and the hardest part is that when they forget to include my widow-ness they are forgetting about Clayton. They are forgetting about his spirit.

Ironic that I remember as a kid during Halloween being worried about seeing a ghost and now here I am hoping to catch a glimpse of one I'd know…

Year 2 A.C. – The Great Anger

November 16, 2019 - Another Trip Around the Widowed Sun

This was my second birthday since Tin passed. Last year I was the big 4-0 and I wasn't ever expecting to be a widow at that age. One year later and another candle on the cake doesn't add nearly enough light to illuminate this shadowy part of the year.

"Be gentle to yourself." Is a phrase I hear often enough and I try to repeat it on the days I just don't want to get up and get moving. I got myself a massage to help but the quiet lowers my guard, which just brings down the busy and his absence fills the room.

I wanted a quiet night to make myself dinner and just watch some tv but a group of people convinced me to go out for just awhile. Reluctantly I got dressed and headed out. I was grateful for the invite and I was grateful for the birthday cake waiting for me upon arrival. As we headed out to the bar, I thought about how this was my first time going since Tin and I never had the chance. It felt more empty since we had repeatedly said we'd go at some point. I took a deep breath and told myself that this was good for me to get out and start to build myself and my life back up. I have gone from being "Mr. Social" to "Mr. I'll Go Next Time".

As the night went on, we shared drinks and laughs. I was feeling a bit more myself I guess. Headed to the bar for another round and a friend said:

"So how are you doing? Are you doing ok?"

I knew he meant well. I just wish he knew to not ask right than on my birthday surrounded by couples as an odd man out but the non-widowed don't see the world in the way that we do - our world through widowed glasses. I had finally let go of my anxiousness to be there in that place in that time without Tin but the Universe wouldn't let me be for just one moment. I tried to keep up the act but the scene had changed. I blamed the time. I blamed the bartender. I blamed my old age of 41 and made my exit. By the time I was home I was in full tears and seeing the start to another year without him…

November 30, 2019 - Thanks-Grieving

Last year I could barely walk through the grocery store during the holidays. Thanksgiving has always been my favorite and the thought of even buying ingredients was too much. This year, I told myself that it wasn't right to stop celebrating. Tin wouldn't want that at all. So I took a deep breath, swallowed what felt like a rock in my throat and grabbed a turkey. My eyes welled up and I told myself to go checkout. I had to go to the store three separate times to buy what I needed because I would hit a breaking point each time. Seasonings, cider, wine, apple pie, butter – God did Tin love butter. Those tears started in the dairy aisle and I had to go check out. All things gathered and I could prep. I had the turkey ready for the next morning and the bread for stuffing drying out in the oven. I was making my way through it all by cooking only my favorites. I felt comfortable as I created the culinary traditions of my

Year 2 A.C. – The Great Anger

youth. I was floating in and out of nostalgic memories full knowing it was only because I was avoiding the reminder recipes - The Guarded Gourmet.

I woke up on Thanksgiving and fought to get out of bed. I had made it this far but putting that turkey into the oven meant I was moving forward without him. I never thought that the closing of an oven door could feel like the closing of a chapter in my life. The sound was deafening as I felt the preheat dissipating replaced by a chill reminding me his warmth was gone. I sat on the kitchen floor and cried.

Hours later, I pulled myself together and gathered up what I was bringing to a friend's. A small group, which helped reduced the anxiety. I moved through the holiday catching manageable memories like compartmentalized condiments off to the side that I could see but choose not to use - but there is always grief in the gravy.

As we wrapped up the evening, conversation lead to how many Thanksgivings it had been since I had been home with family. I couldn't remember so I started counting back and realized it was a road map though my loss. This was the second without Tin. Then the first. Then his last. Than our first in our new found beach life. Our last in Atlanta. Our first together. My last before we met.

Now I find myself Thanks-Grieving…

December 14, 2019 - I Choose to Believe

A week ago I was given an opportunity at a big event to share with my essential oil community about inclusion, community and growth. It amazes me what has come into my life in the past year. Part of my oil journey is the loss of Tin. I share about him in every speech I give. I share about Soaring Spirits and I share about the widowed Facebook support group, A Widow's Valor, that gives those in the Young Living oily community a place to be surrounded by other oilers. Talking about my loss isn't easier, it's just different. I'll always be a work in progress and, as I practice reflection and present time, I can pull myself from the tough days to look at the big picture of my journey and rebuilding. When I stop and take time to look at my journey I can see that I have accomplished something amazing – I survived and now I'm beginning to thrive.

All of our journeys look different but something we all have in common is that our journeys have highs and lows. It's what I do in my lows that I want to share with you because it brings me back to neutral and I can begin my forward growth again. I have had to learn (which is always a changing landscape) that when the hard thoughts pour in I can control the intensity of the storm. I can't stop it, the emotions are strong but the ability to slow its winds is empowering. I never deny how I am feeling. I accept it. I accept what has happened. I accept my loss and I accept my grief. Fighting it only makes the storm worse for me and I lose control. They say that knowing your enemy gives you the advantage so when I acknowledge

Year 2 A.C. – The Great Anger

the storm I can predict its path and move out of the way. Some storms hit harder and I don't move fast enough but there is always the opportunity to get back up, grow stronger and be ever more ready for the next storm.

When I take this approach I begin to feel grounded, forgive myself for falling back, release what I cannot control, bring myself to the present time, feel my strength return and I just believe. I believe in whatever small bit of hope I can. It could be as small as telling myself that the next breath will be easier, the next minute will be calmer and I choose to believe.

I've looked into many ways to manage my experience with grief and loss. I couldn't find the right resource or book that spoke to me. While at my event last week, a friend said she felt called to tell me about a book she had just read and implemented called "Super Attractor" by Gabrielle Bernstein. I downloaded the book and listened along the 5 1/2 hour drive. By the end of my drive I had not only heard the words, I felt them fit in a way that I have been searching. For me and my spirituality, I can't believe that everything happens for a reason and that I control my destiny, those 2 mindsets oppose themselves and strengthens my storms. So I choose that everything happens for a reason and surrender that to the universe and look for signs that I am being guided.

I have been missing Tin more this week as the holidays approach and I have no family near me. The storm of lonely sent an approaching chilled breeze to kindly warn me it was approaching. I felt myself get heavy and instead of tensing up I leaned into the feeling and asked the universe for some sign. Shortly after, I walked into my office and stopped in my tracks at the sight of my coworker's wedding ring on his desk. He never takes it off. I felt those feelings you'd expect the widowed to feel seeing a lonely wedding ring. It symbolized everything difficult for that week and than the thought hit – Although I couldn't see my coworker I knew he was still around. Chills ran through me and I accepted the wisdom I had just been given. Just because I can't see Tin doesn't mean he is not nearby. I smiled looking at that ring and felt great gratitude for the change in my perception. It wasn't a reminder I was alone, it was a reminder that I'm never alone as long as I remember to just believe…

December 21, 2019 - The Ghost of Christmas Past, Present and Future

Thanksgiving was a beast in itself but Christmas can be the kraken in unicorn's clothing. I love parts of Christmas like the lights, smell of Christmas trees and giving others gifts. It's the other parts - families gathering, couples under the mistletoe, Hallmark everything that always ends up like a fairytale…

Tin was 1000% in with Christmas. We had decorations everywhere and so many lights that 9pm felt like 9am. He lit up at the chance to decorate and wrap presents and I loved sitting on the couch and watching him wrap gifts by the tree. I just can't get that image out of my mind every time I get a gift for someone and think of wrapping it. A chill runs and I know I'm being visited by my Ghost of Christmas Past. I want to love Christmas again but that healing is in the hands of Father Time.

Year 2 A.C. – The Great Anger

So ensues the expected question:

"What are you doing for the holidays? Are you going home?"

Attempting to hold in emotional expression, "No. Not this year."

"So your family is coming than?"

Again maintaining a neutral reaction, "Nope."

And than it hits:

"So you're spending the holidays alone this year?" with a clear saddened expression.

I can't control the shoulder shrug. It's automatic to look down at the floor so I don't have to see their reaction but more importantly I don't want to see my own grief in reflected back in their eyes. In an effort to search for a solution for me they continue:

"Oh well what are you doing? Going to a friend's?"

"Ah. My friends are with their families or out of town."

The conversation awkwardly ends and I feel worse but I'm not sure if I feel worse for myself or for the person that was just asking a "normal person's life" question. It's a double hit when your loss causes others to feel bad in a time when they are just looking for conversation and connection. They are less likely to reach out next time and I fight daily to ward off the cloak of widowed lonely.

Then there are the beautiful friends that see me for where I am and invite me into their home. I want to go but the opposite happens and I fear the moments when they are opening each other's presents and I fade from sight like a Ghost of Present Time.

Now I wait. I wait for the arrival of the Ghost of Christmas Future. Is he wrapped in chains of holiday grief or is he lifted by the spirit of the season?

December 28, 2019 - Already A New Year Without You

I'm halfway through this winter warfare others call "the most wonderful time of the year". The annual arrival of the four holiday horsemen. Just as one battle ends another commences giving us barely enough time to heal the wounds and gather back the troops. Thanksgiving with grief in the gravy. Christmas' hallmark heartaches. Now the approach of a New Year further away from our yesterdays with the final horseman named St. Valentine charging into battle just a month after.

Year 2 A.C. – The Great Anger

The birth of a new year and new opportunity does not pass without the reminder of that you have passed Tin. The world celebrates renewal and couples kiss at midnight. It's a reminder that our last New Year's kiss is another year farther out of reach behind me. In one hand I hold hurt and in the other hope. Already about to start a third time around the sun without you here by my side but in fleeting moments it still feels like yesterday.

They tell you when you're young to not rush life and that, one day, you will understand. I just didn't know that day would happen so soon, so fast, so young and it still feels so new that I can't believe I'm starting another year without you...

January 4, 2029 - Long Lost Pineapple Shorts

I'm laying in bed and I'm only 4 days away from heading to Hawaii. I post on Facebook about the trip. In the post I ask who am I going to see there?

Within moments of me posting, I hear something slide and fall in the bedroom closet. Roan (my dog) gets off the bed and goes to the closet, looks at me, walks in and out and walks over to me. He looks at me and than towards the closet and back to me. I have a sudden feeling about Clayton. I get up and look in the closet....

I see that Clayton's yard stick that reads "Antiques and Beyond" has slid down the wall towards the shelves. That yard stick has been there for almost 2 years. I look up towards the shelves it is pointing towards and see something that I had entirely forgotten about....Clayton's pineapple shorts! He had

bought those shorts about 2 years ago and wore them to the aquarium on his last visit there to see his favorite penguin.

There is no explanation for me to post "who will I see in Hawaii ", his yard stick sliding for no reason after 2 years of nothing and leading me to find Tin's pineapple shorts that I forgot I still had. I truly believe these are signs...

Tin is always with me and I feel that something incredible and amazingly positive is going to happen in Hawaii ????????

This is 2020 - My year of clarity!

I know I'm not the only one with these things happening. What signs have you seen????

Year 2 A.C. – The Great Anger

January 18, 2020 - Divine Dimes

I have been more open-minded and openhearted to try and see signs from Tin. Some say that it is just circumstance but it helps me. It is really interesting how we have preset thoughts about certain things and "superstitions". For my whole life I always heard that if you find a penny than it is a penny from Heaven -A small shiny token to tell you that there are others watching out for you.

My Grandfather was big on this and loved to find and collect pennies. When my Grandfather passed away, five pennies were placed on his grave to represent each of his children. Nowadays, if we find pennies than it's Grandpa saying hello.

This week I found a dime. Not unheard of but not as common. Perhaps people lose pennies easier because of their lesser monetary value. Who really knows? All I know is that there I found a dime. I had been struggling in my mind about a business issue I had and I just couldn't figure out what to do next. I looked down and there was the dime. Automatically I thought "Thanks Grandpa. This is you telling me you are here times 10! I felt better. I felt less alone. I felt like I could relax and stop worrying as much about my business decision. I took a deep breath and took a photo because I felt gratitude for my mind shift.

I posted the photo on social media in hopes I would bring positivity to others. People commented about pennies, feeling a sense their loved ones were around and other signs they get. I felt good sharing about the dime. Near the end of the day I had a friend leave a surprise comment …."Ten = Tin". I started to tear up. I was so focused on pennies from Grandpa that I almost missed a message from Tin. Had I not posted, I would not have realized that perspective. Life moments don't have voicemail and texts for you to rewind and look back on. Give yourself time to see your world and the messages you are being gifted…

January 24, 2020 - Social Media Inspiration

After awhile, our friends and family don't get the daily loss reminders we do. I get these strong urges to post on social media and remind them but those posts have evolved into a way to try and help anyone who needs it. This week, as I sit in my car, I just started writing.....

It's been almost 2 years since Clayton passed away. Sometimes it feels like yesterday and sometimes it feels like an eternity.

Until you've been through it, there is no way to truly understand what it is like to be widowed. Even within our own community we all have different experiences that shape us as we move forward because we never "move on". Our person always remains part of us. Some of us lose our person unexpectedly and some of us know it's coming. Neither is easier. For me, caring for Tin with terminal liver failure was not just emotional and not just tiring. I gave myself up but I wouldn't change one second of it.

Year 2 A.C. – The Great Anger

When you care for someone, knowing that the days are tightly numbered, you release all sense of who you are and pour into their needs in hope their last days are as full as possible. No one warns you that after your person has passed on you find yourself with all the time in the world thinking about who you don't have anymore. The most startling part is that you also don't know you.

After weeks, months and even years you start to focus more on discovering, learning and accepting who you now are on the other side of the trauma. You find new fears have been born and new walls have been built up. Where you once stood in a clear path of self-awareness, you now find yourself in a maze with no map. It's taken me almost 2 years to feel like I am finding my way through new thoughts, emotions, self reflection and enlightenment. I'm slowly feeling a bit grounded and not so lost. As I gather more footing, I know that the new man standing is not the one he used to be. The only way I can explain it is sometimes I feel like I'm my own stranger. I spent so much time not checking in with me through it all that now I need to learn who I am all over again. To start, taking care of Tin I gained 20 lbs and stopped focusing on my health. Since January 1st, I have lost 6lbs and have focused more on decisions that are right for my wellness. Doesn't seem like a big deal but 2 years ago I could hardly get out of bed. Grief can easily imprison you...

Last year was mostly fog but this past year I have begun to travel my new road. The animals will always be a huge part of me but I'm learning to bring more balance to all aspects of my life. I know that I have the strength and determination to create my new wellness and I am very aware that part of my growth and happiness is helping as many others as I can.

So here is to 2020! A year of self focus, self care and sharing unapologetically about my journey from the pain to positivity. I know there are negative individuals that have their opinions but those people can just continue to sit stagnant not making a difference in this world while I move forward towards positive change. I wish them well and I'll be here if they find they need me.

Sharing my story can be hard but I know there are many who can find hope within it and if sharing helps just one more person not feel alone than it's worth it...

Year 2 A.C. – The Great Anger

February 1, 2020 - Skeletons in the Closet

Well it's almost 2 years now and I finally gave in. I haven't really gone through our closet since Tin passed away.

Each time I'd go in the closet I would feel like there were skeletons about to grab me. I'd choke up seeing a jacket he wore, a scarf he wrapped, a shirt that was there for a special event we had together. Sometimes I just need to get things out of my sight or they will keep haunting me so, soon after Tin passed, I went into the closet and pulled out most of his clothes to donate. I cried hysterically pulling those memories from their hangers in fear that I would forget them or him or us or some unreasonable thought in that moment but felt so true as I put Tin's stuff in a bag to be handed away forever. I got through shirts and shoes but my body gave in, I sat on the floor and sobbed uncontrollably. He was really gone…

For the past 2 years I have rarely gone in that closet. My clothes go in the hamper, into the laundry, onto the chair and I re-wear them. Something about that closet haunted me more this week than ever but it felt different. It didn't feel full of skeletons. It just felt empty and eerie. There was a calling but no voice. A pull but no hand. Something in me told me I had changed and moved forward.

I began to pull stuff out one by one. I caught myself slowing down and a little voice said to grab it all at once and get it out of the closet. I grabbed handfuls of all our clothes and threw them on the bed. Something about getting them across the threshold changed me. I felt lighter, relieved I guess? I began listening to music and separating out what needed to stay and what needed to go. When I'd catch myself pausing on one of Tin's items my new response was to remind myself that holding on to it wouldn't keep him here or bring him back. That's not the job of objects. That's the job of my head, my heart and my voice still speaking his name.

Tin wouldn't want me to be buried in fabric memories suffocating in sadness. The closet is now just mine. It doesn't negate that Tin existed. It just means that I've taken another necessary deep breath and step forward on this new path cleared of skeletons in the closet…

Feb 6, 2020 - Someone Else's Memories *sigh*

Just an ordinary widowed day. Get up, brush my teeth, look at the dishes and laundry I didn't have time to do, *sigh*, take the dog out - Pretty standard these days. Roan and I start our walk grabbing a bag because we pick up after ourselves. Well actually I clean up after us. Just me. No one to help. *sigh*.

We walk the same way every morning around the apartment complex, past the trees, past the parking lot and over the grass. *sigh*

Year 2 A.C. – The Great Anger

I've stopped looking around. I just check my phone to see who's posted what, who's going where. Flipping through seeing everyone else complaining. *sigh*

Every once in awhile Roan tugs on the leash but today felt different. He stopped and waited while I kept walking. I looked back to see he was staring up at a Jeep wagging his tail and sniffing excitedly. *sigh*

Tin always took Roan on drives in his Jeep…

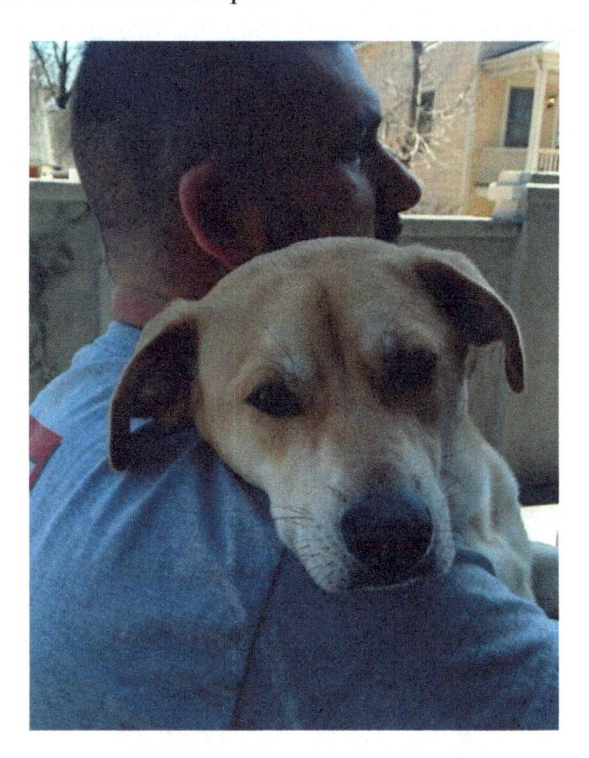

February 15, 2020 - Moving Forward…

My second Valentine's without you. The first one was a fog. The second one I'm wide awake with full clarity to feel all the feelings. To say today is fine would be dishonest. Today is hard but I know that I'll be ok. I am safe.

Since Tin's passing, I have found that my open sharing of this journey has provided a voice for many others that just aren't ready to share, don't know how too or feel they are completely alone in their grief. They just need to feel safe. Sharing my loss doesn't make it easier, it just is different. It doesn't mean that I am "moving on". I can only move forward...

For those of us that are widowed, we know all too well that you feel a tremendous weight bearing down making it so very difficult to stand. The energy it can take makes it even hard to lift your head some days. We struggle to understand where this new weight has come from. Is it loss? Is it hopelessness? Feeling unsafe? The odd thing is that those feelings are

Year 2 A.C. – The Great Anger

due to lack and that doesn't explain the feeling of weight. Through sharing my journey I have discovered what is weighing down on us is actually gifted wings...

I never asked for them but the Universe has a plan so I have been given the wings of the widowed. Heavy, but hauntingly beautiful, these wings weigh us down at first but, as we move forward we strengthen, stand and stretch. It's up to us to realize these wings are there and embrace that they can help lift us up. We can't give them back. We can't hide them. We can only choose how to use them. I can either stay hidden under their cover or trust they will help me soar safe. I choose the latter. When we take our struggles and see them as a potential gift, it gives us the opportunity to change our worlds. My life has changed drastically by shifting my mindset. There are many of us that carry the different wings of the wounded. Whatever YOUR wound, your struggle can be your biggest strength if you choose to use it. Sharing your story empowers you to help yourself and help others. That is uplifting!

Today, on the day that so many others are posting about flowers, candy, arguing about where to go to dinner and aggravated that all reservations are booked, stop and think if there is anyone in your world that might be hiding under their wounded wings. Reach out and offer a hand to help them stand, stretch, strengthen and start to soar. Sometimes a simple "I see you" can help reassure them that they are safe. Feel free to share this post because there is probably someone you know that this resonates with.

Now I want you to let this next statement sink in -

It's ok to show the world your wings...

February 22, 2020 - Smoothing Out the Sea Glass

The intense emotions of losing Clayton are fewer these days. I don't know if that's a blessing or a curse. Double-edged sword I suppose. On one hand there is constant aching you can expect day after day. On the other hand you find reprieve from the bands of meteorological mess. Joy slips in, you drop your guard and the next "feelings front" sneaks in under the radar to pull you off the path soaked in sadness widowly waiting for the visibility to return.

Just such an unpredicted event happened yesterday. Ahead of the game with chores I decided to tackle one more project I should have left well enough alone for a more somber day.

Year 2 A.C. – The Great Anger

Rummaging through my paperwork to organize, I found a notebook that looked familiar but I couldn't place it. I opened it randomly in the middle to find random shopping lists and "to dos".

"Might as well check the beginning of the notebook too"

In the comfort of my home and the turn of a few pages I instantly found myself in the middle of a first page weather front. My chest clenched, my breath stopped and I swear I heard my heart crack like the sound emotional lightning. I remember this notebook now. I brought it to Clayton in the hospital so we could go over his dying wishes. There in front of me, blurred from the torrent of tears, were Clayton's last desires. Who he held dear in his life and what they would take in memory of him when he was gone. A beautifully complicated life whittled down to just a list of who and what. No piece of paper has ever cut me so deep and the pain stayed all day. My smooth appearing exterior now had a new rough-edged wound that I couldn't hide.

After the first big widowed storm subsides, your left covered in shards and sharp edges. Along our new path we are hit time and time again with widowed weather. Sand whips our faces and the crashing waves throw us tumbling in the tideline while each emotion erodes our rough edges slowly smoothing the surface. Like a treasured piece of sea glass, we appear beautiful on the outside but a surprise emotional earthquake can break us open turning us back into a sharp object others avoid. Now it's more widowed waiting for the sands and the waves to smooth my newest rough edges…

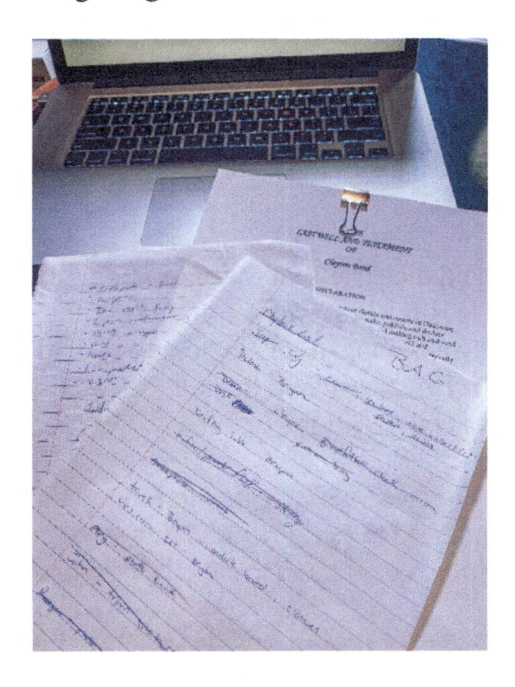

Year 2 A.C. – The Great Anger

February 29, 2020 - Two Unlikely Companions

Boarding my plane to attend and present at the Soaring Spirits LGBTQ widowed event in Los Angeles this week and feeling more nervous than I have ever felt speaking. I have presented in front of audiences over 500 people about a variety of topics from penguins to being widowed. Broad range of topics but my life has always been unique and a bit eccentric. I was given the middle seat on a flight from Atlanta to San Diego. I can only hope that my neighbors on either side are good humans.

With only a few minutes before departure, I have the row to myself until a very winded young woman waves her hand to inform me that she is in the window seat. She is rapidly talking on the phone to someone I can only assume she is in a relationship with:

"I'm on the plane and just got to my seat."

"I almost didn't make it."

"I'll see you soon. I love you"

Here I am sitting in a middle seat, alone, heading to speak at a widowed event hearing a conversation I pray I could someday have with someone.

Stay calm Bryan. Stay calm.

It's jarring when it seems the oxygen gets scarce suddenly. If people only knew how often something is said and it silently takes your breath away. Those basic conversations in life that escape those who now speak widowed words. I know better than to let it fully get to me. I know that I'm here on this plane for some reason. Dear Universe please point out a reason sooner rather than later.

The doors of the plane close and the aisle seat is empty. I shift over and feel the space I've gained. A bit emotionally safer is the best way I could describe it. What appears to be just an empty seat to some, so clearly represents to me the opposite ends of the world I feel this young woman and I are living. I'm gearing up to isolate myself with earphones and time wasting tasks when she begins conversation.

She is young, energetic and very sweet. She begins to tell me that she almost missed her flight and that she is getting married to her girlfriend this weekend. Universe what are you trying to tell me? I'm 10,000 miles up, I can't escape her pure joy and it is beginning to hurt.

I continue cordial conversation and it becomes my turn. How I hate sharing my loss with someone who is headed towards fulfilling their heart. Guilt gathers with grief in so many forms. Nowhere to run and my only option is to release the truth. He's gone and I'm headed

Year 2 A.C. – The Great Anger

to spend time in community with others who have lost what you are about to gain. I'm so very sorry for this bit of shade I cast onto your bright journey young woman.

Then the Universe answered "why" in such a loud response that my heart was struck with pure wonder. Her fiancé has been sick and may have a terminal illness. That giant gap between us was actually space for us to come together in a way I never expected. She shared how deeply she was in love and it reminded me of me when Tin was diagnosed. Like a reflection I could speak too. How in the world can it be a coincidence? She spoke truths about her feelings of unconditional love just as I had given to Clayton. She shared her partner's insecurities and guilt for being ill just as Clayton had. I have never had that conversation with anyone and there this young woman was speaking my heart out loud for me to hear for the first time.

Now I write these words as I am flying over Texas, where Clayton grew up. I'm looking around and other people's video screens are playing different movies but all with weddings. Life is to be celebrated so I bought her a drink and congratulated her on her wedding. Aboard a flight traveling to speak of losses, I am suddenly filled with hope. Thank you young beautiful woman for sharing your inspirational joy with me today. You kept me from guarding myself, showed me more than you know and I am so very grateful…

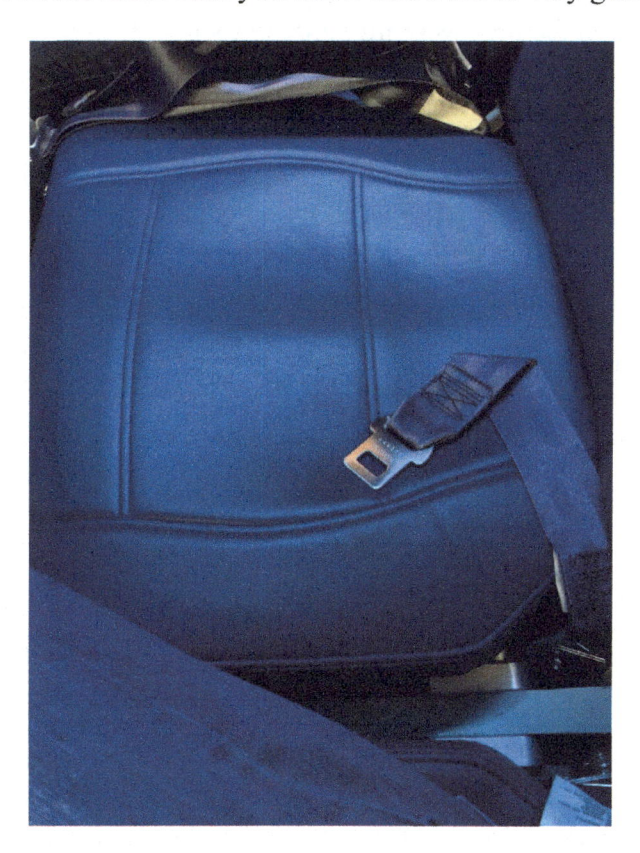

Year 2 A.C. – The Great Anger

March 7, 2020 - Arriving in Community

Until last Saturday, I had never been to a Camp Widow event. I watched as a team of dedicated, compassionate and talented people created a space for the LGBTQ widowed. Held at the beautiful Los Angeles LGBTQ center, was the first ever event for my subgroup in the widowed population. If you've attended an event, you know the work that the Soaring Spirits Team pours out for months, weeks, days, minutes and seconds to get things organized. With this being the first ever pop-up camp, I watched in awe as novel situations presented themselves and the team effortlessly navigated the new waters. I wasn't sure what to expect myself. I gave myself permission to be fully present and feel however I wanted minute by minute.

I jumped in to help with registration and camper check-in. I was nervous but than realized the gift I had been given. I was the person to welcome these other widows into a space we all desperately needed. Some greeted me with smiles while others could barely speak their name without starting to show signs of deep grief. I had the honor to greet them exactly as they were and hold them in their sadness. With the initial emotional release, space was made within them and I watched sadness give birth to a sign of relief and joy. I was the one greeting and comforting them on the outside but on the inside they were helping me acknowledge that my own feelings were mirrored in their tears and that my deepest fear of being alone was being replaced with beautiful community.

Campers were of all ages, types and at different places along their widowed journey. Those seasoned widows providing a look at a hopeful future. Those new to their journey (as little as 2 weeks before) arrived reminding all of us about our starts and the strength it took to take those first steps along our new normal. Everywhere I looked I saw inspiration, hope and felt deep gratitude.

The opening remarks from Soaring Spirits creator Michelle, was a call to community and an assurance that this space was safe for all. Talented interior designer Nate Berkus was the keynote speaker who, in a fantastic interview style, spoke openly about his widowed experience. For those of you who have been following this blog, you know that my partner Clayton was an interior designer. The book Tin was reading during his illness was written by Nate. Flipping through the book, Clayton had dog-eared the page where Nate describes the moments before losing Fernando. It was like Clayton knew the storm of emotional tragedy I would be caught up in and showed me someone else I could relate and look to for inspiration. I brought the book with me just in case I had an opportunity for Nate to sign it and it was taken to the Green Room. Part of me felt so nervous not having it in my hands but I new in order to continue to heal, I needed to trust. Seems a little funny now but in the moment I felt like I was letting go of a big part of who Clayton was and fearing it would be gone forever. That's the part of widowhood where I'm realizing holding on to material possessions don't validate that Tin existed. Book or no book, Clayton is in my memories and heart. There was a sense of relief to give that trust. After Nate's talk, I had the honor of meeting him, sharing a little about my journey and sharing a deep moment of understanding that I never thought I

Year 2 A.C. – The Great Anger

would have from the man I saw on the book cover. I feel like I have gained a new friend who has written a beautiful message to Tin and I. How does one verbalize gratitude for that level of gifted connection?

The rest of the day I found myself surrounded by stories about loss, dedication and love. I heard my own story in the words of others and I felt like pieces of me I had lost were returning. From stories of other caregivers, LGBTQ individuals that felt discrimination on their journey to a group of 5 guys named Bryan (Brian) the magic connection moments were everywhere I turned. Being widowed is sometimes a haunting gift. We have a greater knowledge of our superpower – LOVE…

I cannot express enough that everyone should make the time and space to attend a Camp Widow event. I also cannot express the immense gratitude I have for all of Soaring Spirits and for all of you. We are each other's wings…

(Above Photo Credit: Soaring Spirits International)

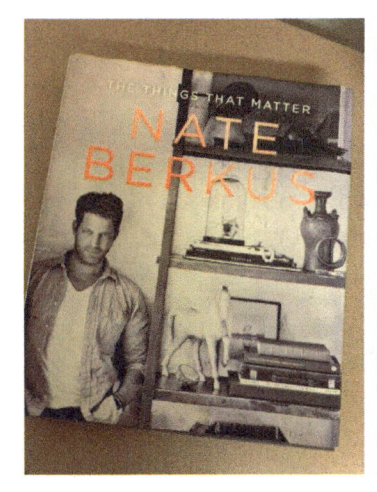

Year 2 A.C. – The Great Anger

March 14, 2020 - Gravely Grateful

"I wished he was dead!" she said.

"I honestly wished he was dead!" she said again with deep conviction.

The words felt like bullets. I gasped, put my hand on my heart and put my head down. A couple was speaking on stage at an event, sharing their journey through his substance abuse and how it had almost tore the family apart. They were raw, open, honest with their struggles and their road to where they were today. Up until her declaration, I found such deep beauty in the commitment they had toward their relationship.

I had to go. I had to get out. I couldn't stop the tears. I couldn't hold in the ball of hurt, sadness, pain and anguish rising in my throat. I was gagging on my grief. Why did she have to say that wish?

I found a stairwell and just sat. There was nowhere to hide and I didn't care. The entire room had heard me share my story about losing Tin and what the loss of your person causes us. Often I'll manage my grief in private but I was done guarding everyone else against the involuntary insult of my visible emotions. Yes there is sometimes guilt in openly grieving. I don't like upsetting people so if they see me upset I actually feel worse. It's a tough balance some days but not today.

I let the emotions come and walked through my feelings. My eyes burned, my hands felt cold and my heart ached. Standing in the middle of the fire, there I met Anger. He has been fairly silent about our loss. I knew he would come. I didn't know when or where but I prepared myself. Instead of embracing his arrival, I stopped and asked him a question.

"Hello Anger. We haven't spoken much and I know that's not ok. You've been through a lot. Tell me, my friend, what caused you to wake?"

"She didn't think about your loss. She should have remembered you. She doesn't understand that death is a dangerous wish. She doesn't understand the hurt she is causing!"

"Anger." I said. "She didn't mean it. She is sharing her struggles to try and help everyone out and her truth is her story. Her intent is good. You're not mad at her. You are mad that you lost Clayton and that is ok but don't be angry with her. She is just sharing the emotions from her trials and that does not negate yours."

"But why does she get to wish him dead and get to keep her person? Why does she get to say those things and take for granted the gift she holds?"

We both felt a change in pressure and took a unified sigh. I felt Anger's fire weaken, smolder and begin to smoke.

Year 2 A.C. – The Great Anger

"Because she doesn't know what it's like to be gravely grateful. Anger, she can only sympathize with us and I don't think we ever want to wish for someone to experience widowed empathy right?"

"No. I wouldn't wish that on anyone."

It was hard to see him now. The smoke had filled the space between us. His voice had weakened. His shape changed as Anger took a seat on the floor of my mind. The calming brought a cool breeze that took the smoke with it and there, where Anger had stood, sat Sadness. I walked over to him. I looked into his deep blue eyes and just held him...

March 21, 2020 - Finding Grief in the Garbage

This is all very strange. The world has come to a slow crawl with this corona virus and it's a bit disorienting. I've had some tough times in life but I choose to focus on the positive outcomes through adversity....

Let's all find gratitude in the garbage.

I am grateful for an amazingly supportive management team at my job.

I am grateful that I am staying home more. Since Tin passed away (only and almost 2 yrs ago) I haven't taken enough time to sit, reflect and hold space for myself like I have this weekend. I was widow worried that my lonely was coming to get me. Surprisingly enough, this has given me time to realize it's ok to slow down. I don't have to keep busy to keep the grief at bay. I have been worried that relaxing would turn into depression but I'm finding it's actually the opposite.

I am grateful that (in this social distancing) we are all actually slowing down together and connecting with one another by phone and video chat. We are actually socializing more in

Year 2 A.C. – The Great Anger

many ways. I have been on long phone calls with friends I haven't actually spoken with in years. Funny how I feel less lonely now during a pandemic. Strange how the fates unfold.

I am grateful that the planet is getting a break from the wear and tear of daily human life. Of course I wish for everyone to be healthy and safe but I'm trying to see positivity in all this. The earth seems to be cleansing and healing a bit. Once all of this is over, maybe we should consider giving the planet a yearly vacation from the people.

If you don't find gratitude in the garbage than you're always looking at a life as a pile of trash. It's hard but placing perspective on perception can take you to better places…

Stay Safe my Widowed Family

March 28, 2020 - Season of Anger

I try to stay pretty positive but I'm already furious at all of those people who are complaining they are going crazy being stuck at home with their spouses and their children. I understand how this weird situation can be on everyone but can they just manage one week of being inconvenienced before jumping on social media to post how difficult it is to be surrounded by family? Could they just think about what gifts they have been given? So many would love to have what you are starting to take for granted. Just shut up! Please just shut up!!

Some people would say to avoid social media right now but that is my main source of socialization since Tin passed. I have no family near and very few friends around. Those friends have families to tend too. So if I don't have social media, I am unbelievably secluded and that's really hard for a lifelong extrovert who loves to make people smile and laugh. I've lost more than Clayton. I've lost me and I'm trying to get back to me but life isn't lining up.

Year 2 A.C. – The Great Anger

I'm so angry and upset with the selfishness I'm seeing. Sorry I don't feel bad that you have "forced time" with loved ones. There are people that have lost their family, children and/ or their spouse and would give anything to have them back. Most of all, don't wish people away because you never know when they'll be taken from you.

I'm always mindful of my emotions and keeping them in check. However, now I really want to lash out. The anniversary of losing Tin is right around the corner. Leaving my house to try and be social is all I know to keep from feeling unbelievably sad and now I'm stuck at home. I can't get away from our apartment and it hurts. I was hoping to find a house to buy before my lease was up but this situation has stopped everything. I'm forced to sign my lease and renew another year in this constant reminder of empty space. He died on the anniversary of us moving in. Every page that needed my initials has April 16th scattered about like all the broken pieces of me I can't seem to pick up.

I have an honest question to ask. I don't ever want bad things to happen to people but are you ever so mad at people's lack of realty that you just want something to scare the gratitude back into them? Is that crazy? Am I the only one that thinks that? Like the whole family is in their perfect car going down their perfect street to their perfect house when a giant deer runs across the road and barely misses them. Then they realize they aren't invincible and that fairytales can be dangerous? That life can be difficult and scary? I mean really difficult. Not that social scare when little Timmy doesn't get a trophy for participating and his life is over. I mean really hard tough life events. Yes I know I am in the season of widowed anger. I just have to weather this part of the storm.

This is the second blog I've written recently where Anger has been the leading character. I see that. I realize where I am in my processing. We all go through our stages of grief on our timeline but does anyone have any advice for dealing with the end of year 2, in the stage of anger, during a quarantined pandemic, for a guy who's fairytale was just to have a family while everyone else is complaining that they have a family?

In these strange days, I'm trying really hard look for gratitude not grievance in this garbage...

Year 2 A.C. – The Great Anger

April 4, 2020 - Please Pass the Salt

When I was younger I rarely said no to food. I liked almost everything except baked macaroni and cheese with stewed tomatoes. Absolutely hated it but it was my Dad's favorite.

"Do I have to eat this?" I said. "I'll eat anything else."

"You'll eat what's put in front of you." said my Dad.

He was raised with 6 other siblings in the old Irish Boston projects so you take what you can get. I'd eat the smallest amount I had to so I could get away from that table. Had I known I'd lose my dad 10 months before Clayton, I would have eaten all the baked macaroni and cheese with stewed tomatoes that he wanted just to spend more time with him at that dinner table. It's funny how the situations of our past show up in our future so many years later…

"I'll have the pandemic with a side of impending anniversary grief please."

"Order Up" the Universe replied.

I never actually ordered that. I have, however, been asking for life to slow down and I guess I got my wish but this isn't what I meant.

Now it's like I'm at a 7course meal and I keep being served crap. I try to be positive about the next course and it's over seasoned, under seasoned, under cooked, overcooked, full of empty emotional calories and cold.

"Excuse me, Universe. I'm not usually the one to send food back but this plate of bland cold life is just not good. Can you run it back to the kitchen and warm it up please?

"Sorry sir but our Executive Universe Chef is an artist and sending it back won't get you a new creation. You'll just have to eat what's put in front of you…"

In 12 days it will be the second anniversary of Tin's passing. How has it been 2 years already? It hurts. What seemed like agonizingly difficult days during his illness are long gone. What I would give to work all day, come home and have dinner with him. At a time that I really need to be around people, I'm forced to be socially distant. What is social distancing anyways? It feels like the world is getting a lesson in widowhood. The life they are used too, the people they want to interact with and everything they love is gone so they sit at home feeling depressed except, in this version of a grief journey, there is another side and they'll get it all back. They'll get to sit down and have dinner together again. I hope they all appreciate it when it all returns and they get the get the chance again to say:

"Please Pass the Salt."

Year 2 A.C. – The Great Anger

April 11, 2020 - Nothing and Everything to Say

As I'm just days away from the second anniversary of Clayton's death, I'm finding myself in all sorts of mental states. The past 3 days I have been happy, sad, depressed, angry, energetic, exhausted, fearful, lonely, hurt, hungry, not hungry, over motivated and under-motivated. I want to talk and I don't want to talk. I guess I'm suffering from quarantine grief disorder. Heck, after all this we will all be diagnosed with PTCD – Post Traumatic Corona Disorder.

I'm so all over the place right now that I really don't know what to write today. There is nothing and everything to say. I don't have a specific focus for this week's blog and I realize that is actually what I should write about. I always try to be present in my submissions and cover all aspects of my journey. I felt like I needed to have something today but it turns out that having nothing to say is also part of the everything. I just don't really know what to say.

Over the past week, I have felt more distant from people despite what I'm doing to stay connected. It's also upsetting to me that people don't remember April 16th is the day but then again I can't expect them to remember my grief-aversary.

The thing of it is that people are asking each other more and more how they are doing and I have so little and so much to say that I can't express it.

"How are you doing with all this social distancing stuff?"

"Thursday is the day I lost Clayton only and already 2 years ago. I honestly don't know."

It says so little and so much all at once...

The Care-Griever Years:
Year 3 A.C.

Pandemic and Self-Passiveness

Year 3 A.C. – Pandemic and Self-Passiveness

Year 3 was the hardest for me. Year 1's fog. Year 2's anger. Year 3 I gave up on me. I reached his third death date anniversary alone in a pandemic. No socializing to help soften the date. The depression was starting to set in. I had excuse after excuse to lay on the couch, eat whatever and drink more wine than I should. Year 3 could have been the year I got stuck repeating had it not been for a new social media app keeping people connected through videos and dancing. A friend reached out worried for my mental health declining. She suggested I join Tiktok because I loved dancing. With nothing better to do, I joined and started scrolling.

I caught myself smiling at the free spirits dancing like no one was watching. They reminded me of me before the grief set in. It took a bit to gather the courage to dance. My first Tiktok on March 15th, 2020 was of my dog Roan speaking. Three weeks later, I gained the courage to post a dance and unknowingly started to create a vibe and a space that would draw in thousands and thousands of others seeking joy, happiness and the freedom of emotional release.

Within days a new healthy habit had formed and my life as the widowed dancer began to unfold. One dance a day became at least two and, in a pandemic in my apartment, my world began to open expand. Stuck at home meant seeing more trends, good and bad, on social media. I watched as the world posted their frustrations, sadness and hurt being from being locked away from a life they missed - a life that felt like it had died. The world was collectively at the start of grief and I was 2 full years ahead. I thought that maybe sharing my dancing could help others start to navigate their new normal and begin to generate joy again.

As great of a plan as it was to help others feel comfort, I didn't realize that I was continuing to avoid caring for myself. If I helped others I would have value but that wasn't true. By December 2020 I had gained 40 lbs, ate poorly, drank too much and my blood pressure was getting too high. What started as a healthy habit dancing turned into an excuse to not take care of me. I had deflected the attention towards helping others so I could avoid helping myself and facing my grief . I was fully submerged in The Care-Griever Syndrome…

April 18, 2020 - The Power of Your Name

Dear Tin,

It's so hard to believe that this week makes the second year I've had to wake up without you. I don't know how to describe how 2 years feels like already and forever ago at the same time. Many people don't understand that grief comes in drops, ripples, waves and flash floods. For me, this week is an emotional ocean. I see you in all the places I go. Others talk, laugh and walk right through the spaces where I see your ghost replaying our memories.

You were so supportive of the dedication and passion I poured into the animals I work with. You were always so proud to tell everyone what I do. You never complained if I had to go in early, stay late or work strange shifts. You always put the animals first before you. I can't

Year 3 A.C. – Pandemic and Self-Passiveness

change the past but I just want to say thank you. Had I known you'd be gone so soon, I would have asked someone else to cover those shifts so I could spend every possible minute with you. Unfortunately, Regret is one of Grief's many complex companions.

I know you are still with me and I know you watch over me. I know you have followed me along the way and on all of my travels. It probably goes without saying that your love and devotion for me is one of the greatest gifts I have ever been given. Although it's hard to talk about losing you I know that our story is helping inspire people to embrace hope through their struggles. I know we are teaching others to feel more gratitude for their everyday. Just please know that you still are doing so much for so many now and I'm so unbelievably proud of you.

So today is the anniversary of the last day we could go out and live life together. We knew time was growing short and all you wanted was to see your favorite penguin Becky so you could say goodbye. We didn't know this would be our last real day together. Tomorrow you'll be too tired and confused to talk. The next day you'll be gone and my world will shatter. I rarely post pictures of you when you were sick. I know you'd hate that but this picture of you and Becky means so very much to me. You talked about her as if she was your own. These are the last moments we felt joy together and I'm so very grateful I have this memory. So in this special place, on this special day, I want you to meet someone very very special.

Clayton, this is Becky's son. His name is Tin…

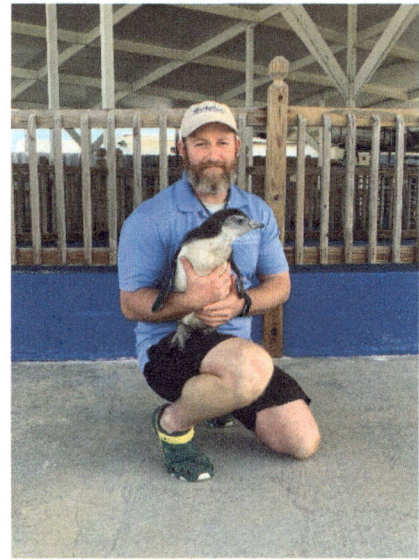

Year 3 A.C. – Pandemic and Self-Passiveness

April 25, 2020 - The Heroic Haircut

I gave myself a haircut at home this week. Well maybe it's not exactly heroic to get a haircut but it took a lot of courage to do it. Not because I might miss a spot or screw up and shave a line across my head but because I had to do it myself. It's been over 2 years since Clayton gave me a haircut. I haven't dug those clippers out of the drawer since he used them. Would they even turn on or have they passed like he did? For a moment I feared that they wouldn't come to life and the grief of Tin's passing began to rise. I almost put them down and walked away. A deep breath and I flipped the switch. The room was full of that familiar buzzing.

I love that sound and I love having my hair cut. It's like a mini vacation. A massage. Nowadays I usually go to a place and have it done. Surrounded by other people and activity that keep me in the present. Not here though. I'm home alone without Clayton. He's not here to wrap the towel around my neck, kiss my head and take care of me. Now that the world is closed, I have two options:

1. Put the clippers down because I just can't navigate the memories. This option means I keep feeling un-kept and that adds just as much to the grief.

-or-

2. Go for it because if I don't do it now I might never have the opportunity and the courage to make it through this milestone.

I stopped thinking and I ran the trimmers across the side of my head. In that moment, I climbed higher than I thought I could. I beat the grief and I committed to care for myself. The more hair that fell the lighter the moment became. I was doing it. I was able to manage the memories. The feeling of the buzzer reminded me of his silly stories when he cut my hair. It reminded me of how it felt when he bent my ears to buzz around them and than I realized that I was smiling…

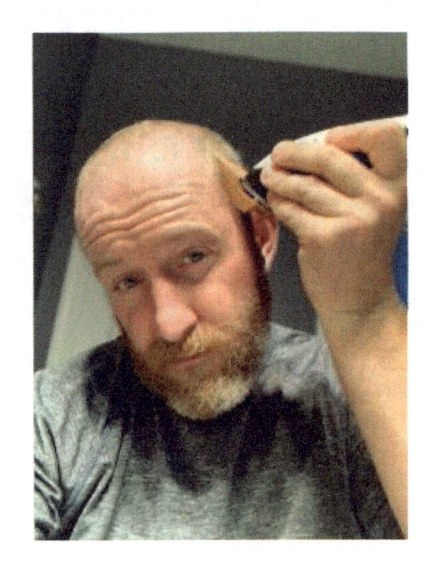

Year 3 A.C. – Pandemic and Self-Passiveness

May 2, 2020 - Quarantined From Closure in a Garden of Grief

We find ourselves surrounded by closures of stores, restaurants, movie theaters, parks and beaches. Those are the closures we can tangibly see but there are so many more emotional situations we are closed off from. The one I'm feeling heavier than any other is a certain aspect of closure with the loss of a loved one and it's echoed in the news. People are falling ill and dying without being able to see their family. Funerals and services are on pause and what would be normal grieving planned event timelines are now being stretched to a new schedule. How sad they can't move through the closure of service sooner but I very much understand where they lay in limbo.

Clayton passed away 2 years ago and we still haven't had a service for him. Shortly after he passed his mother had a stroke and was moved up to her family cross-country. She was in no position to handle having a service for him. A year later there was a last minute desire to have it on his birthday with no notice to family and friends. There was no way we could pull it off. I'd have to drive his urn up to Illinois or ask the funeral home to ship him. The thought of mailing my dead partner and the risks that his urn would break makes me physically ill. I said no.

Now his birthday is approaching. There's talk of having the service this year but the country has been in closure. Things are slowly opening but what happens if we shut down again? His mother is in poor health. Does bringing people together to celebrate his life risk hers? He wanted to be buried next to her. Do we just wait? That's an uncomfortable thought to wait for her to die to finally hold a service for him. It would feel different if he wanted me to keep him but until I can fulfill his wishes. This is a new patch of widowed weeds growing in my garden of grief.

All our gardens grow differently as we tend to them in our own unique ways. Trimming back encroaching vines full of thorns, raking up the leaves of fallen dreams, removing the dead brush, watering the new seeds in hope they grow and fill the empty spaces left from our past. We used to be allowed out to walk our new paths to just check in on our garden here and there depending on the day. Now I am locked in unable to get rid of the old debris. I find myself quarantined from a milestone in my closure surrounded by a garden of grief.

Year 3 A.C. – Pandemic and Self-Passiveness

May 16, 2020 - One Stood Up Widow

Dating is hard enough as it is but adding the layer of "Oh I'm also widowed" changes the landscape drastically. For some of us, we don't even think about dating and for others we have reached a point in our life where we can begin to date again. I know Clayton would want me to be happy and that no one will ever replace him in my heart. So I have started to put myself out there more and more.

Of course I started to see a guy just before the pandemic hit. We kept chatting until he just stopped returning messages. Social media posts updated me that he was probably pursuing another guy. I'm fine with that. We're not a match but could you at least have the decency to tell me? Guess not…

Well fast forward a few weeks and a friend introduced me online to her single friend and we hit it off. A weeks worth of conversations and texts lead to planning a virtual "first date". We would grab takeout, a bottle of wine and have dinner together to get to know each other. It was last Saturday. I had the day off and planned around the date. I even waited to write my blog last week to be able to share how it went. Well there was no blog post last week because there was no date.

I had my food all set, computer ready and thirty minutes past the time we set I texted him. He saw the message and didn't respond for a while. I texted again and he finally came back telling me he fell asleep. No attempt to call or big apology. We haven't talked since.

So my pride was a little hurt being stood up (as anyone's would be) but it's the fact that he knew I was widowed and that dating has been a hard situation to navigate. Dude! You stood up someone who is widowed. What in the actual hell? That takes a special kind of not caring. His loss and I dodged a bullet. Now to get back out there and hope to find someone who wants to be with me for everything I have to offer including my widowed wisdom…

Year 3 A.C. – Pandemic and Self-Passiveness

May 23, 2020 - Lost Belonging

When I was in high school, I had one guy friend named Matt. He was the only guy that gave this outgoing, unconventional kid a chance. The feeling of belonging holds tight space in my heart. I was supposed to have lunch one day with Matt but he didn't come to school. At the last class, the principle got on the PA system and asked each teacher to read a statement he had given them. My teacher struggled to start and began to read. The world faded away and there I was alone without my friend. He had died by suicide. Matt, I didn't know home was so bad. I didn't know. I wish you told me. I don't know what I would have done but I would have done anything to help you. I lost my belonging.

I still think of Matt often. Our short friendship and my loss had a huge impact on my life. Every time a streetlight strangely goes out I know he's here. Losing Matt left a deep mark on me. I am very sensitive to the conversation. Seeing his family going through their grief and knowing my own, I just want to help everyone see positivity and light in hopes it helps just one more person feel they belong.

Inevitably, when Clayton passed away, a number of my friends and family asked that question:

"Are you ok? No but really are you ok?"

It's understandable. There were definitely days that I didn't know up from down but the dark gift I was given early in life reminded me that I bring light to others and that light needs to stay lit. So I honor where I am in my journey knowing heavy days get lighter and I will continue to shine for others in their dark. When I lost Clayton I lost my belonging. When you are widowed, you sometimes don't feel like you belong in lots of situations and that's ok to feel that way at times.

I always share where I am in my journey be it bright or dull. I'm grateful to say that the journey gets easier and lighter each day. I have had fewer blog entries and social media posts on the grieving side because life just seems to be getting more abundantly positive. My grief will always be there and revisit me sporadically but I see changes in me. I can talk to Clayton now without tears. As a matter of fact, there was a man behind me at the post office yesterday. I noticed the box he was shipping had Clayton's exact handwriting, very distinct, block style of a designer or engineer. I looked up and he stood Clayton's height, same build, similar tattoos and warm smile. A year ago I would have immediately looked away and choked down the emotions but my heart was flooded with good memories and I smiled at him. Something that would seem so simple as a friendly smile to that man was a monumental step along my journey. You just never know the impact you can have on someone.

That being said I had an opposite reaction to a simple statement on a social media post. I had made a fun dance video. I love dancing and people gain joy from my posts. Part way through the comment thread there sat a side thread. A woman had exclaimed that I reminded her so

Year 3 A.C. – Pandemic and Self-Passiveness

much of the actor and comedian Robin Williams. Dozens of others commented back agreeing we looked similar and I just was the guy who was always happy and bringing positivity to everyone. For many people, that would just be a compliment but for me I was immediately reminded of my friend Matt. My heart dropped. Her comment unintentionally brought up old grief. I felt stereotyped as the "happy guy on the outside" griever. Being widowed comes with a lot of novel social judgments that most don't recognize. So now I wonder,

although everyone sees me being positive, are they stereotyping me and internally asking "But really? Are you ok?"

I'm widowed. I'm learning my new life. I'm learning to live with grief. In some situations I have lost my "belonging" but - Yes. I am ok.

May 30, 2020 - The Fear in Forgetting

A regular weekend morning cleaning the house and my phone rings. It's Judy, Clayton's mother. I haven't been able to get her on the phone in months. She had a stroke two weeks after Clayton passed away. She was never able to back to her home. She was flown up to Illinois to stay in a nursing home with all of her belongings and memories quietly resting here in Florida.

Calls with Judy are not usually long. She has always been active and ready to move to the next thing. I had sent her photos of animals from work with a letter and my phone number incase she lost it or forgot it. There is always a little anxiety picking up the phone because so many of our calls result in her crying. I'm a big trigger for her emotions and it hurts me to think what her life has become in the past two years. Lively and opinionated, Judy genuinely cares about my family. She always asks about them. I've called almost every week since our last conversation in the Fall. I sent flowers for the holidays and just recently I received a

Year 3 A.C. – Pandemic and Self-Passiveness

letter from her apologizing for forgetting my birthday in November and forgetting to talk to me at Christmas. I'm not mad at all that she forgets. I understand she can't control it but every time she doesn't answer the phone or remember a date I feel deep sadness for what her life has become.

An outgoing, wonderful woman in her 70s who served in our military, Judy has lost her only son, can't go home, can't use her left side, has trouble speaking, trouble remembering and is in a nursing home surrounded by people who she doesn't connect with. Every call she talks about taking a trip to come down to her house and get things but always follows that with the fact that people steal stuff at the nursing home. It hurts to hear her new normal. It hurts to know she grieves Clayton in solitude away from her home and friends, It scares the hell out of me that I could end up in a situation like that when I'm her age. All alone just going day to day until there are no more days. I'm crying while I write these words. Loneliness hits me so hard and the fact that I can't take that feeling away from her hurts my soul.

We wrapped up the call and I took a deep breath. She didn't start crying this time and I had a sense of peace that perhaps she has moved forward in her grief to be able to talk about Clayton without crying. That is huge in our grief journey and I smiled thinking she was better. I called my mom to say hi and tell her about Judy. During the call Judy called again and left a voice message. I feared she had called back because she was upset and would be crying but the voicemail hit an entirely new emotional level:

"Hi Bryan. It's Judy. I'm sorry I forgot to ask Clayton how much he needed for rent this month. Call me back and I'll write you a check for his part."

Judy hadn't cried on our call because she forgot that Clayton was gone…

Year 3 A.C. – Pandemic and Self-Passiveness

June 6, 2020 - What Do You Say to Someone Widowed? Exactly What You Say to Anyone Grieving…

There is just no way to gather the words to fully express the way current events are falling all around us. A pandemic, lost jobs, social upheaval and deep pain from racism. My broken widowed heart hurts for so many and it often takes my breath away leaving me speechless. So many of my friends have said they don't know what to do or say right now to help their friends. Many are worried that they may say the wrong thing and make it worse so they stay silent. However, silence makes the problem worse. Silence is where the evil is hiding.

I often refer to being widowed as a dark gift. Painful but, as I walk forward, I realize I have been given insight and intuition that I never had before. I have been graced with the gifts of empathy, grief and loss. I know it seems strange to consider these as gifts but since Clayton passed away I have gone from a nice guy to one who outwardly shines a light for those in the dark. We all have the choice on how we walk forward. We all have different journeys. As I put myself back together and the future begins unfolding, I want to bring as many people with me towards better days. I would not be doing what I am doing now without my dark gifts and for that reason I am grateful.

Right now, my gift of loss and grief is helping me to navigate these strange social waters. So many people don't know what to say to the hurting people in their lives. For a bit, I was taken aback and had no words. Now that I have had time to process everything occurring, I immediately know what to say. We all remember when we just became widowed. People don't know what to say. They don't want to say the wrong thing. They don't want to upset us but what is it that we tell them? They don't have to say anything except that they are here for us. That is all anyone needs to hear right now. You don't need to say something amazing and profound. You just need to say that you are there for them

We, as the widowed, have unique emotional superpowers that are rivaled by no other. Right now, we can use our dark gifts to help other see the light by simply stating the only thing we wanted to hear on day 1 of our widowed walk…

Year 3 A.C. – Pandemic and Self-Passiveness

June 13, 2020 - A Better Busy Bryan

Just after Clayton passed, I was forced to get a second job. I started up an online business which allowed me to work from anywhere. I wasn't locked into a schedule, at a location with someone else's requirements. I worked extremely hard to quickly get to a point I felt financially safe again. I hit that mark and continued to maintain that level of busy.

I realized that I had needed to be always "on" not to maintain the business but because slowing down and sitting in quiet would bring huge waves of paralyzing grief. I distinctly remember that when I hit my first real goal I told myself I could completely take a day off with my phone on silent. I slept in, got up, made coffee, sat down with my dog and the intensity of pure silence in just sitting caused me to lose my breath weeping. I had been so busy that I hadn't processed much of my grief from losing Clayton and my dad. It was overwhelming, painful and dark. That place held very scary fears and I refused to let myself sit in silence so I went back to "Busy Bryan". I wasn't ready to sit comfortably in my new normal's quiet so I avoided it.

Through the rest of year one and all of year 2, my time was filled to the top and overbooked. I had a full time job, my side business, 2 different blogs to write weekly, travel to speaking engagements, communities to help foster, the gym, my dog, social media and any other excuse I could find to be busy. Even during the worldwide quarantine, when everyone else is stuck at home, I had to work full time, more people came to my side business and I was on zoom calls for all sorts of groups and virtual events.

Now that life is getting back to it's new pace (whatever that really is), my life is starting to slow down a bit more. I am starting to really pay attention to myself, my wellness and my quality of life. Yesterday I felt the heaviness of constantly moving. I received great news involving projects I was working on and I could take a huge breath. Without thinking, I just sat in that moment feeling positive, accomplished and I thanked Clayton for helping me achieve some monumental goals. It was quiet. It was relaxing. It was safe. I took the day off with little distraction. Somewhere along the way, something changed. The fears that flooded me 2 years ago were nowhere to be found. I felt at peace. I felt balanced.

Up until that moment, I kept reminding myself to stay busy to keep away the quiet. Without thinking, I gave myself the permission to sit in calm and found I had grown tremendously since that huge panic attack almost 2 years ago. I don't really like to sit still but at least I know now that constantly being active is no longer a self-preservation mechanism. I've become a better busy Bryan…

Year 3 A.C. – Pandemic and Self-Passiveness

June 27, 2020 - Just Reality That Hasn't Happened Yet – A Letter to the Year 2020

Dear 2020,

We are in an abusive relationship and I'm going to have to ask you to please stop. Some days you bring me amazing exciting happy events and than the next you throw a curveball of stress or sadness at the state of the world right now. I think the hardest part of our relationship is that you know I need a good bit of positive growth. I miss Clayton everyday but the emotions of this year are really starting to add more widowed weight. I need some days that are not extreme downs emotionally because it's exhausting. I'm losing inspiration to even find things to write about. I can't keep my thoughts together and every time I turn around the scene has changed for good or bad. You are making me feel bipolar but I know there isn't anything wrong with me. It's you. It's you not me so we need to work on whatever this relationship is.

I have dreams that I want to achieve. I have goals for my life and I'm being forced to do it all without Clayton. That's the hardest part of all. My dad was taken, Clayton was taken and right now you keep dangling my dreams just out of reach. My business goals just out of reach. My health goals just out of reach. My relationship goals just out of reach. My travel goals just out of reach. This is a vicious cycle you have me in. When I reach for one goal, I have to back away from others but if you just finally let me grab one or two of them than I'll be able to reach them all.

So 2020, I'm telling you directly that I want the rest of this year to be full of wonderfully positive amazing success and no stress in all areas of my life. Some people would laugh at that request thinking negatively about our relationship but I know you have it in you to turn this thing around and get us back in the right direction. I have had so many dreams taken away. I deserve the ones I have now to come true immediately. So I'm going to adjust my wording moving forward. These things that I see in my future are no longer just dreams. They are my realities that just haven't happened yet. I appreciate you moving forward in support of me and I'm excited to accept their arrival soon…

Thank You

- Bryan

> It's not a dream. It's a reality that hasn't happened yet.
> -Bryan Martin

Year 3 A.C. – Pandemic and Self-Passiveness

July 4, 2020 - Trying to Fake the Fourth

Happy 4th of July everyone. I hope it can be the best you can make it! I'm trying over here but I'm not very successful. Today would have been Tin and my 6th year anniversary. Three years ago I celebrated the last 4th of July with Clayton. We were up in Massachusetts for my father's funeral. It was a difficult time but I was surrounded by family and friends. This year is entirely different.

Sitting here alone on my porch typing grief onto the screen as I see family's heading to events and smell a neighborhood of grills. Somewhere a dad is asking everyone at the cookout if they want a burger or a dog. Somewhere a husband just brought his husband a new beer and hug. It really is the little things that you miss more than anything when they are gone. I miss them. Where did it all go?

So here I find myself inside another holiday hurricane. I know I'm allowed these days and these feelings. I know later today will probably be easier and tomorrow is new and full of possibilities. I have to be honest. Having days like this really upset me for two reasons. Obviously losing Tin and my dad but it's the other reason that I struggle with managing. Now that I understand deep loss and how short life really is, I get angry that I'm possibly wasting another day and not cherishing it for all it can be. I know Tin and my dad would not want that for me but I also know that it's ok to have these days. I'm learning to hold space for all those competing emotions and to not judge myself so harshly for just stopping to breathe.

I do so well until I hear those fireworks. Clayton would stop everything to watch and now the sound of them just stops my heart. A holiday for celebrating our freedoms but I never wanted to be free from him. I have hope that someday I'll find the one that will make me smile at fireworks again…

Year 3 A.C. – Pandemic and Self-Passiveness

July 18, 2020 - Remembering You on Your Birthday

Tuesday morning I woke up and wasn't sure how to navigate your birthday. I went to work. I did the things. I stressed wanting to stay calm and collected but also find a way to celebrate you.

If you were here, I would have today off. We would have a lazy morning with Roan. We would go paddle boarding or fishing. We would have lunch with your mom at Red Lobster. We would have your birthday dinner at Giovanni's or Olive Garden. I'm sad to tell you Giovanni's (our favorite date spot here) has closed forever. Anyone who knew you knows how much you loved your food.

I didn't have time for fishing. I didn't have time for paddle boarding but when work ended I made sure to take you to get your birthday memory meals. I stopped at Red Lobster and ordered you coconut shrimp and garlic shrimp scampi. Of course there's cheddar bay biscuits ☐ I toasted you with a glass of wine while I waited, sat and remembered when we paddle boarded past here wishing we owned a house right on the water.

Year 3 A.C. – Pandemic and Self-Passiveness

This next blog was the first official posting on social media. I had made some posts about my grief but not actually shared my blogs regularly. I was scared to put it all out there, but the pandemic had sent everyone into Year 1 of grief. I saw so many similarities from my loss and the world's loss. I was 2 years ahead. Sharing could create a space for honesty, authenticity, openness, normalizing grief and just feeling safe. What I was unaware of was how on point my intuition was. Up until now people on social media seemed to follow me for animal posts and my dancing antics, little did I know I was collecting a community that needed much more…

July 25, 2020 - I Have A Sometimes Invisible, Often Chronic, Incurable Condition – I Have Grief.

Hello,

For those of you new around here, Hi I'm Bryan. I'm a director of animal care at an aquarium. I'm passionately obsessed with essential oils and environmentally safe products. I'm a son, brother, uncle, cousin and a friend. I love to dance. I love to make others smile. I want to make the world a better place everyday in whatever way I can.

Some days the world is better when a kid learns that recycling can save the ocean and that plastic straws can really hurt sea turtles. Some days the world is better when a new friend uses a natural product that gives them results and they toss away chemicals that are disrupting their body chemistry. Some days the world is better with a silly dance video. Some days the world is better with a nephew video chat. Some days the world is better with a smile and holding the door for a stranger. It's not hard to help make the world better but that doesn't mean life doesn't have the hidden hard moments. I find that making others smile helps keep down the inflammation.

You see, I have a chronic, incurable condition. I suffer from grief. I'm widowed. Two years ago I lost the man I thought I would spend the rest of my life with. I lost myself and I gained a whole new emotionally chronic condition. Grief is hard to explain because it affects us all differently. Sometimes it stays with just the infected individual and other times it spreads like wildfire. Grief is and isn't contagious.

Grief can be invisible and also acutely apparent. Grief can lay dormant yet appear as full triggered emotional inflammation with a simple thought, a picture, image and even just speaking one word. I live with grief every day and there is no cure. Once you have been infected with grief, you will always be a carrier. Sometimes you can move through the symptoms and put it to rest. Sometimes new grief brings up old grief and you relive what you thought you had made peace with from your past. Loss of your person reminds you of all the failed relationships you've ever had. Even down to that boy in high school you just adored but couldn't tell him because you were gay. However, someone told him and so he stopped talking to you. Lost love lasts a lifetime and grief creeps in unexpectedly.

Year 3 A.C. – Pandemic and Self-Passiveness

So I move forward through the flare-ups, through the tired days, through the days with loss of appetite, through the nights of emotional eating, through the lonely days, through the memories. My grief is even triggered when I see others suffer loss. I'm reminded of those first few days after Clayton was gone. A storm of emotions and wondering if I will make it. I am reminded of that phone call. I'm reminded of the loudest sound I've ever heard – my heart breaking.

So I do my best to help make the world a better place because that keeps the chronic emotional inflammation down. You don't get over grief, you can only manage the symptoms.

Hi! My name is Bryan. I care for animals. I care for people. I'm widowed and I suffer from grief.

August 1, 2020 - The Keeper of the Lighthouse

Grief's gaze. I knew it as soon as I got it this week. It's that look you get from someone who has just suffered a new great loss. It conveys so much with so little. It's so very different from the look they give to others all around them. Yeah it's quite a powerful look and you totally get it.

You remember being there yourself. Instantly you are transported back to your beginning, back to your first few days. It's been years and it hits like it was just yesterday. Those first days of seeing the world from under water because the tears just won't stop. Not sure what you're doing in the next minute let alone tomorrow or next week. Begging for the universe to throw you a line so you can anchor to anything and stop the spinning even for just a moment. You search the crowd and you see a lighthouse - A person that understands and can help you try and make some sense of it all. You gaze at them in hopes they can ground you. Then suddenly you're snapped back to the present and standing in front of you is your friend who has made his way over to you and you realize you're his lighthouse.

How do I explain it? They know that you have suffered a difficult loss. They know that, of everyone in the room, it's you who understands where they are in this exact moment. It's you who knows what the first few days of the grief journey feels like. It's you who has made it

Year 3 A.C. – Pandemic and Self-Passiveness

past this initial stage of shock and knows what it's like to walk forward. It's you, standing there as living proof that they can survive this stage. It's you that now represents their future. It's you they can talk to because you get it. You provide safe harbor. You've become the keeper of the lighthouse.

It's not a position you ever thought you'd be in but here you are a light in the dark for those new to sailing the storm. You just never know who will need your light whatever their grief may be…

"Hey"

"Hey. Thank you for all of this you guys did for us. It's perfect. "

"No thanks needed. We just want to help in anyway we can. If nothing else this gives you a break from all the crazy the past few days. You guys can just walk around, enjoy the beach and eat a relaxing meal."

"Yeah. It's a lot. All these people here. It's going to be harder though when they are all gone and back to life. "

"I completely understand. My loss is different but I get it. The first few days is a whirlwind but it hits when everyone leaves and you're in your new normal. It's good though that you have your wife and that your family lives here. That will help with the navigating. I'm really sorry you lost your son…"

Year 3 A.C. – Pandemic and Self-Passiveness

August 8, 2020 - The Gates of Grief

I realize I have gotten to a point where I go through my week, head down and pushing things back to keep grief at bay. The weekend hits and my first day is full of errands and obligations but my second day is dedicated to allowing the gates of grief to open when I write this weekly blog. Throughout the week I have my moments where the creaking doors threaten to break and spill into my now.

"Not now, later. Just hold tight for later"

I'm trying to manage the gates and control when I'm allowed to grieve. A set time and place where it's ok to let it all out. Well that's not healthy, that's not fair to me and that is not what I tell other people to do. I very much know that one should feel the emotions when they arrive and not to have them wait for you to invite them in. They are called feelings because they are supposed to be felt. Isn't it funny how we help others and than we don't allow ourselves the grace to follow the same self-caring advice. I've been trying to be more mindful of myself. I put it out in the universe this week that I needed help in order to better help me. Well a few days into the week and I certainly got the message.

A Wednesday, after work and headed to the gym I got the most unbelievable, out of nowhere craving for frozen yogurt. I like it but Clayton was obsessed with it. He would get it all the time and he especially wanted it more when he was sick. My plans were derailed and I turned into the parking lot. I stopped and looked at the place. I haven't been back since the last time I brought Clayton here. Can I even go in? Am I ready? This is sudden. Should I plan to come back so I'm prepared and I can keep it together? That way I can control the grief.

"You're going to be ok. Open the door"

The wave of sugared air met me like sweet welcome and my mind filled with memories of Tin's excitement. What flavors? What candy? What would he fit into that cup this time? I smiled and I asked him "What should we get?" I grabbed a cup and looked up to see a flavor I had not seen there before – pineapple. That's the one! I filled my cup and noticed that the craving had disappeared. I actually was indifferent to eating. No other flavors necessary. No candy. Something else was up so I paid and I sat down outside.

No one else around and the feeling of lonely drifted in on the breeze. I started to feel sorry for myself. I looked down at the melting swirls and the gates broke wide open. I started to sob. My heart hurt. I couldn't breathe. The scene for anyone passing by was a sad, 41 year old man, sitting alone on a hot summer day with pineapple frozen yogurt melting and tears streaming down his face. No one would know what I had just experienced. No one would realize that an unplanned trip to a frozen yogurt place would be one of the hardest things someone widowed could ever do. I let it out. I sat with my emotions and I took a deep breath. Then I noticed the craving was back. I suddenly had the realization that my fear stopped my drive to fulfill a need, a craving, self care, personal growth, moving forward? Well I can now

Year 3 A.C. – Pandemic and Self-Passiveness

see that I might be doing this in other aspects of my life. Bad things happen but I can't walk through life worrying when they might strike. Fear keeps away the magic in possibilities.

Once I realized the big picture, the overall experience was unbelievably powerful. There's great beauty in this chaos and sometimes it appears in ways that can only be described as divinely poetic. There's no way I would have gone in there without that unexplained craving. I have avoided going for over two years. I can't know for sure the reasons my week unfolded the way it did but I knew I was not accepting some things. I know I hold me back sometimes because of fear. I did outwardly ask for help. So what seems like a simple task to some was a huge step in my emotional journey thanks to a nudge from the universe and a little bit of pineapple frozen yogurt.

I see you Tin…

August 15, 202 - Gazing Through Grief

So many things have triggered my grief. It all comes down to five senses. There are the predictable ones that stand out like catching the scent of his cologne lingering in the breeze from a man passing by or the lyrics of a song that strike the strings of my heart. The taste of his favorite food the first time I had the courage to actually eat it again. I've been able to manage some of the triggers. I've packed away all of Clayton's cologne. They are there if I want to smell him again but I don't need them to be the first thing and last thing I see each day next to my toothbrush. I can change the channel if the wrong song comes on at the wrong time or I can turn the volume up and let the words wash over me.

I expected those kinds of typical triggers but it's sensing the surprise ones that you'd never think of until they happen. Going through my phone and hearing his old voice messages. That startling feeling when a friend took my hand for the first time and every part of me

Year 3 A.C. – Pandemic and Self-Passiveness

wanted to squeeze and hope it was Tin's. The different feeling my bed has when I wake up without him there stealing the sheets or the quiet of the house lacking his voice, lacking his goofy big footsteps. Not the first ones you think of but understandable. However, there is one sense that has struck me so deep because I never thought it would ever happen – seeing him in person again through Grief's Gaze.

I don't mean in photos, dreams, videos or mind drifting memories. I mean for a split second thinking he's actually right there in front of me alive and looking back. It never occurred to me that I would ever see someone who resembled Tin so much that I would do a double take. A typical morning workout before work with the same people nodding "good job for getting up and getting to the gym." I set my towel on a machine and scanned the scene. Same height and skin tone, same kind of hat, same arms, same legs, same stance and tattooed spots. His shirt hung the same and his mannerisms from the back were almost identical. He turned around and began to walk towards me. My stomach dropped. Same walk, same eyes, same smile, same age. Not an exact match, but close enough when you're gazing through grief. He nodded as he passed. I smiled back then quickly looked away and fiddled with the weights.

"It's like he's right here but doesn't know me. What a confusing feeling. Deep breath Bryan."

So many new thoughts ran through my mind. I could and couldn't look at him. Do you know what it's like to want to cry and smile at the same time. Did you even know you could simultaneously have contradicting emotions cloud your conscience? His goofy lanky walk made me remember Tin's awkwardness. His big shoes reminded me that Tin's feet were like paddles. I'd joke they were the reason he was such a good swimmer. This familiar stranger's height and long arms caused me to fight back tears. Clayton would always stand behind me and put those arms around me. One around my waist and one over my shoulder with his hand resting on my heart. Grief's gaze brings back the deepest desire we widowed can never sense again, holding our beloved just one more time.

Grief and loss cause a lot of emotions and a lot of unique thoughts. It's not crazy. You're not crazy. I'm not crazy. We just deeply miss and want so terribly to have that sense of touch again. I don't know this guy and I'd certainly never ask him but in that moment deep down I heard my inner voice say:

"Hey. I know we don't know each other but could I ask you a favor? Could you just hold me for a minute? Just one minute so I can close my eyes and pretend that I can have the one thing I can't ever sense again.

Year 3 A.C. – Pandemic and Self-Passiveness

August 22, 2020 - Beautiful Failures

A part of being widowed is that you are forced to remember all of the relationships that didn't work out. That sting when your first crush doesn't like you back. That feeling life is over forever when the big high school sweetheart breakup happens. College brought a whole new world. I was getting more and more responses from girls that wanted to "just be friends". Coming to terms with being gay, trying to navigate that entire new world and my first real boyfriend breaking up with me because I was "too sweet." - The usual failures.

Thicker skin and more self-preservation, a 10 year relationship that began with good intentions and ended in disaster. Faults on both sides but one half crossing the line and shattering sacred safety. I held back sharing the reasons for leaving and lost friends. I should have told them that he threw things. I should have told them that he would repeatedly tell me:

"You know all our friends only tolerate you because they like me."

I never told them what he said for fear it was the truth. Instead, I kept it to myself and they chose him. Unfortunately, validated fears. – An Unfair Failure.

At this point in the romantic film of my life, in walked Prince Charming to take my hand and help me up:

"I'll never treat you like he did. I promise."

Two years of building trust, he gave me a ring as a promise for our future. We chose to move to a new city and start fresh. We found a new landscape, new adventures, new people. He found new temptations. I found new deceit and a new failure. I wasn't good enough for my friends last time and this time I wasn't good enough to be enough for him. Shattered dreams and a broken heart – A Fairytale Failure.

A couple years of healing and the heart of a hopeless romantic, I tried again. Wholesome, secure, sweet, our families loved us. This was it. It was all fitting. It was unfolding like the storybook dream I always wanted. Then we had a typical weekend night, typical comfortable dinner and he said an untypical statement:

"I'm sorry but I thought I'd love you more than I do by now."

I said nothing because I didn't have any air left in my lungs. The words stole my breath away. I packed up my things at his apartment and headed back out onto the road I hate traveling alone - A "better as friends" failure.

Time moves forward and after awhile I have a date or two with a nice guy but there were no sparks. Instead he gave me an invite to a pool party where I find you. I just know that it's you. It's easy. It feels right. I let down my fear of failure and you stay. I realize that us is all

Year 3 A.C. – Pandemic and Self-Passiveness

the good things from all of those past failures. In that moment it makes sense that had anything in my past been different, had my begging with God to just let them love me than I wouldn't be here with you. All of those relationships suddenly became beautiful failures. It was so hard in those moments to have faith that you were on your way. It's truly a gift when you are allowed to see the Universe's Why but just because you see it one moment doesn't mean things remain clear.

A new life in a sleepy little beach town, a career I have dreamt of reaching and holding you, Clayton. After all of those failures, I was finally getting my turn at what so many others have and take for granted. This part of my life was so beautifully written and then the page turned. You left me but not like all the others. An acute disease with only 8 months to do everything I could to hold on knowing you would go – A Heart-Shattering Failure.

Now I sit here and write out the storybook road my heart has had to endure. Fairytale endings are not as common as they are in books. I write to share the hard truth in hopes my lines give words to others who can't put their emotions on paper. I write my lost relationships so if all of these tragedies are part of a bigger plan than others learn some hidden lesson that's intended for them. Than hopefully all is for not and, at least to others, my story and I become a beautiful failure…

Year 3 A.C. – Pandemic and Self-Passiveness

August 29, 2020 - Grief's Rewinding

It has been 866 days since Clayton past away, 867 days since I said "I love you" and kissed him on the forehead for the last time. Those first few days after he died felt like years. Every minute was the first of that minute without him. Every day was the first Monday, Tuesday, Wednesday without him. Once the first week was over, the second was easier but it was still the first day back to work, the first May, the first summer, Halloween, my birthday, Thanksgiving, Christmas, no New Year's kiss, empty Valentine's without him. Then, suddenly, I found myself only and already at the first anniversary of our goodbye. Back to Day 1 and Grief's rewinding.

I thought the first year would be the hardest. Finding myself back at Day 1 in Year 2, I was going to be saved from having to fear the arrival of the "firsts". What I didn't know was that Year 2 brought the arrival of clarity. The immediate emotional storm of Year 1 subsided, I wasn't dodging falling birthday branches or trying to stay sheltered from the sting of sideswiping widowed holiday winds. I had made it and thought the worst was behind me. What I didn't realize was the widowed rewind is like watching a movie again. You notice things that you missed the first time. That silly poster on the wall, a stranger bumping into the main character foreshadowing a later meeting, the ghostly figure that walks past in the reflection of a window. You miss all of those the first time but you catch them on the rewind. Some bring a laugh and others bring deep fear. Year 2 revealed a lot from the background in the scenes of Year 1. It never dawned on me that part of moving forward also meant having to go backwards and being forced to look at everything again. I thought Year 1 was painful but Year 2 solidified that he was really gone.

I'm 135 days into year 3 and this second rewind has been even harder. I'm seeing deeper into the background now that Clayton isn't sharing these scenes with me. There are lots of questions and shadowy figures in the distance ahead. I'm catching myself trying to freeze the scene and walk backwards in hopes I can return to the first frame because I'm worried how the credits will read when this movie is over. Does the leading character live happily ever after? Does he succeed in his quest and celebrate? Does he just fade away into the sunset and his story forgotten? The Grief Rewind has brought me to the fear-of-the-future stage in my journey. It's unsettling. It causes anxiety but I can't stop the movie from playing. There is no intermission. There is no script for the next scene of my story. Life is improv. All I can do now is walk on set and be me as best I can without Tin to help set the scene…

Year 3 A.C. – Pandemic and Self-Passiveness

September 5, 2020 - Do You Know or Do You Believe?

We fall into our patterns and the longer we are in them the tighter they stick. It's not necessarily a bad thing. Peppered into our day are all sorts of habits. It's the repetition that provides us comfort. We say good night and close our eyes until the next day when the sun returns. The question I have for you is do you know or do you believe that the sun will rise tomorrow?

Many of us would automatically say "I know" which makes sense because every day for as long as there have been days we can depend on the pattern of the planets. It's when we think about it deeper that we realize, despite your belief systems, every night we go to bed with a dash of faith and a little bit of hope that tomorrow will come. No one knows for sure that the sun will absolutely be there. Even though little orphan Annie sang her heart out about it, no one can promise us that the sun will come out tomorrow. Could there be a solar storm, an asteroid or some manmade disaster overnight? All those possibilities are scary but even now we are looking outward because looking inwards is even scarier. So let me ask the question again but from a different viewpoint.

Do you know or do you believe that you will rise tomorrow? Do you know or do you believe that those you said "good night" too will have a tomorrow?

I have dealt with loss throughout my life. All of my grandparents, a friend in high school who couldn't stand the pressure and died by suicide, my father trying to manage lifelong pain, Clayton feeling a little under the weather and than gone in 8 months. The uncertainty of tomorrow is very apparent in my thoughts every day. It causes me to stop and pause to feel both gratitude and fear. What if my tomorrow doesn't come?

I don't dwell on the thought or let it consume me but it is always there. Some days it makes me nervous. Some days it makes me more adventurous because YOLO right? Some days it makes sense when the thought hits and some days it's entirely unexpected. I want to share with you something that happened last week that I did not tell many people about. I was making coffee on a regular morning and it hit:

"Here you are making coffee by yourself. What if you never have someone to make coffee with again? What if you got really sick and there was no one here for you? What if you had a heart attack right now? There is no one here to try and save you. You could die today and no one would check for a few days."

The overwhelming fear knocked me to the ground. Hyperventilating, holding my chest and tears running down my face - I was having a huge panic attack. It had been years since my fiancé and I separated that I had my last attack. Strangely enough, I felt gratitude that I knew what was happening. I could feel the feelings of fear knowing they would wash away verses the first time when I thought I was not having a tomorrow. Soon after, I felt relaxed enough to stand but was exhausted. I told a few people what had happened and took a nap to recover.

Year 3 A.C. – Pandemic and Self-Passiveness

I'm not telling you this so that you feel sorry or worried for me. I'm going to be ok but so many have gone through this journey staying quiet and that can sometimes make the walk harder. I write these you to know that we all have these fears. We all have doubts. We all have difficult days and it's normal to believe that the sun will come out tomorrow…

September 12, 2020 - Future Gifts

People will often ask how I'm able to keep going after such difficulties losing my father and than my partner within 10 months of each other. Well here is the secret...

I just keep trying.

Yup that's it. I keep trying. That is the magical answer I have for you. Some days are fantastic and other days I can feel frightened but each new day I try.

The thing I've learned is that every day is another chance to find purpose. One day's purpose might be to take care of sea lions and penguins, the next might be educating people about oils followed by a day to spend with my dog, a day to motivate people, a day to do a news interview, a day to make a Tiktok, a day to grieve or a day that includes any, all or none of those things.

What I've found is that trying in itself is purpose. When there isn't something I can tangibly show myself I've accomplished (because we all feel like we have to have visible substance to prove our work other thing I've learned is that my past difficulties has help to shape my future and directed me down roads I never would have ventured without a cosmic nudge. Hindsight can be a blessing depending on what lens YOU choose to look at it through.

Year 3 A.C. – Pandemic and Self-Passiveness

So when you are faced with difficulties or the memories of difficulties past than remind yourself to see the gifts that have resulted and know that our difficulties right now become our future gifts...

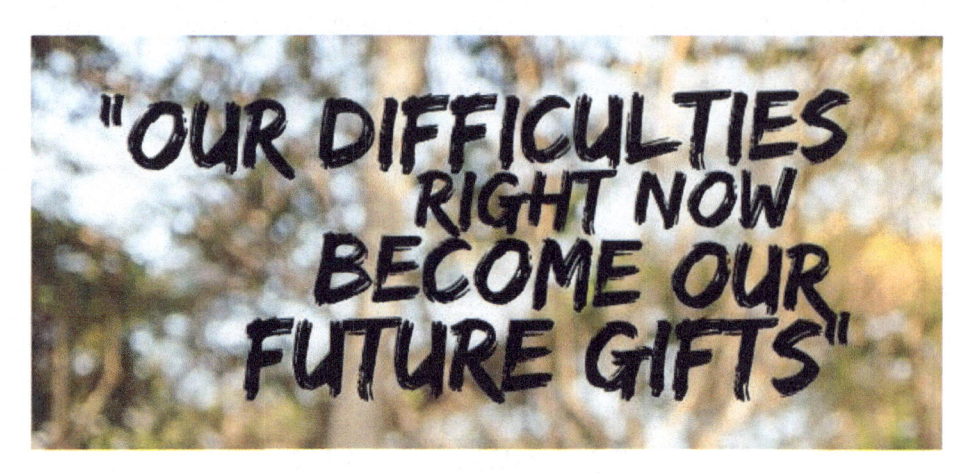

"OUR DIFFICULTIES RIGHT NOW BECOME OUR FUTURE GIFTS"

September 19, 2020 - Widowed Weather

Almost three years ago, I flew home from a convention in Mexico. We had to fly around Hurricane Nate. I got home. Clayton and I prepped the apartment and planned to go to his mother's house. He wasn't feeling well and I wanted to take him to the hospital but he said we should wait until after the hurricane. Nate passed and 8 months later so did Clayton.

This week, Hurricane Sally was supposed to miss this area but decided to stop and visit. I was as ready as I could be but you're never quite ready. Flooding, delays, loss of power - I can handle all of it. I'm good in tense situations and wasn't anxious, that is until I saw my extra set of keys on the counter. My friends that watch my animals had given my keys back so I had them available for visiting relatives. I forgot I had them. Now I had to go to work to help but I wasn't sure what the storm was going to do. Would my dog and cat be ok? Would my apartment be ok? Would I be able to get back home?

"I should have more keys to people. Damn it Bryan. Why didn't you think?"

None of my family live nearby. None of my neighbors answered their doors. Clayton wasn't here for me and I instantly felt completely alone and scared. What do I do? How do I manage this? Why do I have to go through this hurt during a hurricane?

I sat down and just stopped for a minute. Wind was whipping outside and matched the swirling emotions and thoughts I had inside me. I took a deep breath and had to put faith that this would all safely pass.

"You've been through worse Bryan. You'll figure it out."

Year 3 A.C. – Pandemic and Self-Passiveness

My coworker was headed to pick me up in his truck so we could get through the flooding. My best hope is that we could make it over to my friends' and get my keys to them just in case. As luck would have it, the roads there were clear, keys dropped off and we made it into work. The storm continued to wrap itself around us and I held on to the goals in front of me.

"Everything at home will be fine. You aren't losing more today. Get your work done."

I kept my focus on the tasks at hand and boxed up my stress, fear and emotions.

"I'll just unbox those sometime later." I told myself.

Sally kept moving and eventually passed. Things were calm enough that my friend was able to go check on my place and take Roan on a walk. I was so grateful for not losing phone service because a simple text alleviated a storm surge of worry. We finished the day at work and I headed home. It took a few hours but the things I packed up and put away for later unpacked them selves without warning.

Standing in the kitchen, I recalled the moment I realized I had my extra set of keys. I began to shake. The rising tide of tears broke through the barriers. I sat down on the floor holding Roan and the loss of Clayton flooded over me. I withstood the hurricane but it was the widowed weather that knocked me to ground…

Year 3 A.C. – Pandemic and Self-Passiveness

September 27, 2020 - I Don't Think I Could Stay

Talking to someone who has lost a loved one isn't the easiest situation. Many people get anxious, some shut down, some unintentionally say the wrong thing. I try to remember that they are hoping to meet me in a space of support by saying something and when that something comes out wrong (which it inevitably does) I search for the true meaning of their message behind the mishap.

Here are some supportive stumbles said to me:

Say - "He's in a better place."

Feel – "So it's better to not be with me"

Say – "Time heals all wounds"

Feel – "No it doesn't because I'm never going to not miss him."

Say – "You'll move on?"

Feel – "Move on? Like I will be over everything and the sun is shining and it never happened kind of thing?"

Say – "You'll find someone new. Your soul mate is out there."

Feel – "Hopefully I can love again but he's going to have to understand he won't replace Clayton.

There is just one thing someone recently said to me that I'm still trying to work through. I was asked what happened to Clayton and how did he die. I explained that it was 8 months of slowly fading until his body failed him. I know that what this person said in response was meant to compliment me for how I handled helplessly watching Tin slowly pass but their words struck an entirely new string in my heart.

"I don't know if I could do it."

"Do what?"

"I don't think I'd be able to handle it. I don't think I could stay?"

"What do you mean?"

"I don't think I'd be strong enough to watch someone slowly die. I'd have to walk away."

Year 3 A.C. – Pandemic and Self-Passiveness

There were days that I was exhausted and felt I couldn't find the energy. There were days that I just wanted his suffering to end but at no time did I think it was too much and I would just walk away to leave Clayton to die without me. I think, well at least I hope, that what my friend really meant (in his message mishap) was just trying to celebrate the strength I found in an unimaginably difficult time in my life. However, if he truly meant what he said than I am here to tell all of you that the loss I feel daily isn't as bad as the guilt would be had I given up and just walked away.

I was hurt by how my friend's sentences strung across my heart. I could hold onto that in anger but instead I will view it as a gift. You see, for the first time since Clayton died, I realized what I actually accomplished is something others might have given up on. No matter what waves washed over me, I stood strong. I didn't give up on Clayton. I didn't give up on love. I stayed…

October 10, 2020 - Return to Me

Today, I find myself in Texas near Houston. A speaking engagement planned almost a year ago. It has been a long time since I have been able to travel, speak and feel the energy in a room of people. This new world we live in can be suffocating especially for a widowed man who sometimes feels deep solitude and aches for big crowds to entertain. I'm very much aware I've lost the person I used to be. I hope he returns soon because I miss him almost as much as I miss Clayton.

I'm honestly shocked at where my life has led me these past few years. Later today I will be speaking about inclusion, diversity and stereotypes. At every speaking event, I share about Clayton. Mentioning his name means his memory lives on and new people get a chance to "meet" him. One of the most important needs for someone widowed is that their lost love is remembered. This trip and this day are a little different. Yesterday I flew around a hurricane to get here. That's not why this trip is different. It's how similar this week is to the same week a few years ago.

Year 3 A.C. – Pandemic and Self-Passiveness

You see, three years ago this week I was in Mexico for an animal care conference. Hurricane Nate hit the Yucatan peninsula the day before I was headed home. We flew around the hurricane and landed. The next day Nate landed. Clayton wasn't feeling well. I wanted him to go to the doctor but we had to wait for the hurricane to pass. With only minor damage and some power loss, we were safe. Safe that is until I got home from work on October 10th 2017. Clayton was on the couch, weak and skin a deep yellow. I rushed him to the hospital and so marked today the anniversary of his terminal diagnoses. So what's on the other side of yesterday's hurricane? For me, there is a fear of the unknown and the unexpected.

Sudden loss has its signature stings, as does expected loss through terminal time. I can only speak of my caregiver grief and having this additional diagnosis day. Clayton was only 42 and in about a month I will be the same age. By the anniversary of his death in April, I will have lived longer. I feel a great heaviness and a deep gratitude. Two emotions can be felt at the same time - That's called a fork in your road. I could have stayed home this weekend and felt my grief alone but I've decided to take the other path and go head first into life on the other side of the hurricane.

Today I get up on stage, share my love for building safe communities and remember Clayton with great pride and love. On this, his diagnoses day, as my words float across the room to inspire others, Clayton returns to me…

October 17, 2020 - Mistaken Manifestations

More and more we are seeing focus on self-growth, motivation, manifestation and talk of mindset. I get the premise and I try to practice the mentality. Yes it can change your day around if you focus on the positive but there are limits. I have to share this topic with you all so you understand that sometimes when you push "your mindset" and "manifesting", it has serious negative impact on grief.

I don't resonate well with cherry-picked philosophies. The "sometimes this works but not all the time" kind of thing doesn't sit well with me. Like there are rules when it works in your

Year 3 A.C. – Pandemic and Self-Passiveness

favor but then it's just haphazard or a grander plan when things go wrong. Where do we draw the line? I need consistency. Manifesting? Or everything happens for a reason? It can't be a combination of the two.

Like I said, I try to be positive and motivating as much as possible but there are rough days. Sometimes I'm told that having a tough day is ok and normal but other days I hear that I must be manifesting the difficulties. That is excruciating for me to try and understand.

"I'm being positive. I'm putting good out there. I don't want bad things to happen."

"Well you must be doing it wrong. You attract what you put out there."

"So I'm causing these things? With all the positivity, I'm still to blame?"

And than comes the harshest response:

"You are the cause of what happens to you. You manifested it."

"So let me get this right, I'm attracting the bad events. I'm actually the reason that these problems are happening"

"Yup! Simple as that."

"So you are saying that I manifested Clayton to get sick and die? That it's all my fault?"

"No that's not what I mean. No that's not how that works. Sometimes terrible things happen for no reason."

"But you said that we manifest our lives. You can't pick and choose. It's either all or nothing."

For those of us who have stayed behind after our loved ones move on, we fight daily with the deep reach of grief's guilt. We'd do anything to have them back. We would trade anything including ourselves. Was there anything I could have done to prevent it? If only I had said something, done something different? We ask ourselves these questions everyday but the hardest guilt for me to manage is if I somehow mistakenly manifested this…

Year 3 A.C. – Pandemic and Self-Passiveness

October 24, 2020 - Washing the Widowed Window

I clean. I clean the dishes. I clean the laundry. I clean the house – Well sort of. I'll admit I clean what's apparent, the obvious and easily seen. Since Clayton passed away, I've been busy with a full time job, a side business and just figuring out life. They say that grief triggers hit at strange times and that is very clear to those of us who experience it. Sometimes I feel like my life on social media is just a window into my widowed world. People walking by and seeing bits and pieces. I feel a deep responsibility to share, not just the perfect photos with the pretty things, but to share the whole world in here. So here's something seemingly simple that hit me really hard this week.

I was vacuuming. A simple task I do every week. Nothing out of the ordinary, nothing tremendously triggering until the vacuum caught the corner of an area rug. I pulled back, the rug played tug-0-war and the vacuum handle snapped. Aggravated and annoyed I moved the vacuum to notice what that rug had been hiding for 4 years – The new carpet that was here when Clayton and I moved in. There in front of me was the stark contrast of my past life I dreamed of and what it has become. I know I have a lot to be happy about, but when it comes to losing Clayton and the emotions that have come with it, I feel worn and faded like that exposed carpet. It hurts, I miss him and I miss me with him. It's so hard to talk about but there are days I don't know who I am and what to think or feel.

A new vacuum and it's time to do a deep clean. I started in the bedroom. I began to clean the obvious and told myself that it was time to move some furniture and clean what's been in the shadows. Headphones on and I was jamming to a fun tune, pulled back the dresser and lost my breath as if the vacuum had sucked all the air out of the room. When we first moved in, Clayton had surprised me by painting the wall one day while I was at work. I had forgotten that he said he didn't bother painting the whole wall behind furniture. It was a waste of time and paint. At that moment I had wished he wasted the time to finish but there on the wall was an empty space without color. The whole rest of the wall, like me, was vibrant except one empty spot that's blank because of Clayton.

Year 3 A.C. – Pandemic and Self-Passiveness

It's been a full day of cleaning. It's been a full week of strong triggers but I know sharing helps others so today I decided to wash the widowed windows so you could see more into this world…

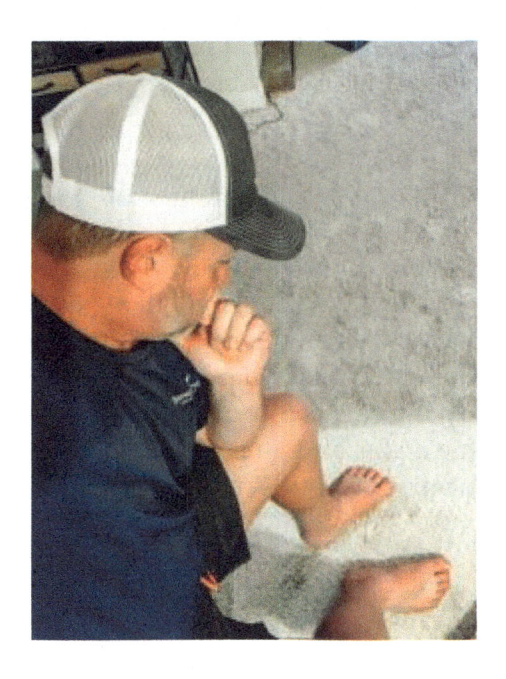

Year 3 A.C. – Pandemic and Self-Passiveness

October 31, 2020 - Tears of a Clown

It's Halloween again. I used to mark my year's passing by holidays and life events. Now that Clayton is gone, my year is filled with reminders written in grief across the days, weeks, months and seasons. My year is a grief calendar.

It's been four years since I really did anything. We dress up at work for the kids to come and Trick-or-Treat but that's not the same. Tin loved Halloween. He embraced whatever costume he poured his excitement into. There is something magically innocent about playing pretend. You feel like a kid again allowing your imagination to run free. I used to feel that way but as people throw costume parties and kids collect their candy, I start to collect my memories of the treats I had before life tricked me. I wish I could have that time back and ironically tonight is daylight savings. The clocks turn back but not back far enough to hold his hand on Halloween just one more time.

Sometimes, when I walk into a place I haven't experienced since Clayton died, I time travel. My mind reverts to the last time I was there and I briefly forget he's gone. It's really hard when present time hits and the heartache returns. I try to get through grief doors on my way moving forward. However, my fear is going through the other side of this Halloween door and finding I stumbled into a haunted house. Monsters in mirrored memories, my lost spirits and skeletons surprising me around a seemingly safe and simple spooky scene while ghosts of Halloween past cause me to gasp for air around strangers. Everywhere I look I don't recognize anyone, they are coming towards me and I can't escape. I finally let my imagination out and now it's got the best of me. I reach for his hand and the horror sets in. He's gone, I'm alone in a nightmare and I can't control grief's rushing return when I remember.

In all honesty, I don't do many things I used to because I'm scared. I'm scared I will get upset and not be able to contain it. I can't feel shame for my emotions but I also don't need them to be on a public stage. There is no stopping the flood when my grief gates break. You see, for me, everyday already has a little dusting of Halloween pretend. A bit of costume and slight of hand, I'm the ringleader and entertainers of my own widowed circus. Some days I juggle, some days I walk the tight rope. Some days I feel like the side show freak, the widowed weirdo, and some days I'm the acrobat or the fire breather. It brings me great joy entertaining the crowd but some nights after the show, somewhere behind the scenes of the big top, there are tears of a clown when there's no one around…

Year 3 A.C. – Pandemic and Self-Passiveness

November 8, 2020 - It's OK Not to Be OK

Honesty and authenticity is where my blog writing begins. There are moments in the journey that spark continuity in the conversation of my condition but there is so much else involved that I don't know how to articulate yet. There is no manual on how to do this. The road is written as its traveled.

One aspect I haven't shared about is professional therapy. There is a good reason for that - I haven't had much. Right after Clayton died, Hospice contacted me to see what support I needed. It took me a bit to speak to someone. I gathered my grief and went to see a man about a complex condition. After pouring my emotions out, he informed me he was retiring and there was no one to replace him. I would have to find someone new.

My search for someone else has not been easy. Providers not available, my own fear and frustration tied in with life's "I'll get to it soon." So I chose to climb the wall of despair on my own. The added stress year 2020 has slowed and caused me to slip. The extra weight exhausting as I kept pushing until the feeling of panic swept in and stopped my climb. I had panic attacks before but not like these. Each building in intensity and striking at more and more random times. Losing my weekends and evenings to high emotions, exhaustion followed by guilt and feeling ashamed.

Many of you reading will instantly offer to be there for me and I deeply know and appreciate that I have so many to turn too. Here is where the grief layers the loss and twists my view. I don't want to take others away from their family. I feel responsible for stealing that precious time. I know what it's like regretting hours and minutes list. I don't want to be the cause of that regret for someone else. It's a vicious untrue cycle. I'm well aware of it.

So this week I found a counselor. She asked what people often ask me to share on stage but this time it's different.

"Share your story."

The words that bring me to speak and inspire others brought me right back to all the moments of loss in my life. Love ones lost, relationships leaving and animals reaching the end of their time all joined in sound and filled the room with a symphony of sadness - Heartbreak Harmony.

She said things I have said to myself. I suffer from depression and have a unique type of grief. I have gone through a lot of deep loss with no time to process it. I coped and worked harder to get past or skip over it.

"You have complicated grief disorder and it's going to be ok."

Year 3 A.C. – Pandemic and Self-Passiveness

Our visit ended with her asking what the rest of my day was like. I planned to go to the gym and run errands but she pointed out it's ok to go home and just feel. This morning I woke up and started coffee. I looked around and saw all the things I didn't do yesterday. The stress built and the room became overwhelming. A pile of clean laundry on the chair is normal but every time I see it I'm reminded that Clayton is gone. Fear floods the room and I'm gasping for air. Minutes later I find myself on the floor tight, tense and terrified. However this time was different. I texted a friend who called and said it will pass but I had to let it happen. In the midst of the storm I remembered I had an official diagnosis, it had a name, I was not the only person who feels this way, people want to help me, I'm not a burden just understandably broken. I finally told myself it's ok to not be ok...

November 14, 2020 - Champagne Dreams and Lost Love Legacies

Yesterday was my 42nd birthday. I'm unbelievably grateful for the outpouring of celebration especially on social media where so many of us are finding community during a pandemic. I decided that the day should start with a toast to lost loves and no better way than a glass of Veuve Clicquot champagne – The Widow's Champagne. In the 1700s in France, a woman named Barbe-Nicole Clicquot Ponsardin lost her husband and had to take the winery they built together forward. From her loss, she created a dynasty. Most likely you have seen this bottle but had no idea that it's origins and the legacy sprung up from the Widowed Clicquot.

Being widowed has all of it's own difficulties but adding this year take things to a whole new level. Everyone's grief journey is unique but I can't imagine what it's like to be just newly widowed world during this time. At least I was gifted normalcy in my surroundings as I learned to take each new step away into my new future. I could have as many visitors as I wanted. I could travel all I wanted. I could choose to be surrounded or alone. Today that basic human support can be drastically withheld.

I can't speak for the newly widowed in a pandemic but I can tell you that, even though I'm halfway through widowed year 3, my healing and growth has been greatly hindered. On the other hand, was I staying too busy to actually feel and is this some chapter in a divine plan to teach me a different perspective? What I do know from biology and the movie classic "Jurassic Park" is that life will find a way.

Yesterday I turned 42. To many, 40 is a big deal so really what is 42? For me, 40 was my first birthday without Clayton and 42 was his age. By April 16, 2021, on the fourth anniversary of his death, I will have out lived him. Yes, he was older so chances were that someday I would go through losing him and living on but never expected widowhood to arrive so very early in my life and our relationship. I am now his death age. That is a heavy, strong dose of my own mortality.

I share where I am at in my head and heart each week because I know there are others that feel the same and these topics have historically been kept in quiet closed-door conversations.

Year 3 A.C. – Pandemic and Self-Passiveness

"Don't air your dirty laundry" said someone back in the day.

Had Barbe-Nicole Clicquot Ponsardin not defied what others thought a widowed woman should be then she would never had reached me centuries later. To some it's just champagne but to me it represents strength, perseverance and, most of all, hope. So I raise a glass, toast our strengths and release us all from the chains of guilted grief. Share your stories so others can find footed grounding and take a step forward. From pain there can be incredible power and hauntingly beautiful healing for you and countless others. Someday someone may read this blog and say "Me too". In that moment, I will have bent time, broken the rules of death and hold space for the future grieving as they heal. That is widowed legacy…

November 21, 2020 - Faith in Fingerprints

Since Tin's passing, many have said he is with me, many have said he's moving things in and out of my path to help make things easier and more successful for me. On many occasions, I have found pennies, dimes, seen cardinals, butterflies and got a call or text just at the moment I needed them.

The thing about signs is that they can be convenient if you are really hunting. I've had many days where I'm just panic-searching for a whisper in the breeze telling me he's near. The hard part is that I just don't know for sure and I just want a sign so distinct that I'm not always chasing insignificant shadows. About two weeks ago, I hit a wall and lost my temper. I had a full unleashing on the universe. I said everything I have been harboring inside about how angry, disappointed and unfair life had been too me. Completely messed up "grand plan" without so much as an explanation or a "sorry I had to put you through that for the greater good". I declared that having faith in someone who keeps hurting you is an abusive

Year 3 A.C. – Pandemic and Self-Passiveness

relationship and I am done. I'm too good of a person to be treated this way. I deserve to be happy, healthy and held in love. Enough was enough and through burning tears I demanded:

"If you are really here to help me Tin, I need to see it!"

Everything stayed quiet.

This past week had turned out quite wonderful in many of the parts of life I have been feeling lost in. I started to revisit how I yelled at the universe as I opened a drawer that's been shut for two years. In it there was a jar of charcoal scrub a friend had made and given to Tin. He loved it so I never used it. I was brought immediately back to sitting in the bathroom and talking as he took his bath. I'm not really a bath guy but he had to have one every night. Eucalyptus in the air, a glass of wine and we talked until the bath bubbles faded away. I smiled remembering a 6'3" guy trying to sink in a bathtub and laughed that I just had a talk about how awkward bathtubs can be.

I smiled looking down at the faded label on the jar.

"I guess in many ways you are here touching my world. I hope you are guiding me on this new journey. I hope you are pointing me in the right directions. You know I get nervous."

I opened the jar to remember the scent of the scene and there pressed into the deep charcoal blend were Tin's prints. Right there, in that moment, his actual touch. Keep going Bryan...

Year 3 A.C. – Pandemic and Self-Passiveness

Novemeber 28, 2020 - The Pain and Possibilities of "Yes"

The first thing I learned to do when Clayton passed away was say "No". I said no to getting out of bed, no to eating, no to showering, no to the gym. No was the safest place I could hide myself. Saying no stopped the world and that is just where I wanted to be.

As time began to pass, I would start saying yes to the basics of life just to function like "normal" out there in the big world. I had to say yes to working (two jobs now). I had to say yes to folding my clothes, washing the dishes and making my bed. Slowly I got my feet back under me and stood up to start walking my journey but, this time it was just me. No advice from Clayton. No reassurance. No map. Just a broken compass in my heart and fear I'd pick the wrong path.

Through the first year, I walked guardedly through widowed mist seeing shadows, hearing strange sounds and continuing to say "No". Friends would call to me to follow their voices and go out. - "No".

I just couldn't bare to step into a space where Tin and I had created a memory, or worse, see others getting to have the memories we never made. I can't. It's painful. - "No".

I've said no to many things over the past 2.5 years because I feared the pain in the possibilities of yes. Yes meant allowing others in and what if I lost them too. I said no to dinners, drinks, dancing. I said no to opening up to new people and I said no to celebrating anything including holidays. What I've realized this year is that being afraid of the possible pain is also keeping me from the possibility of creating another fulfilling life. I've been feeling trapped in this crushed kingdom and my only choice is to say "No" or "Yes". Now it's time to start saying yes and not fear the possibilities of hurt, rejection and failure. I've already endured the weight of all three of those possibilities but I have to have faith that muscle memory will keep me standing if the weight returns.

I've started to say yes to the one thing that can help me find my new world. I am saying yes to trying. I'll try and I'll keep reminding myself that you can't fail if you don't try but you can't succeed either. The past month has been a whole lot of diving in and saying yes to trying. I said yes to date someone but that has fallen back to being a friendship. It's ok because, buried in the possibility of failure, was actually a gift - The knowledge that I could say "Yes" to trying to find love again.

Yesterday was one of the hardest "Yes" moments of my widowed wondering. Staying with a friend for Thanksgiving put me into a scary situation. Holiday decorating happens next. Three years ago to the day, Clayton, my mom and I went shopping. I stood back and soaked in what I knew would be a beautifully painful memory, Clayton and my mom searching for that one special tree – His last one. I haven't decorated since.

Year 3 A.C. – Pandemic and Self-Passiveness

All day yesterday I replayed that memory. I had moments where tears wanted to well up but I focused on "yes". Even if I cried my eyes out putting up decorations, it was going to be the best try because it was my first try. So as I picked up a decoration to hang, I paused, hesitated and then said "yes". I placed the silver ornament on the tree and stood back. I had done it. No one in the room realized what had just happened but I realized I was ok. A monumental event bathed in lights alongside laughter, holiday music and all possibilities…

December 5, 2020 - Table for One? No Thanks. I'll Just Wait At The Bar.

Some may love going out to eat alone but for me it is emotional. Even waiting for takeout can be tough. Grabbing dinner this week, I sat at the bar and got an awkward look from one group. I'm sure it was nothing but that doesn't mean my feelings weren't valid. Whatever it was that they were thinking about me was their reality and it made me feel very uneasy.

Ever see that guy having dinner by himself and wondering why he's alone? Where's his family? Doesn't he have any friends? Maybe he's crazy? I feel bad for him…

When I was younger, those are the things I would think seeing someone alone. It's always pointed out in conversation and depicted as negative on tv and in the movies. I certainly didn't realize when I was younger that I was looking into my own future. My perspective of the scene created a perception that went from feeling sad for the guy to thinking that maybe there was something wrong with him or that he might do something wrong. I had no reference for my stream of thought except what I learned - Alone means something is wrong with someone.

We are taught at a very young age the golden rule of being a good person. Treat others as you would want to be treated. Don't judge. Walk a mile in their shoes. Give the benefit of the doubt. However, if you are unsure, fill in the gaps with whatever truth suits your opinion and your perspective because ultimately it's up to the other person to change your perception of them.

So now, when I'm out at a restaurant by myself, I'm the guy at the end of the bar that, by default, has something wrong with him. All those patrons have no idea that I work two jobs just to feel safe. They also work two jobs, it's just masked as a relationship with someone

Year 3 A.C. – Pandemic and Self-Passiveness

else who brings in additional income - future security in a spouse and kids. You'll have people to help you later in life. Sounds a bit cold but it is biology at the root of it all and easier for society to accept.

Even just meeting new people can go south fast. A few week's ago another guy sat at the bar and started to talk with me while we waited. He asked if I was married, probably just to share something in common in conversation. I told him briefly about Clayton. I could very much sense him feeling uncomfortable as he focused more on his phone. So I stopped sharing and kept to myself. No chance to even change his perception. He didn't want to talk to the weird widowed gay.

What people don't understand is, all the little things they have in everyday life many of us widowed have lost. As I sit and wait for my food, I overhear conversations about the wife, the husband, about the kids, what to do about replacing the hot water heater, complaining about the in-laws coming for the holidays, weekend plans free from a second job. I don't have any of that filler stuff in my life and the pandemic has added a whole new layer of complication many don't even think to consider. I'm the guy at the end of the bar everyone should avoid just in case. They don't know the strength it takes to do "normal" things like sitting in a restaurant. They don't know I write a blog to help others feel less alone. They don't know what I've done to create spaces for others to feel welcomed and included. None of that counts. How ironic that the guy who seeks to build inclusion feels so passively excluded so often.

Some may tell me that I have the wrong perception but the fact is that this is my widowed reality. Others would say "who cares about their opinions" but the burden of other' perception is on me. I guess I'll just stick to delivery from now on. It's just easier…

Year 3 A.C. – Pandemic and Self-Passiveness

December 12, 2020 - The Woven Widowed "What" in the Fabric of Life

"What was I just doing? What was I about to say? What is that person's name? I've known them for years. Damn it Bryan! What is wrong with you?"

For a while, I thought that maybe I was a little crazy. I was struggling to understand why my thoughts were so scattered and why I couldn't get simple things done. Start to fold laundry, bring stuff to the closet, start to make the bed, turn and see dog toys all over the floor just to look up and remember I was supposed to be folding laundry and that was 20 minutes ago. I get frustrated with myself, overwhelmed at all the things I couldn't or didn't do and give up. The "What" turns from confusion to "what's wrong with me?"

Bereavement brain. I never knew until Clayton died that it's actually is a thing. In our world it's "Widowed brain" but grief fog shows up in many forms. Sometimes you don't even realize your head is in the mindless mist. It can be minutes, hours, days, weeks before your realize you were doing something. A full stop and change in direction leaving behind something you said you'd do. It's only when you suddenly are reminded, you realize widowed "what" is now woven through the fabric of your life - Stitched sadness in unpredictable patterns.

This week, as I pulled out holiday decorations (I wasn't sure I could even look at), I opened a drawer that had remained closed for over 2 years.

"Where did I put those? What did I do with them?"

I pulled the brass handles and stitch slid into my past. Shortly after Clayton died, a dear friend of his asked for some of his shirts and sweatshirts. As I went through his things, I happily set them aside knowing how much their friendship meant to both of them. Part of me was sad that his things were leaving me just as he had but I knew they were going to be loved in their new home. I set them aside in a drawer for safekeeping as I emptied out our closet towards closure.

The fog suddenly lifted. There in a drawer were Clayton's things I thought I had shipped over 2 years ago - Forgotten fabric. I lost my breath. Seeing them brought me back to his last day. I paused, caught my breath and lost it again realizing my widowed "what" had kept me from sending her meaningful memories. The feelings of loss, guilt and failure swept over me. I sat on the edge of the bed and cried. It was unintentional but I was disappointed all the same. I forgot about sending them, which, in my heart, turned into "I forgot about him." You can see how quickly something simple as a woven "what" can knock you off the road. We aren't on solid pavement. It's tough to balance bereavement brain when you're walking on grief gravel. Unsure footing and failure is now a part of my life's fabric.

Year 3 A.C. – Pandemic and Self-Passiveness

So my only goal today besides writing this blog is to sew up this tear. Forget the laundry, forget the dishes, forget the gym. The most important thing today is getting out of the mist and sending a wonderful person a box of memories.

Year one was a fog. Year 2 was the realness of loss. Year 3 seems to be me stitching up the last 2 years worth of "whats" in this tattered tapestry…

December 19, 2020 - Bitter, Bland and Forgotten Flavors

This year has been nothing less than bipolar. Severe ups, downs, twists and turns I could never expect. Year 1 and 2, I could keep busy, keep moving and face the loss of Clayton when I wanted too. Now, year 3, in a pandemic with the world halted, I'm forced to taste the truth and it's bitter – He's not coming back.

I've had more time to sit and stew over my thoughts and widowed worries then I really wanted. I feel like a kid at dinner that can't stand the meal but can't leave the table until his plate is clean. Every spoonful is excruciating. Tormented by the taste. Ironic that when we are kids our parents force us to eat things we don't like because they are good for us. Here I am at 42 fighting the voice of my father telling me to fork down the fear so I can move into the future. Over-seasoned servings of reality and I can't help but gag on the grief.

Clayton was more often the chef. I knew I'd come home to some amazing meal or the house filled with whatever fantastic food he decided to bake. He loved food. He loved sitting down for dinner. Now that he has gone, I find myself grabbing fast meals, eating while standing in the kitchen or just forgetting all together. I've come to the realization that I have lost my joy for cooking and eating. Every step of the process now comes with a serving of palatable punishment. Why pull out all of the bowls and utensils to make a meal that would remind me

Year 3 A.C. – Pandemic and Self-Passiveness

of him? Only to follow with the fact that if I do sit down, it's just me in the quiet. It's just me to clean up. I can't enjoy that sadly seasoned scene. Why whip up gastric grief?

If you read my blog each week, you'd have known that recently I opened a drawer and found some of Clayton's clothes I forgot about. This week, I opened a kitchen cabinet to grab a dog treat and the bag tipped. I opened the other side of the cabinet to reach the bag and there were all his forgotten flavors. Poultry seasoning from our last holidays, cocoa powder for his cakes, stale spices and seasonings I pushed to one side almost 3 years ago. I remember going through cabinets after Clayton's death and I remembered not being able to throw those out as if he would be mad they weren't there for him to use. I kept them because part of me hoped I was just having a bad dream and, when I wake up, he'd be back in our kitchen.

I thought that keeping them would somehow help me and I could slowly sprinkle and stir them back in but, the fact is, I forgot the flavors and it turned out to be a recipe for disaster. Seeing them now, I taste the baked in bitter and I've lost my appetite for the day. I'll just send myself to bed without supper…

December 26, 2020 - The Day After

The day after your diagnosis.

The day after our last holidays.

The day after your death.

The day after all of the "firsts" without you.

The day after all the seconds, thirds, fourth, fifths, sixth and, trust me, on the seventh day after there isn't rest. Every day is a new "day after".

Funny, that I'm writing this blog the day after Christmas. Most people refer to centuries as "BC" (Before Christ) or "AD" (Anno Domini). Interestingly enough AD means "in the year of the Lord" yet many misinterpret it as "After Death". Doing that skips an entire 33 years of

Year 3 A.C. – Pandemic and Self-Passiveness

human history. The ironic part is now being widowed brings another melancholy marker in my historical timeline. I now live in year 3 AC (After Clayton).

I'm honest about all the aspects of my journey through this new "After Clayton Calendar". Most of year 3 AC has been more fog lifting, more venturing out, more random recalling of memories, more tries and more tears because each day is still the new day after.

The difference now is subtle but exponentially significant. This year I've been grief gifted with reflection. In the years 1–2 AC, I was unable to look back and learn. There wasn't enough separation between where I had started and where I now was. Now, when I look back down my road newly traveled, I see a much longer distance walked. The path surrounded by enough tangible terrain, I can physically feel the space from that hallowed horizon.

The past 2 years was a fog of grief. All I could see was in front of me so I fixated on the road ahead. Go towards that widowed-wished mirage ahead and hope you find life saving waters. As the fog lifted, I could start to see to my left, my right and the distance behind me. As if my emotions were painted into the landscape as I walked past, there was a hauntingly beautiful view full of widowed wetlands, vicious valleys, positive peaks, singing streams, barren beaches, thawed tundra, metaphorical moors, jarred jungles, plains full of possibilities and mountains coated in emotions. Minute by minute showed me no progress but, in time, I have truly have moved through a grief geography I never new existed and that I was the actually creator of my world.

What I didn't realize is that mirage I was walking towards was actually me. I am my own oasis. So now I know, when I have a difficult day, I can reassure myself there is always the day after…

Year 3 A.C. – Pandemic and Self-Passiveness

January 2, 2021 - Letting Go of Leaving

I have had an amazing time the past week with my family. A much needed reconnect. The interesting theme was everyone's "sorry".

"Sorry we can't visit." "Sorry there is nothing to do." "Sorry we can't hug."

Funny how we take on the weight of "sorry" when we shouldn't. As everyone was "sorrying", little did they know I have held secret - a very deep sorry.

A huge fear growing up (which I still struggle with) is when I am out of sight I am out of mind. Forgotten until I'm there in person, on the phone or, yes, in a social media post. I know it's from my childhood. Classic case of the "different" kid picked last in gym but picked on the rest of the day. I kept my head down and hurried along in hopes they wouldn't see me. I would stay out of mind. I wanted to be included yet escape. In college, things calmed down but I couldn't wait to start my career so I finished early for my dream job. Friends were upset I wouldn't be there the last semester and when graduation day came around, the welcome back was a bit chilled. I had left and I lost meaning. Fears reinforced. Just dive into the career.

Years of working weekends, holidays, saying "yes" to strange hours and "no" to a normal social life all to build value. There were times I could have put work to the side and said "no" but in such a competitive field, if I took time away then I feared I would be forgotten and miss out on growth. I've reached an amazing goal now but was all I choose to give up necessary? Many times in my career I was present and still overlooked. There's an even amount of responsibility spread across my doing and their withholding but, to the managers out there, keep in mind your decisions and just how heavy they can be on your staff. A seed won't sprout with a thumb pushing it down. If a flower is failing, we don't get a new flower. We caringly enhance its habitat to increase its chances of success. In animal training, all animals deserve us trying to set them up for success, but I digress.

I have also always dreamed about finding the one and getting married. There have been a handful of good tries but they ended up ending. Fears reinforced with the hardest ending of all, Clayton. In the other relationships, it was a choice to move on but with Clayton there was no expected exit.

My return home brought up that deep secret "sorry" that always weighed heavy on my heart – I left. I left my amazing family and friends. I left home to chase enchanted employment. I poured into an endless career cup and I missed so much. Perhaps I feel this because I'm widowed or that I wasn't around to help my family more? The "what ifs" weigh heavy. "What if" I could have helped my father or does everything happen for a reason? The veil between guilt and grief lays thin. Perhaps I feel called to share these words because others hold this weight as well. We are taught to chase after our dreams, be successful and live

Year 3 A.C. – Pandemic and Self-Passiveness

happily ever after. What they don't tell you is that the sacrifice you make leaving can haunt you.

So on this visit I returned back down my street, past the bus stop I was bullied at, to see the house I grew up in, the beach where my dad taught me how to skip stones and the park I would sit at dreaming of how wonderful life would be when I could leave. There I sat with 12 year old me acknowledging his fears and reassuring him that he has done his best. I told him that people leave and come back while others leave to make room for new people. I told him about all the amazing things that have happened in our life because he took the chance and I thanked him. Had that young kid stayed, I never would have met Clayton.

His decisions meant no harm and the time has come to forgive leaving…

January 9, 2021 - "The Upside Down"

I have always had trouble when I'm told that there is no way out and no solution to things. Apparently, looking back at my writing, that fact holds true even in loss and grief. I didn't realize at first but it explains my anger when I was hit with the regular "whys?" and the "what nows?" - No answers.

Through life we travel over and through a variety of terrains. I had hit an impasse and the only thing around was a hole in the ground. I looked to the left and right hoping to see a little white rabbit show me the way. Instead, life pushed me from behind and I fell. The shear fear from the death drop and sudden impact of losing Clayton knocked me unconscious. Months had passed and I woke up disoriented with no way to climb up these widowed walls. I felt trapped. So I stopped and asked myself a novel question:

"What if the reason it feels hard is because I am trying to turn around the down?"

Year 3 A.C. – Pandemic and Self-Passiveness

I decided to stop sitting at the bottom looking back up with insatiable longing and began to dig down. At first, I thought I'd dig forever but that ditch eventually broke through to a gateway, an epiphany opening leading into consciousness caverns. I was met with a stale warm widowed wind and I realized what was happening. In "The Divine Comedy", Dante's journey is of a widowed man guided by a shade named Virgil as he descends through the levels of Hell in hopes to make it to his lost love in Heaven. My understanding of what was happening became clear as I stared into the darkness of the grief gorge. Like Dante, I was about to head through Inferno. Somewhere softly from the down, Virgil was calling to follow.

If you've never read Inferno, at the bottom Dante finds not fire but ice holding the most egregious of sinners - the traitors. Here Satan lays frozen and Dante is guided by Virgil to begin climbing down Satan's chest through a hole in the ice. It is there at true center where Virgil reverses direction and begins to climb up Satan's leg. Dante becomes disoriented being suspended in two truths. Virgil points out that from the center all ways can become a new ascendance. Like Dante, I had to travel down to the center of icy torment. There I discovered I had damned my own journey by punishing the past. I felt the universe had betrayed me and so froze my future.

As I sat holding creation in contempt, I realized I do not have the right to know the reasons behind my endless "whys". I can't punish the Universe (and myself) by staying frozen demanding answers. To move forward I have to let go of the need to know. I can only choose my "what now". So here I am thawing at the true center of loss and, just like Dante, my "upside-down" has become my new "right-side up"…

January 16, 2021 - Under This Widowed Weight

Throughout caring for Clayton before he died, I felt the weight of responsibilities. The weight of being a caregiver and the weight of working full time, the weight of making sure

Year 3 A.C. – Pandemic and Self-Passiveness

medications were dosed and delivered on time, the weight of his comfort and the weight of emotions. Heaviest of all for me, the weight of what was to come.

There were so many weights to handle that I had to leave a few behind. The weight of my fear, the weight of my sadness and the physical weight I was adding. I didn't care about me. I just wanted him to be free of any weight I could take on because he was carrying the heaviest of all – Knowing he was dying.

After Clayton passed, I felt lighter without all of those responsibilities but that left me feeling vulnerable to the emotional elements. Sudden exposure from the lack of pressures caused panic so I started to pile on work weight, busy weight and more physical weight. Distractions distorted the devastation. There was safety in being buried alive under self-imposed burden.

I remember being in that space. I had accepted I would forever have to hold on to the heavy. This third year of widowed walking has brought forth something I never thought I'd reach. I had so much on my shoulders that I just kept moving forward without turning back. When you carry a boulder, the widowed weather brings tough stormy days and you don't really notice grains of grief that crumble off. Each storm's passing erodes the stone into subtle sand. I didn't acknowledge that the burden had grown lighter until I finally heard a happy memory behind me. It caught me off guard and I found myself looking over my shoulder for the first time. There I was standing up straight again no longer bent under a boulder of bereavement. The happy memory had started tipping the scales away from solid stone sadness.

I will always carry grief for losing Clayton but now I can start to stretch and breathe again. These first few years, although heavy, have built my strength so I keep moving forward a little lighter each day. Through the sunshine, pouring rain and stinging sleet, this journey continues to carve and smooth me. Despite what they say, time cannot heal all wounds. Even time can't remove these sovereign scars. I still have distance to travel but at least time is helping take off the layers and slowly freeing me from under this widowed weight…

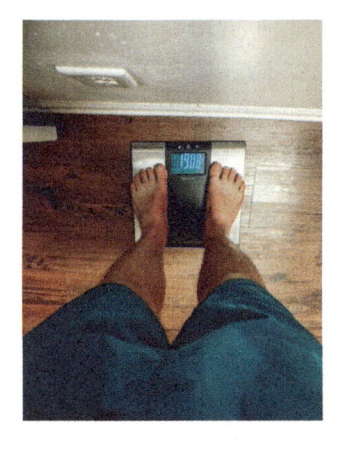

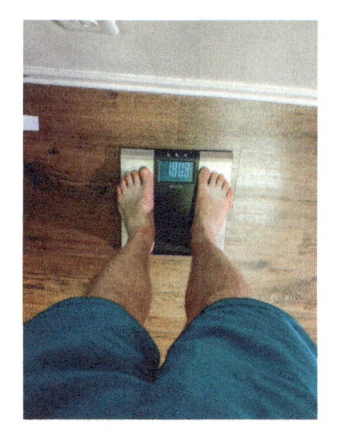

Year 3 A.C. – Pandemic and Self-Passiveness

January 23, 2021 - Worries and Whys

Growing up, I suffered from severe asthma, allergies, etc. It was common for me to take medication daily. I can recall the shear panic if my wheezing started and I couldn't find my rescue inhaler. I couldn't do what the "normal" kids did and I was bullied, left out and judged. As I got older, my asthma decreased. Under doctor supervision, medications were reduced and now I just have a rescue inhaler. I'll probably always have one. Today I'm in my 40s and I have witnessed another side of medication that has created new widowed worries and whys. I lost my dad to opioids that resulted in alcohol use. I lost my partner Clayton to a medication that destroyed his liver in 4 months.

I said part of my journey was to dig deep and get into parts of widowhood that are rarely shared so here we go. Here's something more personal, I am deathly allergic to PREP (Truvada). For those of you who don't know, this is a medication that reduces the chance of getting HIV. It has become an extremely popular and easy to obtain medication. Friends suggested I start taking it just in case. I was extremely worried but the doctor said it was very common and most people did fine on it so I started taking it. Better to be safe right? I was moving forward and being responsible. After 4 days, I had debilitating pain all over. I had severe kidney and liver reactions and was immediately taken off of it. The doctor said I was not a candidate for that type of drug. I could go into liver failure just like Clayton. Now, it's emotionally difficult for me to even take an aspirin. Pharmacaphobia - The fear of medicines. Yes it's a real thing. It's very real for me and believe me when I tell you that people have shown no respect for my fears.

This dives deeper than just taking medication. It dives into the complexity of grief, dating and even feeling I belong in the gay world. With that "magic med" people engage in dating more freely without all the worry. I'm happy there are advancements but many forget that advancements don't work for everyone. It's becoming a norm of the culture and, if you don't fit in, the discrimination and judgment flow fast and freely. When I've shared that I'm not comfortable dating someone positive, I can even explain why before I'm accused of being uneducated.

"Ah, hello have you ever heard of PREP you idiot?" (Yes that was an actually said to me)

When I get a moment to explain, I tell them how I lost my dad, lost Clayton and that I'm severely allergic to the "magic" medication they think I know nothing about. That usually ends the discussion on the spot without even an option to be friends. For such a "love is love" and "open and understanding" community, we sure know how to not support each other. I'm just being responsible for myself but it apparently doesn't matter what you've been through if it's not what others want to hear. For me, medication, side effects, adverse reactions and death are all very real things. I don't want to be a part of a community that doesn't want to accept me because I can't do what the "normal" kids are doing. It's back to being bullied, left out and there isn't a rescue inhaler for these social symptoms.

Year 3 A.C. – Pandemic and Self-Passiveness

So here I am trying to move forward. Dating is hard enough and I don't fit in with all the changes, trends and the new "no-worry" pills. I don't feel like I belong anywhere anymore. Why am I the one who has to be allergic? Why do people have to be so judgmental? Why am I even bothering to try? Why did all of this have to happen? I wouldn't even have to think about any of this Clayton had you not died. Some days I get so mad because you're gone and I have o deal with all these new worries and whys…

January 30, 2021 - Pets and People Years

Everyone has a set time here on this Animal Planet. When we take in a new family member, we know there are good chances we will be there for their whole life and still be here when they have moved on. It's a normal part of life and we buffer our emotions by planning ahead for the inevitable with common questions like:

"How old are they in dog years?"

Every time we ask, we are making ourselves aware their existence here (as we understand them) is usually faster then ours. It's a mechanism to prepare us early for what's to be lost. I'm hit with it more often than most. Earlier this past week I was at work a little worried about my cat's recent behavior when a little girl at the penguin exhibit asked me:

"How old are they in like dog years? I mean, you know, like penguins years? Like it's 7 dog years for a people year."

A common simple question from a curious guest, I appreciated her thinking beyond "cute penguin" and (just so you all know the answer) I've loved penguins that have lived into their 40s, so it's about 2 penguin years per people year in good care.

Year 3 A.C. – Pandemic and Self-Passiveness

My life has been filled to the brim with countless animals coming and going into my life either by natural timeline or a change in jobs. Saying goodbye is never easy but this week was a rogue wave. I had been making a lot of extra wishes for the safe keeping of our kids by throwing a lot of pennies to the bottom of my widowed well but time was ready to come and collect some of the dues.

Clayton and I have 2 children together - Roan, our dog, and Stallone our cat. Both were rescues. Clayton adopted Stallone before we were together. A last chance at adoption for a severely malnourished and abused black kitten with F.I.V. and, in pure Clayton fashion, he had to help the underdog (or should I say "undercat"). Stallone would hide all day and only come out to eat under the cover of night. When Clayton and I blended families, it was amazing to watch how quickly Roan and Stallone took to each other. A brotherhood was born. When Clayton was near his last days, he worried so much about our boys and I promised I would take care of them.

Two days after that little girl asked "How many people years?", Stallone suddenly stopped eating. I brought him to the veterinarian hoping he just had something that could be treated. Three hours later they called to confirm why animal intuition was tugging on my heartstrings with thoughts of goodbyes. We always knew that his FIV would shorten his "people years" but never thought it would happen so soon and so fast.

So there I was holding our son who, just like his other dad, was hit by an acute onset of his time ending. We couldn't talk about his fears. We couldn't talk about his confusion. I couldn't explain why we weren't at home. I told him how much he was loved, how glad we were that he was part of our family and to not be scared because he'd just fall asleep, leave his suffering behind in my arms and wake up healed in Clayton's arms.

It's never easy to loose a loved one. It's never easy when you know it's that time and the right thing to do. I'll miss you my little boy but the hardest part is I can't explain to Roan why his brother, just like his other dad, won't be coming home…

Year 3 A.C. – Pandemic and Self-Passiveness

Feb 6, 2021 - The Peter Pan Perspective

I couldn't wait to grow up. I can distinctly remember being in 5th grade and telling myself I only had to deal with this for 7 more years and then I'd be free to fly. I've always been a big dreamer. At times my imagination would create beautiful worlds and outcomes of grandeur. I'd have great hopes for the future but that active imagination would also turn dark and create some intense fears out of nothing.

I can remember being so upset by the littlest things and my dad would say "Do you really want something to cry about?" He wasn't being threatening, he was providing perspective that there are harder things in life and everything didn't need to be a "trigger". No one told me that the future I was wishing to get to would be filled with things much worse then 5th graders. Those 7 years felt like they dragged and all of a sudden I'm 42 and widowed. I didn't want to be this kind of grown up.

I have had many days since Clayton passed wishing I could have paused time. Just to be able to hang up my shadow and be carefree. Some days I've played pretend and lived in a fairytale where everything was fine. Some nights I'd go to bed hoping it was all a bad dream. I'd just wake up back in my bedroom a much wiser 5th grader. No rushing and way more respect for the process.

I can't go back so all I can do is share my perspective in hopes that others will slow down their rush. You never know what that next big thing is and my dad was right, it might really be something to cry about.

For the past three years I have searched and searched in all my imagination. Although at times I truly feel like "a lost boy" I've looked everywhere and I can't find a way to get to Neverland. Peter Pan never stopped by and I'm well aware of my shadow…

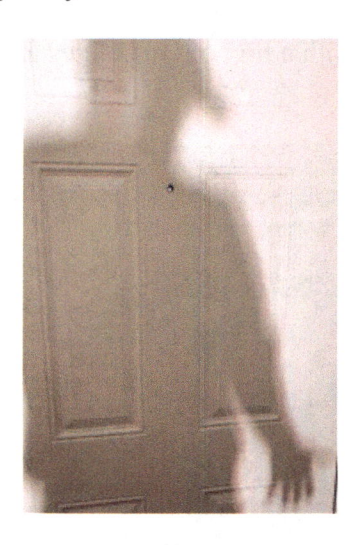

Year 3 A.C. – Pandemic and Self-Passiveness

Feb 13, 2021 - Wid-OWED

This week has been tough. I have had conversations with probate court to try and finalize Clayton's Will and picked up Stallone's (our cat) ashes back from the veterinarian. Now he and Clayton sit on a bookshelf until we can figure out a funeral for them. I'm coming up on 3 years since Clayton died with so much missing closure. On top of all that, I can't walk through a store without pink and red hearts "Valentine vomited" everywhere. This week, while others savor the sweets, I keep biting off more bitter.

It's very common for people to tell me to hold on and that things are going to get better. They say that good things happen to good people. Others say that life isn't fair, move on and hard work pays off. How do you balance honoring your emotions but also putting on your big boy pants and moving forward? This week, "Everything happens for a reason" leaves a terrible taste in my mouth. This week I feel like a kid forced to sit at the table until my plate is cleaned while the rest of the neighborhood is outside playing. It's just not fair.

Dear Life, when is there a block of time without difficulties, reminders, holiday hardships and heartbreaking hard work? I'm tired. This week I am more worn down. I don't think this is a matter of feeling entitled. I feel owed.

"Life, I would like to speak to your manager please. I'm Wid-OWED."

I know that declaration doesn't change anything but I just have to say it out loud. I am very aware that my life is not all difficulties. There are many others who have similar or other challenging life experiences but, again, it is ok for me to be fed up and say it out loud. These feelings will pass. I will eventually find myself walking through grounds of gratitude again but not this day, not this week. This week I don't want to see people holding hands happy. This week I don't want to hear people talk about their family plans. This week I don't want to know that a couple just got the house of my dreams because they have two incomes. They'll get to celebrate together with a box of chocolates and I'll be here alone with this box full of my broken heart…

Year 3 A.C. – Pandemic and Self-Passiveness

Feb 20, 2021 - Safety Behind Locked Doors

Safety. It's the basis of all our primary needs. Safety, security and stability, when any or all of these are threatened, we go into survival mode. As someone who is widowed, these are in constant fluctuation for me. I have had calm days, stressed days and anxious days. The fear of being unsafe is something I've carried my whole life. Unfortunately, it has been repeatedly reinforced and manifests itself in strong ways. My life revolves around locked doors.

Maybe it started with seeing "monsters in my closet" as a kid. What I do know is that it was exponentially triggered when I was robbed. I had moved to Atlanta to be with my fiancé. We lived in an apartment and signed a lease to rent a home. Shortly after that, we had a heartbreaking breakup. I moved into that house having to start all over. I felt so alone in a new city, in a new place. The only safe place was my new house so I didn't really want to go anywhere. A friend of mine finally convinced me to spend the day at the lake. Reluctantly I said yes and I had a great day. I was being reassured that I could enjoy things again. When I got home that night, I walked into the house to find the back door open, a window was shattered, my belongings were gone and the contents of the refrigerator spilled all over the floor and furniture. The police arrived and told me "This isn't really your neighborhood" and left. There I was alone, surrounded by my damaged life, no help from the police and feeling horrifyingly unsafe. I couldn't move out for another month so every night I laid on an air mattress in the living room with all the lights on and a knife next to the bed. To leave for work in the morning was scary but the return each evening was worse. I walked around the house to see if it was broken into before I'd enter. I'd check every room, behind every door and in every closet with a knife in hand.

When I finally moved out I noticed something new. I'd lock my apartment door and check it. Then I would check it again. Then I would walk down the hall and a great fear would come over me so I would go back and check the door again. I had days where I would leave in my car and have to turn around to check one more time. I started video taping me checking the door so I would be able to watch it throughout the day.

Over time, my anxiousness died down and I could lock the door and walk away until Clayton passed away. Here I was again, alone with my safety and security threatened by his death. I was robbed of him. I distinctly remember the first morning leaving for work after he was gone. I locked the door, walked away and a panic attack started. I had to rush back. I had to check. I had to be sure it was locked. What if someone broke in right after Clayton died? What if someone took my dog? My heart couldn't take it. In an instant I was back in that house with a knife, on an air mattress unable to sleep and full of fear.

"Safety first" they say. So now I check all the doors and I check them again and again. I check the door to my house and the doors to my car but losing Clayton has added one more to the list – the door to me. It's always been a tough door for others to open but right now it feels safer if I just recheck the lock…

Year 3 A.C. – Pandemic and Self-Passiveness

Feb 27, 2021 - The Dentist is in the Details

For many who are widowed and many who suffer extreme loss and grief, the start back to "normal" is a long and winding road. Even tasks that we consider "everyday automatics" can be pushed aside or delayed. Some days it's hard to just get out of bed let alone brush your teeth. Each thing you do after your person dies is highlighted as "the first time I've (blank) without them". We don't think about our teeth because we stop talking, eating and we certainly don't smile so it's "out of sight, out of mind".

There were plenty of days just after Clayton passed where I would sleep in until the afternoon, get up, go the bathroom and go back to bed. Why bother brushing my teeth? You don't really care about cavities when there is a huge one in your heart.

This April will mark the 5th year Clayton and I would have been here. Just before we left Atlanta, I went to the dentist for my regular cleaning and had to find a new one once we settled. Year one passed and I hadn't made it a priority. Year two was other things on my mind. My mother had beaten breast cancer but my father passed away. Four months after my father passed, Clayton received his diagnosis that we would only have 8 months more so I poured everything I could into him and nothing into me. You guessed it – no dentist.

Year one without Tin and there were days I forgot to brush my teeth. Year two and I honestly didn't care what my health was like. It's now year three of widowed winter and I've started to stir from the hibernation. I began to eat better, exercise more, drink less alcohol, go to doctor checkups and allow myself to start feeling less guilty that I'm here and Clayton isn't. I'm learning it's ok for me to go on living and it doesn't mean I'm leaving him behind. That right there is a profound statement for me to say and, although sad in it's inception, brings me lost comfort.

Year 3 A.C. – Pandemic and Self-Passiveness

So this week, after 5 years, I went to the dentist. I knew of the potential consequences and the fact that flossing and I do not get along well. The hygienist asked me when was my last cleaning. She asked why and, as always, I was very honest and shared my loss. She shared her condolences. As the x-rays began and the cleaning commenced, I couldn't help but go back to feeling firsts. This was the first dental visit post Clayton. As the hygienist scraped away, she had no idea that she was helping me clean the slate. Lying there, I realized my appointment was taking away actual and symbolic buildup from the past few years.

Cleaned and polished, the dentist came in to inform me that after 5 years of being at the bottom of the priority list, I had excellent teeth. After all that they had been through and the little care showed towards them, they stayed strong. Seems to be a theme in my journey and that (along with a good cleaning) makes me proud to start smiling again…

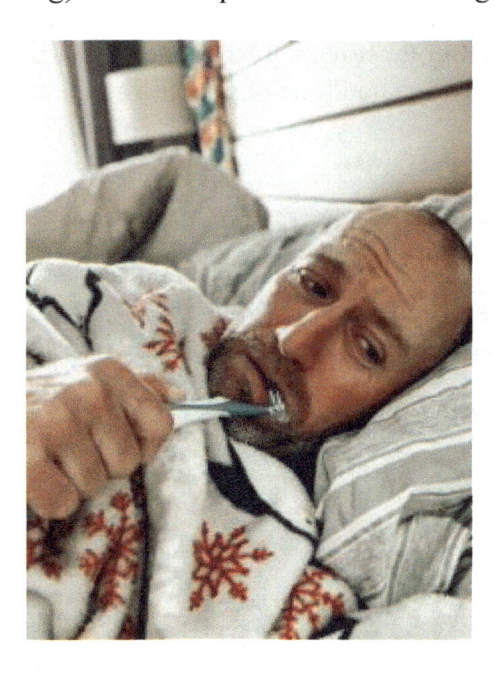

March 6, 2021 - The Escape Room

Part of my widowed journey is getting the opportunity to get away from home. Staying in the apartment that Clayton and I both lived has its benefits and its challenges. He hung up the art and organized the furniture. Everything here holds whispers of his style and view of interior design. I'm coming up on renewing my apartment lease and, although I can get out of it and move at any time, I feel a bit trapped.

Every year my lease renews on April 16th. Clayton's death anniversary is also the anniversary of us moving down here.

So I've been entertaining the idea of buying a place. Starting fresh and moving forward but real estate prices are jumping. I don't want to settle or rush and buy something to buy something simply to get out of this reminder rental. That's not fair to me now that it's only

Year 3 A.C. – Pandemic and Self-Passiveness

me. I've got pre-approval for a mortgage and next we see if the house I'm manifesting shows up sooner rather than later or I sign another year in the widowed walls that Clayton designed.

Before the world shut down, I was able to do quite a bit of traveling for work, fun and public speaking. Some trips were long but even just a weekend getaway would sweep me off to a land where I was not widowed. I could just be me in the space I was in without returning home at the end of each day to the emptiness greeting me. Travel was a healthy break to connect with life outside of the daily reminders. Unfortunately trips have gotten scarce and I find myself increasingly growing trapped so I find myself going to my escape room.

When we found this apartment, we wanted to have a second bedroom for people to visit. What I didn't know is that after Clayton's death I would be a visitor in my own home. On the nights that I don't want to sleep in our bed alone I play pretend. I pretend that I'm away on a trip and I stay in the other bedroom. It feels fresh, different and, most of all, it doesn't feel like our empty bed where Clayton should be next to me alive and just asleep…

Year 3 A.C. – Pandemic and Self-Passiveness

March 13, 2021 - Grief Gifts

One month away from the third anniversary of Clayton's passing and some moments it feels like it was just yesterday. Each year has had its challenges and this year I've lost our cat Stallone. I've written before that it's the build up to certain dates that's worse then the actual days themselves. Each season has its sewn in sadness. While others stir with spring's warm welcome, I watch as life renews and it feels like a taunting. Clayton doesn't get to come back but the date he died does.

April 16th is always going to hold that feeling. The day my life changed and I had to start walking forward alone again. The reminders are often and unique. Every year taxes are due on my sister's birthday and my lease is up the following day. I remember being with Clayton on April 15, 2018. He wasn't making sense with his sentences and was too weak to really stay awake. I knew goodbye was not far away but I just needed him to remember it was Stephanie's birthday for just a few more hours. It was her day and I just hoped it stayed that way. He smiled, whispered for me to tell her happy birthday and I felt a shift in his energy.

At 3am on April 16, 2018 I woke up suddenly as if someone had rushed in the room. Stallone, our cat, and Roan, our dog, were both standing over me side by side. I knew Tin had moved on but in his passing he gave me my first grief gift. He had waited. April 15th would stay sacred for Stephanie.

Since that day, messages and items have appeared from unexpected places at just the right times. Surprise flowers, cards and one of my most treasured is the painting my beautiful friend Marta made. I have posted about it before. Marta had taken a photo from my Facebook and painted Clayton and Roan on the beach.

This week I began to feel the tension of April 16th's arrival. A friend of mine came over to have a social night and in the middle of wine, cheese and episodes of The Golden Girls (Clayton's favorite show) she handed me a thin box and said she had a friend who could draw. Her friend had gone through my Facebook pictures and created Clayton meeting Stallone on the rainbow bridge. Her thoughtfulness and his talent created a physical image for me to see what I held in my heart.

I didn't know what to say. All I could do was look through the gratitude tears at my new beautiful grief gift…

Year 3 A.C. – Pandemic and Self-Passiveness

March 20, 2021 - Bachelor of Grief

I never wanted to apply and enroll here at Widowed University. I've always been opened to learning more in life but I never wanted this education. Like I said last week, the build up to Clayton's death day is one of the hardest times of the year for me. Two years last April I got my WU associates and now I'm almost through my junior year headed towards my bachelor of widowed degree.

"What do you want to be when you graduate Bryan?"

I've gained knowledge but where do I fit in now out in the big world? You don't graduate from the grief. You graduate with it.

It's Spring, people are talking about weddings, getting engaged, having babies and finding partners. I have none of that and no one knows if I ever will have those chances again. No one can say for sure that I won't be a bachelor for the rest of my life. No one can say that there's a guy out there that the universe plans for me to meet. What if Tin was it and the universe just plans for me to be alone for the rest of life. That's a real possibility and it hurts.

Always just a brides-man never the groom, the fun uncle but never the dad, the guy that's there if you need him but "out of sight" unfortunately feels like "out of mind". It's a constant struggle to feel happy for others and sad for myself at the same time – a bachelor of balancing being bereaved and begrudging. As they walk down the aisle, babies take first steps forward, couples buy their dream homes, I just keep seeing people walk away together without me. What happens when everyone is gone?

Does this degree mean I'm destined to just be that lonely old gay guy full of widowed wisdom – A Bachelor of Grief.

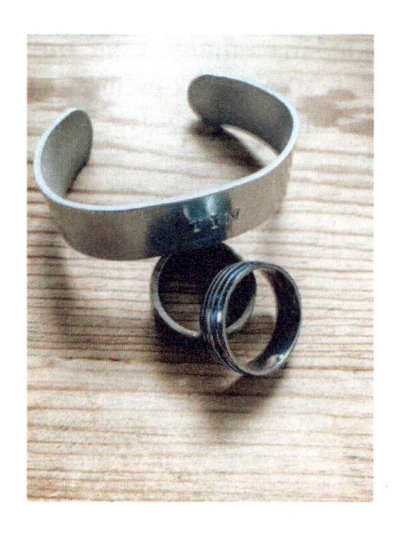

Year 3 A.C. – Pandemic and Self-Passiveness

March 20, 2021 - The Grief Keeper

For almost 3 years, I have been writing each week. I missed a few here and there but that's life. Year 1 was a fog. Year 2 was sharp realizations. Year 3, I finally accepted that Clayton was not coming back and it was time to focus less on losing him and more on keeping me.

Everyone's journey is different but in many ways grief and stages are very similar. I keep hearing "me too" when I share and I'm starting to see that I've been walking on a more worn and kept path than I realized. It's there in those shared moments that I find small bits of healing. Many ask "have you moved on" or they make a statement like "it'll be better when the grief is gone". These are meant to be supportive but I'll always keep missing Clayton. I'll always keep wishing things were different. I'll always keep his memory alive. I'll always keep sharing where I am along this path.

This year has taught me so many different things about me. I have made a conscious decision to be my first priority and advocate for myself verses allowing the grief to be my guide. When I shifted my perspective on the grief managing me to me managing my grief, the path widened. The road started to be less of tough terrain to travel. Being honest with myself about where I was at and really diving in to think about why I was walking through my days the way I was gave me the insight. I have been letting my grief lead me but was that the way life would now forever be? It'd didn't fit right or sit well.

A big part of my grief has been keeping so busy that I don't have time to think. Another big issue that weighed heavy was I kept feeling guilty I'm here and Clayton is not. Those are normal things that many of us do but at some point we either keep them or let them go. So at the start of this year I had a deep conversation with my grief. Grief was always going to be here so we had to work on our relationship. I get that the things he kept me doing were to help protect me but he wasn't letting me breathe and grow. So he couldn't keep me overworked. He couldn't keep me scared. He couldn't keep making me feel guilty. He couldn't keep making me emotionally eat. He just couldn't keep me.

So I'll still have days where all I want is for Clayton to come back. I'll still honor every feeling and memory that comes to me. Maybe this is all part of the process and it's a natural 3 year milestone but the grief no longer runs my days. Now I am the grief keeper…

Year 3 A.C. – Pandemic and Self-Passiveness

April 3, 2021 - The Better Place

"It's so hard to lose someone but remember he's in a…"

I've always struggled with religion. I was raised Irish Catholic and being gay was not accepted the way it is more openly today. I'm not sharing this to start a discussion on religious beliefs but to paint a picture of this aspect of my "widowed place".

Growing up, I was always the well-behaved kid who did his homework, treated people kindly and stayed out of trouble. What no one knew was I feared I had already failed. I couldn't shake the idea of finding the man of my dreams, which was against the rules of the "other place." I spent many nights apologizing to my ceiling asking for my feelings to be put in a "different place".

I spent my growing up telling myself I'd eventually move my heart out of the "wrong place". For the time being, just deny it or I'll end up in the "hot place." Keep it to yourself so you'll end up in the "good place."

College opened up to a bigger life. After trying my hardest, I accepted that there was no way I good be such a good person and a predetermined cosmic mistake. Luckily, friends and family celebrated me. I had found the "safe place".

All grown up and life moved me from east to west, from the big city to this "coast place". Each location, for a time, felt like the "right place" but locations could never match being with Clayton – the "best place". Meeting at a bar but in different timelines, we carried on until we met again at my loft pool in a "surprise place."

Years later I find myself in an "unexpected place". People try to reassure me that he is now in an "amazing place". My heart hurts each time I hear those words because it means being in "another place" is a "wonderful place" rather than being with me. There have been times where that young boy resurfaces, lays awake looking up at the bedroom ceiling thinking what if Clayton dying is to put me in a "punishing place."

No matter how wonderful we may think of the "upper place", Clayton being with me will always be the "better place."

Year 3 A.C. – Pandemic and Self-Passiveness

April 10, 2021 - My Grief Ghost Visits the Week Before Widowed

I knew he was fading away faster and faster. I knew that Tin's last day was soon but you don't know until you know. We fit in frozen yogurt, going out to dinner, the beach and visiting the aquarium just one last time. I didn't know it was the list of lasts. I didn't know it was my week before widowed.

To say the last week was full of us trying to live life to the fullest would be a Hollywood fairytale. That last week was one of the hardest. Clayton was fiercely independent and hated being told what to do but his condition was doing just that. He couldn't move much on his own. Before getting sick, Clayton would spend every night taking a bath in the guest bathroom. I would sit down next to him and talk. There he was, my handsome future husband asking me about my day not realizing I was in awe of him, so strong and so sensitive at the same time. Then I blinked and we were in the last week. All he wanted was a bath. So I held him up as he walked, undressed him and stood behind him in the tub to lower him. Warm water from the faucet and from my eyes filled the space around him. There I sat in awe of my handsome, soon to be late, husband as he asked me about my day.

Two days before Clayton died, we went to see the animals at the Gulfarium one last time. We went to eat at a local restaurant he loved, The Gulf, one last time. As we sat and ate, I noticed his appetite wasn't what it normally was. I knew he felt weak and I knew he was hiding it to save me. His illness was telling him no more food and it was getting him frustrated. Before we left he needed to go to the bathroom and he couldn't lift himself out of the wheelchair. I helped him up, set his clothes and lowered him down. I could see the frustration in his face through the tears in my eyes as I watched him sigh in defeat. I looked at him in awe, my brave dying partner.

He wanted to visit our apartment that night but it was getting late. We said we would make the trip up the three flights of stairs tomorrow. He sat relaxed in the passenger seat and held my hand.

Tomorrow arrived but Clayton didn't have the energy. I went over to his mother's to be with him. He could barely open his eyes or breathe and I sat looking for the last time, in awe, of my handsome fading partner. I didn't know that this was our last sit. There was no way to know that this was the end of my week before widowed…

For some, it's the anniversary day while others have trouble with holidays or birthdays. My week leading up to Clayton's death anniversary hits harder than any other. The guest bathtub waits dry and the passenger seat of the car is empty. Memories are marked in places and travel forward to the present time. They bring him back to life in those spaces right before my eyes. All around, people walk by. He looks at me knowing that only I can see him and for a moment we sit. Tears fill my eyes as I look in awe at my beautiful passed partner. My grief ghost always visits the week before widowed…

Year 3 A.C. – Pandemic and Self-Passiveness

The Care-Griever Years:

Year 4 A.C.

Self-Generated Joy

Year 4 A.C. – Self-Generated Joy

Year 4 turned out to be my turn around year. Up until this point, I was searching for something or someone to turn my world around. Nothing and no one arrived. I had finally understood that great things and great people weren't going to pull me out of the shadows. It took me four years to realize that I was the person I was waiting for. Once I accepted the sole responsibility for my growth through grief, the world began to open up. I poured into myself. I lost 40 lbs. I started to feel better physically, emotionally and mentally and it showed in all I did. My social media began to explode on Facebook, Instagram and Tiktok. People began messaging me to thank me for sharing my all parts of my journey. I was invited on podcasts and celebrities began sharing my dancing. I was reinforced even more the mindset that if I took care of myself I would generate enough positive energy to pour over others.

A Tiktok I posted in remembrance of Clayton's birthday caught the eye of someone new, Devin, who would turn out to be my fiancé a year later. Year 4 truly is the year I realized I had a magic within –

The ability to self-generate joy and joy is contagious.

"WE ALL HAVE THE ABILITY TO GENERATE OUR OWN JOY WHEN WE MAKE TIME TO DO THE THINGS WE ENJOY. WHEN YOU ARE JOYFUL YOU HAVE ENOUGH TO SHARE AND THAT'S WHEN THE MAGIC HAPPENS BECAUSE JOY IS CONTAGIOUS..."

- SEALIONBRYAN

Year 4 A.C. – Self-Generated Joy

April 17, 2021 - The Grief Tour

This week, my week before widowed, I took a trip off the main path of my journey and doubled back to the places I saw you last. My head said "yes" but my heart said "no don't go". It's been 1,098 days since I could actually touch you, hear you and see you in person. Today marks Day 1 of year 4.

This week's weather matched my emotions. There were dark clouds, heavy rain and furious lightning filling the skies and in my heart. I have felt sad, depressed, lonely and angry but the one thing I can't feel anymore is denial that you're gone. So this week I walked in places that we walked. I ate at places we ate, I sat in places we sat.

I went to the last place we ate together, The Gulf. I wore your hoodie and your pineapple shorts. I ordered a drink and sat in the same chair as last time. I pulled your chair out for you and I remember helping you sit and stand that night. No one knew I wasn't alone. The bartender stopped and said she liked my shorts. I choked up and said thank you. She asked if I was ok and I told her about our last dinner. I thanked her for "seeing" you.

I went to Olive Garden and had a glass of wine in your honor as I waited for our takeout. I ordered your favorites and started to tear up. The waitress asked if I was ok and I was honest. I told her I was ordering dinner for you. She shared her condolences and I heard her share my story with her coworkers. The staff's energy changed and it was like they gained perspective on just how their day was. You gifted them that and they "saw" you.

Yesterday was your angel anniversary. I woke up crying because minute by minute I'm further away from the last time I saw you. The day was going to be whatever I wanted it to be so we had champagne and key lime pie cheesecake for breakfast. Roan and I sat together on the couch talking about you. He still looks for you. We cuddled under your favorite penguin blanket and I still wear your favorite sleep shorts and the sweatshirt we got from our first trip to see my family.

Before I went to lunch, I drank a beer in your honor. I burst out laughing and my eyes welled up in the store when I saw it had your favorite saying. Not my first choice but I couldn't say no to you.

Lunch was at our favorite little French restaurant, The Bay Cafe. We wanted to sit outside but the weather continued to match my emotions. The Staff said the outside dining was closed and my heart hurt. I shared that we were there together on your angel anniversary and they immediately arranged for us to have a private table outside to ourselves. I looked across the water at the building you dreamed of buying to create a bed and breakfast. The waiter came out to check on me and saw my tears. He gave me a gentle smile and I knew he saw my love for you.

Year 4 A.C. – Self-Generated Joy

The toughest stop on the tour was next. I hadn't been to your mother's house in over 2 years. I had gone a few times after you died to help her and check on things but since your mother had a stroke and was moved to Illinois to be in assisted care, there was no reason to go. This year felt different. The lawn was overgrown, the house stale and everything still exactly where I remembered it. I looked at the bathtub where I last helped wash you. I walked around the yard that you so lovingly landscaped. I sat in the same chair I did the last time I saw you and looked where your hospice bed used to be. I found your favorite bottle of cologne and for a moment I could smell you.

I left the house just as I found it and went over to get us frozen yogurt. It wouldn't be your day without it. Along the drive I held my hand out in hopes you'd grab it and I could feel you again but my hand just hung there empty as the passenger seat where you used to sit. As I searched the flavors, a spunky young woman asked me why I was so picky. She knew I was thinking really hard about my choices so I told her about you. She smiled and said "That's beautiful you are remembering him like this" and right then, in a world full of loss, a stranger gave me a hope filled hug because she saw you.

Today, like every Saturday, I sit and write this blog alone in our apartment. Every day I see you in the pictures. I see you in the designs. Although it's not in person, just know that I still see you. All week long, friends and strangers have shown me great kindness. They've given me gifts beyond measure because they "saw" you.

On this tour called life, I'll keep sharing our love story in hopes that others are gifted the opportunity to see you too…

Year 4 A.C. – Self-Generated Joy

April 24, 2021 - Heartbreak Hangover

Last week took me on an exhausting emotional tour. The week before being widowed hits me harder than any single memory or special day. The emotional stress is heightened to such a level that when it starts to subside, I can physically feel the effects – Tired from lack of sleep, disturbed by nightmares, sore eyes from bouts of tears and silent migraines blurring the way forward. I've been left sore, battered and bruised again. The week post-widowed the past two years has been time to retreat and recollect myself but this year provided no break from life's push forward.

This week was full of positive events at the complete opposite end of grief. There was no break, no time to unwind from widowed. Competing waves began crashing into one another, churning up life and my steadfast self-stability. I didn't know what was going on around me and couldn't sort the swirling in my heart and head. I looked for direction. I looked for

Year 4 A.C. – Self-Generated Joy

distraction. I looked for relief. I looked for reassurance. I pushed and persevered as much as I could but the storm was strong. I finally gave in and walked right into the rising tide.

This week, the week post widowed, I hurt. My heart hurts, my thoughts hurt and my body hurts. Once again, I have to find the strength to recover, stand back up and restart this journey without you. I just wish you were here to nurse me back to health from this heartbreak hangover.

May 1, 2021 - The Tangled Widowed Web

This week hit hard in a way I never expected. My Instagram account was hacked and a social media storm ensued. I started to get notifications from Instagram and friends that something was strange. I was completely locked out with no options to change my password and get stuff back. The hacker started to email me threats and demands. I was sick to my stomach thinking someone could post or send horrible content to friends and followers. After three hours, the hacker made a mistake, I had an update email that I had to translate from Turkish, which gave me a way to hack the hacker back. Password changed and my account back under control, I started to hyperventilate, my heart was racing, tunnel vision, tingling lips, I thought I was going to pass out. I was shaking and in disbelief that my life was returned to me.

"It's just a social media account. You can create a new one and start over."

Many have told me that maybe I post too much and check too often. They don't realize that social media was a savior for me after Clayton passed away. Facebook and Instagram kept me connected with friends. They would check in on me and fill the empty space that Tin's voice and arms used to fill. A friend was in the room when I regained control. He asked if I was ok and I started to cry. I shared that my social media holds much more for me than fun animal pictures, dancing videos and my widowed blog. My grid holds my grief. I couldn't hold it back and I just let it out:

"I wouldn't be this upset about being hacked because I wouldn't care about social media if Clayton wasn't dead." I started sobbing. I felt so violated and angry. Losing control of my account meant I just lost him and myself again. I've worked so hard to try and regain me.

Until you go through what I've gone through (and I pray you never do), you will never understand the immense stability social media has played in my moving forward. When I was younger, people were expected to take pictures and put them in important albums. Now, we do it all online. My social media isn't just for "likes", it's a reflection of the road I've traveled and a reminder that I am strong. On my toughest days I can scroll through my posts and remind myself that I can do this. I can move forward after losing him. Maybe someday I won't need this tangled widowed web so much but for now while I rebuild my life, it is a safety "net".

Year 4 A.C. – Self-Generated Joy

Down here on Earth, technology continues to advance. I keep trying to message Clayton but he's not responding. Maybe someday we can connect to those who have passed. Until then, does anyone have the number to Heaven…

Clayton Allen Bond

2:22 PM

> I miss you 🖤😢
>
> Where are you? 😢
>
> I wish you were here 🖤
>
> I miss your voice 😢
>
> Are you alright wherever you are? 😢😢😢
>
> Today is hard. I need you 😢😢😢😢
>
> I hope you know wherever you are how much I love you 🖤
>
> What's Heaven like? Have you found my dad there yet? Will you tell him I miss him too 😢

Year 4 A.C. – Self-Generated Joy

May 8, 2021 - The Widowed Willow

When I was younger, I used to think that hardship and emotion showed a sign of weakness. That smaller, shorter, thinner-skinned Bryan was just always going to always be "Crying Bryan". It stung to get bullied and it was tough to see others feel hurt. What I realize now is that those difficulties were toughening up my outer layer like the bark on a tree, each event and year adding a ring of experience and strength. I realize that those layers are how I got through losing my dad and Clayton in the same year. Knowing I could handle the now and mourn it later meant I could stand strong through that terminally tough time. It sounds strange but I hold space and gratitude for the early grief. I continue to grow.

Its not always the biggest trees with the biggest branches that stand strong after a heartbreak hurricane. Even the thin weak looking weeping willow holds it's own. Rough roots take anchor in the wet ground the willow finds itself stable in. Its treetop tears stream down its bowing branches ever repeating the cycle of self-care watering. Sharp winds try to tear it down but the flexible boughs ignore the environmental attempted insults. The most amazing thing is willow branches that break off can regenerate into a new tree spreading the same wooded wisdom.

I could try and pretend to be a tall strong sequoia but I stand as who I am – The Widowed Willow. Deceiving in size, the widowed willow still provides protection and offers others comfort with sorrowful sap symbolically abundant with emotional aspirin. I used to worry so much about the future, "whys" and "what ifs". I used to be the "worry willow" but my dad used to say "big things come in small packages". He'd always assure me that there was no need to worry about what hasn't happened. He'd respond that worrying about something that might not happen was a waste of time and to "take it one day at a time." So often I ignored Wayne's wisdom but now I see that tough love was dad pouring nutrient rich dirt.

So I embrace the earth I find myself in. I might not be the tallest. I might not have the strongest branches or the deepest roots but I am the widowed willow and I'm still standing here showing others they can grow through grief…

Year 4 A.C. – Self-Generated Joy

May 22, 2021 - Just-ified

"Just" - What a powerful word.

"Were you just partners or where you married?"

The word "just" has the power to completely negate every thought, word, blog, good deed I've ever done in Clayton's honor. To some, we were "just".

Clayton and I were planning on getting engaged and married. If you are planning to get married then you are engaged right? Or do we need the ring, proposal and money spending "just" to validate that it's real? If that's the case than I strongly suggest you tell your children this fact right after you tell them that Santa isn't real.

If your relationship isn't tangible in some materialistic way that you can actually hold in your hand then it "just" doesn't count.

"You, your feelings and your relationship don't / didn't actually really matter to the rest of us." – Society's Norms

I pour my heart and soul into sharing so others feel less alone. When someone chooses the wrong wording, I try to give them grace that they don't mean it but it hits hard. This hit harder than ever this week.

Just a couple of days before someone on social media said "just", I was at the beach. I go often to sit, think and talk with Clayton. I always tell him I wish he was here and there it was, a ring in the sand, a man's wedding band. I don't know if it was lost, tossed or placed there by the "powers that be" for me. All I know is it seemed like it "just" was there but to me it wasn't "just". I picked it up and it fit.

I don't know why it was there. I "just" know that I found it and a few days later someone asked if Clayton and I were "just"…

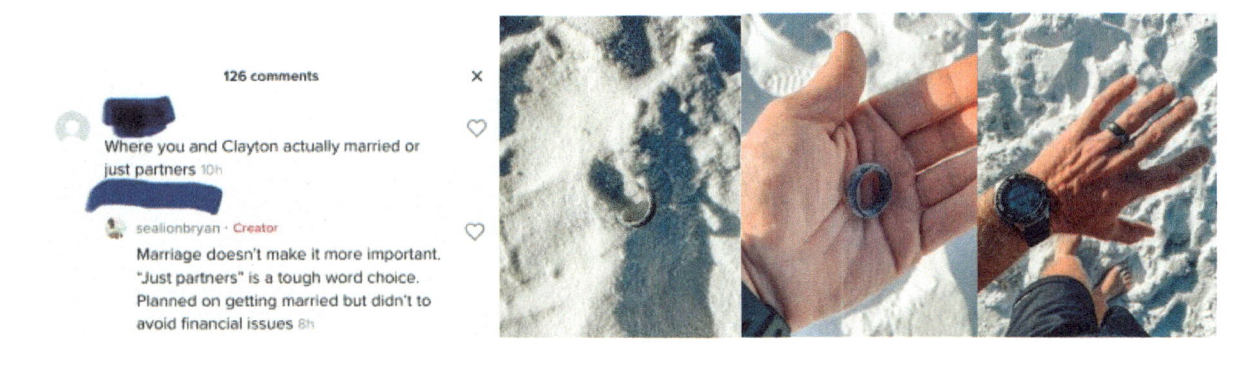

Year 4 A.C. – Self-Generated Joy

May 29, 2021 - Toxic Perception

Bryan, what does growing through grief look like for you?

I appreciate this question because it gives me an opportunity to share that my life looks very different each day. Overtime, my weeks and months have expanded in many directions.

I posted on social media earlier this week holding a flower and sharing that I have to plant positivity in the grief soaked ground around me. I had a comment suggesting that I was pouring toxic positivity on my widowhood. I realized that he was doing something we have been conditioned to accept immediately. He judged what I posted without hesitation or looking into my overall journey. He, unknowingly, used toxic perception.

Gone are the days that people give each other grace and the benefit of the doubt. Too often I have heard someone demand benefit of the doubt for them selves yet turn and burn their neighbor because:

"Their perception is your reality."

I hate that statement and I don't use the "h" word lightly. I have had past employers use that term to manipulate people and I refuse to honor it. The intent is to make others bend to "your rules and viewpoints".

I could have easily lashed out and responded aggressively but I gave the commenter the benefit of the doubt. They were reacting in a place of dark grief. Don't get me wrong, I am mad at the comment but I'm not mad at that person. I'm mad they are in so much hurt and sorrow. I just wish I could take it away but that's not within my power. It's us and us alone that can choose to plant positivity in our own grief gravel. All I can do is be an example, a full example that there are many shadowed moments where the widowed veil blocks my view. So I commented back that I have a widowed blog and I share the happy and the hard. I reiterated that my post said "grow through grief" but just in case it helps others to know my journey isn't simple...

I can't take Clayton's last name off the label in our mailbox because it's the only place in the whole world that our names are together on paper...

Year 4 A.C. – Self-Generated Joy

June 5, 2021 - Finding Change

I've written about finding coins before and there was a long time I didn't find any. This week it seemed everywhere I turned there was a penny. I think I found 8 total and 3 in just one day. They go in my pocket, I forget until later and it's like I've found them all over again.

Year 1 of widowed and dropped coins brought falling tears. Year 2 with similar circumstances like finding coins had a different effect. Instead of getting upset, they were reminders to keep picking up lost pieces and reinvest them. I kept my head down in hopes I'd find pennies telling me I was on the right path. I was missing everything around me because I did not trust my own steps through the sorrow.

Year 3 of widowed, I had a huge crash in my "self stock". I became extremely depressed and anxiety attacks hit. It was official, Clayton wasn't coming back and I was a tarnished, tossed aside shell of myself. I didn't think anyone would find value in me and want to pick me up. So I gave up. I ate too much, drank too much, slept too much and exchanged excuses for myself too much. I had no worth to myself.

In December, I saw a photo of myself and was shocked. I couldn't recognize whom I was seeing. I had a poverty mindset about me. I was outwardly wearing what I felt was my widowed worth. I realized I was "self broke". I made a decision right there that I couldn't let myself give up. So after three years of trying to salvage the old Bryan, I declared "self bankruptcy". I forgave myself for the self-doubt that created "self debt". I had to rebuild self-credit. No one could find me and pick me up except for me. So I stood up, polished myself off and started reinvesting one foot in front of the other.

This year has held a lot of personal revelations. I've started to pour more of my energy back into myself and I'm seeing huge growth in the return. Thursday night I put on shorts and there were pennies in the pocket. I smiled, took them out and went to sleep. Yesterday, I woke up and stood up out of bed. Like most mornings, I looked back in hopes the past three years were a dream and Clayton would be in bed still sleeping. Of course he wasn't there but in the bed where I had slept was a penny right next to Clayton's penguin blanket. I swear I emptied my pockets the night before. Maybe I missed one? Either way, 1 year ago, 2 years ago, 3 years ago seeing a penny in my bed would have made me crash hard.

I've noticed, along my grief journey, my experience has come with less emotional expense. The grief doesn't go but I am growing with it. I have been investing more in my "self savings account". So what do all these pennies mean? Good luck? Angel messages? Heavenly hellos? Or just lost coins? I don't know for sure. All I do know is it seems I'm being sent signs that I am surrounded by change…

Year 4 A.C. – Self-Generated Joy

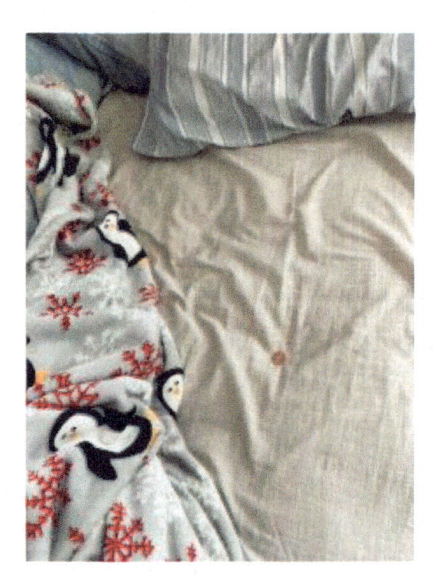

June 12, 2021 - My Road to Return

I have been having a near death experience. You know, where your life flashes in front of you, all the memories, sights, sounds and smells. That rewind reminder, which puts your whole past into a present perspective. No, there wasn't an accident or anything sudden, my near death experience has been almost undetectable. How so? It was slow and stretched out across the last three years. Let me explain what suddenly occurred to me this week.

Since Clayton died, I've spent plenty of days remembering all our time together but I have had lots of old events randomly rise from some forgotten corner of my mind. This week I had more memories surprisingly surface. Good memories that made me smile but I couldn't seem to understand what triggered them. There was nothing said, no sound or sight obviously contributing to my consciousness. I've learned to ask myself "why". Why do I feel the way I do? Why did I have that thought? Why everything? So I asked myself why those thoughts came into my mind when they did. My answer for everything happening now: "Because Clayton died."

The connection made no sense until I asked myself to go deeper: "But why?" I answered myself honestly: "When he died, part of me died."

There it was, my answer to the rewind riddle -"part of me died". That was anew piece of the grief puzzle that had been missing. It makes sense why so many old memories seem to surface without a specific trigger. I thought that a lot of me had died but this year, as I grow through the grief, I have brought parts of me back to life that I thought were gone forever. Not all of me died, just part of me. Instead of the normal "near death" experience, mine has played out in subtle slower scenes.

Year 4 A.C. – Self-Generated Joy

Coming back from the "dead" can be overwhelming. For a while you don't know if you will wake up again. I felt numb, cold and feeling like a lost soul. I could have stayed in that headspace for the rest of my life but I missed me and wanted to come back. No one else would be able to shake me awake. I had to revive myself. So I chose to change my mindset. I choose to open my eyes. I chose to warm myself. I choose sit up and take a deep breath. I choose to stand and I chose to put one foot in front of the other.

It's taken me over three years but I'm waking up from the hit of heartbreak. I still feel sore and there is pain from the bereavement battle but I am healing. I know these widowed wounds will scar over. One day they will serve as memories of how far I've come. They will remind me of this epic journey on my road to return…

June 19, 2021 - The Care Griever

Summer has hit on the beautiful stretch of Florida beach I call home. The area is buzzing with tourists and that means I'm hanging close to home for the busy season at work. My career is animal care. This week I had friends staying just a bit to the east of me about an hour away. They were here for a fun retreat and graciously invited me to join them for the all the days. I could go during the day but each night needed to be home to take care of my dog Roan. The drive out was full of excited anticipation seeing friends. I was so excited that I missed the scenery driving out the first day. Alas, grief's grip holds tighter under the twilight.

The ride home full of glee and gratitude, I had let my guard down. On that dark highway with just a few passing headlights, to my right a bright building begged my attention. I glanced past the empty passenger seat at the hospital where they decided Clayton would not survive and the widowed wave rushed through the window. I couldn't do anything to save him. All the times we road this road late at night, all the meds I laid out, all the moments holding his hand in hope. I couldn't care more for him than I did but, ultimately, my care wasn't enough to defend him from destiny. There I was driving alone just like when I had to leave him overnight at the hospital. Feeling guilty, but I had to get home and be responsible for all the

Year 4 A.C. – Self-Generated Joy

parts of our lives. That's the curse of a caregiver. How in the world do you balance your "life" while someone you love is losing their own?

Loss plants each of us in the Garden of Grief, our roots diving deep down desperately trying to hold us firm in the ground. Those who lose their person suddenly grab the gravel differently than those who slowly watch our person fade. Neither is more egregious. Both are life shattering. Caring for others brings me meaning and purpose. As a caregiver, not being able to stop Clayton's terminal-time creates natural (and normal) questioning. Did I do enough? Could I have done more? Should I have tried differently? Did I miss something that could have kept you here?

I'll never know if there are actual answers if my care was flawed or if it was a one way fight with Fate. I just know that Clayton isn't here anymore and it serves no one if I pour that kind of care into a cup of bottomless bereavement. It's taken 3 years to realize that the one who needs the most care right now is me – The Care Griever…

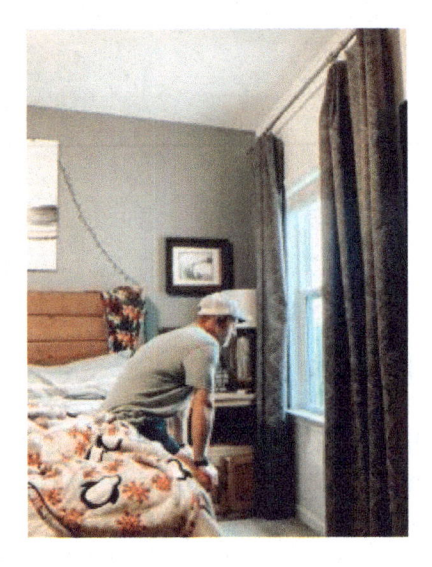

June 26, 2021 - Levels in Life

Clayton, I gave the bike away. The one you gave me for Christmas. I was going to ride it to work but life. Right? You got sick. I needed to have my car so I could get back to you as fast as possible each of every "our last days" and then you died – Life right? The gears of that bike just collecting grief's grit, I thought about getting rid of it but I felt grief's guilt. If I got rid of it, you might somehow be mad so I just left it.

This year, a friend went through a really difficult relationship that ended. He moved out to start moving forward. He is grieving the death of the person he thought he knew. In many ways, he is bearing a version of widowed wounds because the edge of Bereavement's blade strike's blindly in battle. We have had some deep conversations about managing the minutes and moments of feeling difficulties, darkness and depression.

Year 4 A.C. – Self-Generated Joy

I offered insight being 3 years ahead on the road of a loss. One of my comments was about letting go of objects that no longer serve you. It's hard but you don't need to keep carrying the weight. Funny isn't it? How we don't apply our own advice to our experience. Later that day, the bike caught my eye and I knew our conversation was a cosmic creation for both his and my benefit. So I messaged a big group to see who could use my bike and it just so happens my friend who is trying to find himself again wanted it.

As we loaded the bike up, I remembered that there was an air pump, helmet and bike lock in the porch closet. I don't even know the last time I looked in there. I opened the door and opened an internal apology to you. I knew that the bike would be better to serve another but a new home means again that you're not coming home to me, at least not in the way I want. I need to remember that holding on to objects aren't the same as holding you. I need to make space in my arms to hold myself and whatever life hands me along this new way…

So I grabbed the stuff and your level slid from the back shelf onto the floor. I got mad. It almost landed on my foot. Seriously there was no reason for it to fall. I didn't need annoyance right now. Or did I? The level reminded me of the time your yardstick moved on it's own towards a forgotten pair of pineapple shorts you had in our closet. Shortly after the strange yardstick situation, I was given a free trip to Hawaii. That certainly is a big cosmic coincidence…

There in the middle of my grief guilt, you nudged a sign that I continue to move forward. I don't know what's next but I do know, with each step, I'm moving towards new levels in life…

Year 4 A.C. – Self-Generated Joy

July 3, 2021 - An Unwanted Independence Day

Tomorrow is the fourth 4th of July that I have an independence I never wanted…

Tomorrow is our anniversary. Fitting that the start of our short journey together would be full of fireworks because that is exactly how I felt every time I looked into your eyes. You lit me up and now I have to find my light myself. My heartbeat so hard for you and was louder than any pop, bang or sizzle shot into the July night sky. All beautiful displays have an ending but I didn't know the finale of your show would end so soon.

I don't do well on the 4th. I feel like an abandoned dog that hides from the bright lights and loud sounds of others celebrating their freedoms. My freedom is full of fears that some of my dreams might just fade like falling fireworks.

Fourth of July hits me twice since I lost my dad and Tin the same year. My father passed away on June 29th and the last 4th Tin and I had together we were there for my father's funeral. We didn't know it was going to be our last anniversary. I didn't know I wasn't going to get another chance to celebrate with you, Tin.

I'm still not ready to celebrate my unwanted widowed independence. I'm still not ready to be at the barbecue and see couples together while a dad makes sure the burgers are flipped. The sights, smells and sounds of celebration fill the air but tomorrow I'll just be doing my best to keep a sparkle of hope in my heart…

Year 4 A.C. – Self-Generated Joy

July 10, 2021 - Marbles, Memories and Recycled Reminders

Some weeks go by and I find myself searching for signs or situations that give me insight into what I should write about each week. I fought looking for inspiration. I felt if i couldn't write about Tin (or my life without him) that I was losing him more. Stressing about sharing sunk stories deeper out of reach so I stopped feverishly trying to find forced words. I put faith that the words would find their way to me. I stopped trying to find unseen signs and unheard messages - that's when they showed up in the simplest ways. Random items would recycle my moment and cause random replay.

This week, walking my dog, I wished my dad and Tin a good day. I found a penny. My neighbor said good morning, I responded with a smile and a silly joke. She smiled. I turned the corner and found a quarter. Currency for my kindness? I started to think about what I would write and I paused.

"Don't worry about it Bryan. They will bring you the words when you need them."

I kept walking and my dog went sideways to an area he was never interested in. A step in front of me was a clear marble. Looking into it, I was flooded with memories finding old marbles in my back yard with my dad. Those memories lead reminders of scuba diving, family trips and his "direct advice" that I shouldn't worry so much about little things - "Thanks dad."

Yesterday I dropped a protein bar behind my dryer. Ugh. This was Clayton's job. His long arms were always grabbing stuff out of my short reach. Clayton would put all our empty cans and bottles on the dryer to recycle them and was always having to fish ones out that fell. I started to get upset but I couldn't just leave the protein bar so I pulled the dryer out. There sat lost Tupperware lids, old cat food our late Stallone had dropped and there was an empty vodka bottle. I choked up seeing signs from Tin and Stallone. Clayton and I would have a drink when I would come home from work. I'd have a "shower drink" while he sat in the bathroom and we talked about our day. I loved that time with him each day. When Clayton was diagnosed, he stopped drinking any alcohol. Here, almost 4 years later, an old relic from our relationship rituals sat waiting for the widowed to stop rushing through his day and just remember.

When you don't force it and you least expect them, life brings you marbles, memories and recycled reminders…

Year 4 A.C. – Self-Generated Joy

July 17, 2021 - Authentic Anger

I'm harder on myself more than people realize. There are times I haven't honored my feelings because I just try to see the bright side of everything. I have a high tolerance for others but sometimes I look the other way more than I should. I have to remember to give myself grace during growth and sometimes growing with grief involves anger. Well, I'll be honest with you. I got really angry this week and let it out. I don't regret it because it was authentic and appropriately used.

This week was extremely emotional. Thursday was Clayton's birthday and all week long I watched others show little to no gratitude for what they have. They showed no courtesy, no one asking others how they were, just asking for more for them selves. All week I felt anger. I hit a tipping point from my widowed anger and it resulted in a strong lesson for a very inconsiderate individual.

I witnessed a woman rudely pour negative attitude all over a scene because she had illegally parked and blocked others. She was asked to move her car because someone had to get somewhere in a hurry. She retaliated by calling people jerks for inconveniencing her. I heard her say she didn't care that others were trying to leave and I finally snapped. I couldn't stand one more person acting selfish. I granted myself permission to let out my anger and use it to create perspective about politeness:

"Well you parking here might be keeping someone from getting to the hospital. Maybe they just got a call that there is an emergency with a family member and you made them miss their chance at a last goodbye. So sorry you're inconvenienced."

The woman and her whole family stopped in their tracks. All the attitude, dirty looks and nasty words stopped. I stared her directly in her eyes. I wanted to let more out but I knew my words hit their mark. There wasn't a reason to unleash the widowed dragon. She already felt the heat from my heartbreak. Burning her further with my bereavement wouldn't help anything and I know later I'd regret going too far - Keep the fire fast, focused and use it few and far between.

"Oh I'm so sorry. I was frustrated with how busy everything is. I didn't think of that." She replied as she looked away, joined her family and drove off.

Some may say I should have let her have it. Some would say that was too much to make her feel bad for the rest of the day. Either way, I'm allowed to be authentically angry sometimes and I'll keep using my loss in hopes it opens the way for others…

Year 4 A.C. – Self-Generated Joy

July 24, 2021 - The Normally Normals

It's been a grief goal for me to return back to "normal". I have put into place fail-safes to reestablish pattern, predictability and self-protection. That's normal self-preservation.

Now I am starting to feel more comfortable in my day-to-day. I have realized my new "normal" has also kept me from enjoying aspects of a "normal" life. Let me explain. I had nothing to do today. I literally had no plans except to write this blog. That is not normal. I went to bed early. I let myself sleep in. I took a long walk with my dog. I made coffee. Then I started to sit in the same chair I write my blog in every week and it didn't feel right. It didn't feel it's "normally normal". That chair has comforted me each week as the widowed words transfer through me to the screen. This week I felt like the chair was holding me a bit too tight. I needed space so I made a decision that was not my normally normal - A pool day.

I packed up my computer, water and a towel. As I walked, I realized there was some anxiousness. I hadn't taken a pool day on my own since Clayton had passed. A pool day meant I wasn't accomplishing things. Guilt for taking time away from responsibility and serving others started to swell up. If I didn't do "this" or "that" today than I was wasting my time. Guilt that I could have a pool day and Clayton couldn't. I started too blame myself for sleeping in and un-normally taking a slow morning – Normal Guilt.

The next wave hit. I stopped walking to the pool for fear I'd be surrounded by couples and families. I'd be surrounded by what was taken from me – Normal Fear.

Wave three came in quick and I swelled with anger that I have to figure this all out without Tin. I started to ask the "normal whys". Why him? Why me? Why is life not fair? - Normal Anger.

The next wave brought something I wasn't expecting. In previously "normal" emotional storms, I would be done for the day. I would give in and the day would have gone back to being blanketed with "normal distractions". Today was abnormal. I told myself that my feelings were valid but now they had to have their place and time. I deserved a pool day. In that very moment I felt something freeing - Normal growth.

So I kept with my plan and went to the pool. When I arrived, there was only one neighbor there and she knew I was working on my blog. She validated the quiet scene and my step towards growth. That wouldn't have happened had I stopped moving forward. So as I sit here and write surrounded by a beautiful pool scene and the calming sounds of water falling, I realize I can acknowledge my widowed worries and my self-strengthening at the same time and neither negate the other. You can feel two things at the same time and that is normal...

Year 4 A.C. – Self-Generated Joy

July 31, 2021 - What Do You See

All week I have had a new thought that I can't shake so I guess I'll ask but I know I might not get a direct answer yet.

They say we are separated by a "veil" that is ever changing. I envision it's like the whole world is covered in some strange cosmic widowed veil. Under it's cover, we can only see what's here and maybe that's why those of us on this side carry our grief. We aren't allowed to see all of you on the other side but you all can see us. For me, that is what makes the tears hit fast and hard. So Clayton can you tell me what you see when you cast your gaze this way? Does the veil change how you use to see our world?

What is it like where you are? Do you see things all the time or just when you check in? What does our world look like to you now that you see and know so much more?

Do you see our blue skies and green grass the same or is the beauty beyond the veil so bright that it outshines what we know here?

Are you standing in the kitchen and do you see me when I'm washing the dishes? Are you sitting on your side of the couch and do you see me lying alone wishing you were right there within an arm's reach? Are you in the car with me and do you see me singing to the radio? Are you there in bed watching me dream you are still here? Do you see the look on my face when I wake, look towards where I thought you'd be only to remember all over again that I can't see you?

When I sit and write this blog each week, are you sitting next to me watching what I type? Do you see how much I love you, how much I miss you and how bad my heart hurts some days?

I guess could ask a million questions but, honestly, I just want to know -

Clayton, do you see me?

Year 4 A.C. – Self-Generated Joy

August 7, 2021 - The Benefit of Bereavement

I've always thought through life on a grand scale - The excitement of positive possibilities. How magical it would be to have an amazing job, a beautiful home and grow old with a true love. I guess the problem with being a big dreamer, now that Clayton has passed away, is that with big dreams can come big heartache.

Maybe it's my personality, maybe it's me getting older, maybe its experiencing deep loss, probably a combination but I know my patience isn't what it used to be. I've tried to go through life giving people the benefit of the doubt. Some would say that I give too much to others and I wouldn't be as frustrated if I held back a bit but I can't help it. I think the part that gets me the most is when others forget to do the math and add up the times I've shown up. I've learned I am a strong person, stronger than I ever knew, but being taken for granted is definitely my weakness. However, it's my decision to show up so I can't fault others for not meeting me half way. Some days, honestly, it feels like a lose-lose situation but it wouldn't feel right to hold back trying my hardest. I just have to remind myself that it's the authenticity in the trying that really matters not in the validation from people who choose to look past my effort. Clayton would certainly remind me to stay focused on the possibilities and not to waste time worrying. It's a tough memory actually remembering hearing him say those words. If we only knew back then that he was speaking his own truth faster than we knew.

I catch myself feeling like I have a shorter fuse now that Clayton is gone. Where I'd hold on and look past what others said or did before, now I catch myself just walking away. You'd be amazed how many times in a week people who know you or what you've been through will forget it and say something insensitive. It's an interesting view on this side of loss. I'm burdened and gifted all at once with this widowed perspective. Through this lens of loss I see many take for granted the things they have and the experiences they haven't had to endure. When your life has little worries, they seem like big worries to you. I know because I used to live there.

I can't push my perception on others yet require their benefit of the doubt. I can't go through life demanding that everyone know and show empathy. My loss is one I wish no other would go through. I also can't expect everyone to remember what myself, and others have experienced. The best I can do is openly share what many of us hold inside. No matter how much time passes parts of us stay broken.

Year 4 A.C. – Self-Generated Joy

On behalf of those who have suffered loss, I'll just ask that anyone who reads these words try to walk through life giving others the benefit of bereavement…

August 14, 2021 - The Grief Dating Game

Well I guess we should just talk about it. Having to even think about dating again after Clayton passed away completely sucks. Dating is hard enough as it is but adding on being widowed, gay and living in the south is a hot mess. There are like 3 gay guys here. Two of them are in a relationship and then there's me. It's a military/ beach town so lots of people just stopping by. Of course there are other guys but nothing seems to click. They are already in a relationship, don't want a relationship or can't understand that I will always miss Clayton which is not a reflection of them. He can't be replaced but that doesn't mean I can't have another relationship again. Some days I feel like I should just go live on the island of misfit gays. Rejection is a beast but I wouldn't be honest by not authentically sharing that some days it feels like something is wrong with me. Broken or built in a way that popular gay culture says they accept but, let's face it, a guy posting a photo in a speedo will get more attention vs. this blog. Unfortunately, I'm not wrong.

Many don't know that I was in a 10 yr relationship a long time ago. It ended very badly with fault on all sides. So I have been through a "messy divorce". I have dated people who have cheated on me. I have dated people who decided we were better as friends. I dated someone who died. They all hurt. They all bring grief of their own. In every scenario, your hope for that relationship is shattered and the person you fell in love with is gone. The dream died and grief was born. You wake up the next day starting over. Some choose never to date again and others give it a go. I know I'm ok alone but I want to have time with someone while I still have time. So I try.

I started to think about dating a year after Clayton passed. That's just the timeline my journey placed me on. I have met a guy that felt more like friends. I have met a guy that didn't want anything serious. I have met a guy that wanted to be super-serious after 5 minutes. I met a guy who stood me up on a virtual date. I met a guy who was using old photos to appear like less of a mess. I have met a guy who was annoyed that I wrote a weekly blog and he asked when I would "be over it." Dating is exhausting and I'm already tired from carrying grief's

Year 4 A.C. – Self-Generated Joy

"dead weight". I don't need someone who's alive to add to it. Recently, I had a guy ask me out. We had a great time and agreed we both wanted a second date. Can't set a second date if they don't bother texting or calling. I could be angry and hold a grudge but that serves no one. The best I can do is give them grace that their past holds some heartache for them too and we are all just trying to figure out the rules of this grief game…

Public service announcement – direct rejection is better than passive rejection. Just saying.

It is what it is. Not everyone is a match but the grief dating game is a harsh one. Friends reassure me that "they aren't the one" but salt in a wound is still salt in a wound. At this stage, the only salt I want is on a margarita being delivered by a good guy. Is that too much to ask? Dear Universe, I'm officially MAN-ifesting him.

August 21, 2021 - The Grief Thread

"I'm only hanging on by a thread."

Such a common phrase we use to express that we are in a place which scares us regardless of the reason for our grief grip. I've said that phrase many times in life. I've said it when I was sick of being bullied in school. I said it when I was going to give up on my career. I said it after Clayton passed away.

There I was hanging by a thread each time but it never dawned on me to look at the scenario from the other side until I recently (unintentionally) changed one word from "only" to "still":

"I'm still hanging on by a thread." - There is hope in that phrase.

When we get hit hard by trauma, we often think the worst but is it actually the worst? All depends on how you look at it. So far I have survived 100% of my hardest days. If I'm am hanging by a thread, I haven't hit rock bottom and if I hit rock bottom I can start to climb. Does that make "hanging by a thread" more comfortable? No but it does give me a chance to think about it differently.

Year 4 A.C. – Self-Generated Joy

If I'm holding on to a thread, that means I'm still hanging on. It's been implied that I might get tired, let go or that the thread will snap but the thread and my grip are still there. So wait, what's the other end of the thread attached too? I guess I've never asked. I wouldn't be hanging here if the other end wasn't being held taught by something or someone…

So I climbed the thread and, at the top, I wrapped up the excess. I continued to follow the trail. That spool of thread started small but soon enough grew. However, the grief still blurred my vision and I couldn't thread the needle so I just kept collecting along my way. Once in awhile the fear kicks in and I check. I pull on the thread to see if there is still tension and I keep walking. It's been over three years of gathering up grief thread as I walk this widowed way. My vision is more clear now so I've taken the time to thread the needle and begin to sew my grief. As I move forward I'm starting to lay down a rope behind me that I've sewn with hope for others who need something stronger than a thread to hold onto.

The pen is mightier than the sword but a needle threaded with grief can mend…

August 28, 2021 - Facing Future Fears: An Open Letter to Myself

Dear Bryan,

I think it's time for us to talk a bit about the fears found since Clayton passed. These thoughts and widowed worries have actually compounded and worsened seasons of our grief. They have been cyclical and fed into one another. Try as I might to break these cycles sooner, I couldn't and I'm sorry. I added to our pain but the worries were overwhelming. I hope you understand that I didn't mean to heighten our heartache. I try not to let them consume us but there are days that I can't shake the fears and I see it in our eyes, I see it in our stance, I hear it in our voice. Sometimes I look in the mirror and I see us but we are little blurry.

Honestly, one of the greatest fears we've hidden for as long as I can remember is being alone and forgotten about. This fear has had us hold on to people we should of let go and also push

Year 4 A.C. – Self-Generated Joy

people away that we should have kept close but the fears of losing them overrode the right thing to do.

Bryan, I know it's difficult to manage but you can't worry that everyone will go away. We can't keep worrying that we will wake up each morning and learn we've lost someone else. We've survived so

many difficulties and I'm so proud of us for the strength and perseverance we dug so deep to find in order to keep moving forward.

I honor our concerns and I give our grief grace but it's time we release the fears and set our selves free to walk through life without these tethering terrors. What if we don't find someone to grow old with? What if we live longer then all of our loved ones? What if we need help and care in our old age and there isn't anyone around? The widowed "what-ifs" will always whisper but we can't let them consume us.

Bryan, I don't have the answers for what the Universe has planned. All I know is we will show up with the strength and courage we need to overcome these obstacles. We will keep growing through this grief and moving forward. Fact is that there will undoubtedly be tough days ahead but why stress about what we don't know? It's time we stop pouring energy into our worries. I'm here for us so take my hand and together let's stop fearing the future…

All My Love,

From Me to Me

Year 4 A.C. – Self-Generated Joy

September 4, 2021 - The Great Shattering and the Holder of the Missing Piece

That moment is unlike any other. Whether you are expecting the grief or it surprises you, there is no way to describe the very second you learn you have a new future. Tunnel vision sets in, you can't catch your breath. All you hear is the loudest sound you've ever heard and it is coming from within you – your heart is shattering like hot glass being hit with cold water. How will you pick up the pieces? The back winds of the storm blow through and sweep a piece of your soul off into the sky. Chase as I might, I couldn't catch up. Exhausted so I rested on the side of my new road. After what seems like dozens of sunrises and sunsets I finally had the energy to stand, still sore from my great shattering. One foot in front of the other in the direction I thought I'd find the missing piece so I started my epic journey to find it again.

It seems impossible at first. I felt like I would never find it again. It is stealthy and any glimpse I caught of it was fleeting. I wasn't even sure anymore if I lost it or it left me. Either way, it is gone and I didn't know if I'd ever get it back but forever forward. Maybe, just maybe, someone ahead will find it and hold on to it so they could fix me in the future. Three and a half years later, I was still thinking that someone out there waiting to fix me. I'd have a thought about better days and suddenly there'd be a rustling nearby.

"Hello. Who's there? Have you seen a piece of me? Help me please?"

He was watching me from a distance ahead on my path holding one hand over his heart and something else in his other hand. He looks so familiar but a faded figure – a shade. I'd catch a glimpse of him and he'd quickly disappear around the bend. By the time I got there all I saw was an empty road less traveled. The man eluded me and I lose hope again. Why was he keeping me from me? Hadn't life been cruel enough?

After all the chasing, I was exhausted. The stranger always seemed to be just minutes ahead in my future. I grew weary and stopped. I had to just take care of me right now. I sat and drank in self-care from the surroundings. I had made it pretty far already and, for the first time since the great shattering, I felt a smile. I sensed I wasn't alone and I opened my eyes. There was the shadowed man holding the lost piece from my shattering. This was the first time I didn't yell to him. I was still smiling. Slowly he came towards me. I still couldn't "see" him. He knelt down and handed me the piece he kept safe – happiness.

"You've spent a lot of energy looking for something that was always close, Bryan."

Year 4 A.C. – Self-Generated Joy

I looked up from my hands and finally saw him clearly. I was looking back at me…

September 11, 2021 - Past to the Present: A Look Back in Widowed Time

Clayton has been gone for over three years now. A lot has changed. On a day to day, I don't realize just how far I have traveled. This week has had a lot of old memories stir but not for the worse, for the better. The week brought about events and memories that could have laid me emotionally flat out for days. As the responsibilities built up and shifted, I stayed calm. I had been in a similar spot before with stress and having to keep myself on course. Deadlines and late nights draining my energy reminded me of being Clayton's caregiver. Eating meals standing up or just too busy to think to eat but I remembered back to the moments I'd be up from 4am until 1am to make sure he had everything he needed. Many things have changed but some stay strongly the same. I still wear the hat Clayton gave me and I'll keep wearing it until I don't wear it anymore. I need to do that for myself.

When the dust settled from busy end of season responsibilities, it hit me that I was much further along in widowed time then I realized. Reminding reflections of just how hard each day was three years ago yet here I sit today with a smile. This week's widowed blog is one that I wrote almost 3 years ago to the day. I want to share it now so that those of you who may need a forward flash of hope can see where I am now verses months after the great grief. It takes a lot of work to start moving down this road alone but along the way life starts to pick up again. The most important thing to remember is that an object in motion stays in motion so always be forever moving forward…

Love,

Bryan

Year 4 A.C. – Self-Generated Joy

September 18, 2021 - Grief Gaps

Love and loss are the great unifiers. Later in life the family seems to only get together for weddings and funerals. The most interesting part of my grief is how separated and alone I felt even though I was surrounded by love and support. I was kept separate from the rest of life by the grief gaps.

A major aspect of being widowed is my fear. Since Clayton passed away, saying "I love you" to anyone was scary for me because the next thought I'd have was that someday they would be gone. What do I do when everyone I love has left? We all quietly know that the tradeoff to love will eventually be loss. They come as a pair but we ignore the pending outcome. I certainly did until Clayton passed away. That flipped my view and the fear of loss overshadowed the joy of love. "Love lost" became my focus verses "love gained". So I just kept telling myself that I loved me and we would be ok.

Last week I lost and old friend. I haven't shared about it because the family wants their privacy. What I can tell you is that Clayton showed up in a way I never expected. This older lady had started to look different to me. There was something familiar in her eyes. In just days, I noticed subtle changes and I knew before she did that her time was quickly coming to an end. I shared my thoughts with her family and doctor. Further testing showed I was right. She was going through the end stages just like Clayton. For the whole week I shared with the family what would happen in the upcoming hours and days. They would hear names of medicines that hadn't been said yet and time was short. It hurt to relive Clayton's death. However, as much as I hate to admit it, because of my grief I was able to give that old lady and her family a gift – enough time to say their goodbyes. That sweet lady passed away shortly after. The loss weighed heavy on my heart and I looked for the lesson.

The timing was too well designed for it to be a coincidence. I have reached a point in my healing that I truly felt I could fall in love with someone again and I have. We were brought together because he had seen a video I made about Clayton. He reached out to me in friendship, which has grown from there. We planned a weekend together just days before that sweet lady started to feel off. After a week of reliving Clayton's last days, he arrived and I felt something I hadn't thought was possible. I can grieve for Clayton and fall in love at the same time. I can honor both relationships equally without having to choose. I can be my true authentic widowed self because I have gaps from grief that I have worked to fill. So, as far as I can see it, Clayton helped orchestrate this beautiful new loss and love…

It's taken me a long time to understand that contrasting emotions can share the same space at the same time. These grief gaps have changed from dusty drop-offs to fertile riverbeds. I realize that if I consistently say "I love you" to myself, there is a never-ending flow that I can share with others. Where I once saw a great divide, I now see a way to cross. With great love comes great loss but with great loss comes great love. As long as I remember that they show up as a set, I no longer have to fear the future. Perspective can plant possibilities. So just

Year 4 A.C. – Self-Generated Joy

remember that roses may wither but rose-colored glasses have no thorns…

September 25, 2021 - Grief in the Grass

Six years ago, Clayton and I took a trip to visit his mother. We were still in Atlanta and she was living along the coast of southern Florida. We had left the city cement behind for a walk along the waves. What I hadn't realized was the subtle but profound stop we took along the way. As soon as we parked the car, Clayton got out, threw his shoes and stepped on the lush green grass. He loved to be barefoot and outside but I had never seen a grown man instantly become his inner child. Pure joy, innocence and fully present in time. All I could do was laugh and breathe in the energy. That memory planted deep inside me by the glimmer in his eyes and his soulful smile pouring over those soft summer blades. He was glad to be in the grass.

Ironically, just 2 years later, Clayton would be helping his mother landscape at her new home. It was there that he picked up an aggressive ringworm infection that went systemic and the antifungal medications hit his liver hard. When Clayton passed away, I felt grief's fog surround me and I started to just drift. I floated day-to-day only feeling what was inside, forgetting what I could feel around me. As the time passed and his death became actual to me, I began to avoid having moments from memories. I refused to walk outside barefoot because I knew that there would be grief in the grass.

It's been three and a half years and I have traveled a long way but I have not stopped to stand in the grass. I've learned that part of moving forward means I have to walk through the weeds. I've also learned that there is a big marsh of misery that is very easy to commiserate in. I can't allow myself to get stuck in the swamp so I kept moving. When most people feel uncomfortable they go with one of three options:

Run from it, ignore it or fight it.

I'd like to give you a fourth option – What if you say thank you?

Year 4 A.C. – Self-Generated Joy

What if, just what if, when you feel uncomfortable you say thank you? Not because of the grief but because whatever it is or was just showed you where next to grow?

The more I share about where I'm at, the more I realize how much others need to hear or read exactly what they are thinking. My grief comes from the loss of my father and the loss of Clayton but there are commonalities in grief regardless of the road. I write keeping in mind others may be in the same weeds. So this week I intentionally did something uncomfortable - I took my shoes off and I stood in the grass. At first, all I felt was my emotions rushing up. The hard truth that he was gone and I wasn't going to get another chance to see Clayton stand in gratitude. I asked "Clayton is the grass really greener over there?" I let out a sigh so the breeze could take it away and I just stood there. I began to notice the feeling of the grass on my feet and the warm sun on my shoulders. I heard birds and I found myself smiling. I forgot how much I loved standing in the grass and there it was again - another one of grief's gifts. I don't think I would have ever connected with that moment this week had Clayton not given me that memory.

So this week I just want to share that it's not "your grief" or 'my grief' it is "our grief" and together we can keep moving forward. In the end, it doesn't matter how you got to your grief, at the end we all walk through the same "gates". Until then, I'll stop taking the grass for granted…

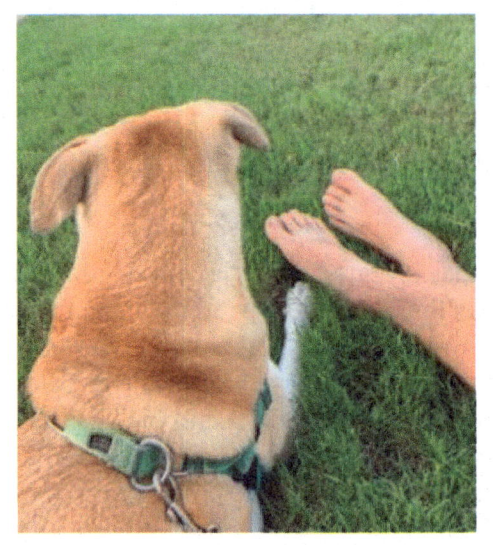

October 2, 2021 - Inflight Fear

I'm afraid of heights. I have been completely frozen on the top of a ladder. I stand back from windows in a tall building and the idea of skydiving is sheer terror to me. Strangely enough, I love roller coasters and I don't mind flying. I think the security in being seated helps combat the fear of free fall. I guess it's not actually the height that I'm afraid of, more so the impact of the landing. Maybe, subconsciously, my fear of falling kept my height to 5'6'.

Year 4 A.C. – Self-Generated Joy

Flying has always been a mixed carry-on bag. It's a good thing it's invisible or I'd probably be charged for extra luggage. Flying puts me high out of my comfort zone. I've always worried that something will go wrong with the plane. I'd say that is normal but losing Clayton has created a new set of in-flight fears as I fly through my day. I fear what happens to others when I'm up on the plane.

Let's start this share but stating that I don't let these thoughts completely control me. Some days the have a tighter grip but I know that they are irrational most of time. That being said, it is normal to have new thoughts, fears and feelings after your loss. Going through a trauma creates an immense new space like a giant galaxy of grief. Light-years between things and you never know what you'll discover. Black holes of bereavement, planets full of potential, confusion causing comets, and intergalactic emotional explosions that continuously generate more room to grow. So as long as you control yourself in space, you'll be able to steer yourself through the stars.

Clayton and my father passed away in their sleep. I have fear first thing in the morning that I'll learn someone I love didn't wake up. Up 30,000ft, holds a similar fear. Yes I know there is in-flight WIFI but messages may not come through and, if they do, I'm still stuck on the plane trapped with no escape. So I keep my phone on airplane mode and beg that when we land there's no sudden life-crashing message.

Three years ago, in-flight fear was very real for me. The second year after losing Clayton and the need to escape my reality over shadowed my fears of flying. I had 13 trips in one year and was feeling freer than ever. Always something to do meant I didn't have to be in that empty apartment until suddenly the world came to a stop. For my third widowed year, I was trapped in the place I feared the most. No escape from myself, my thoughts or my grief but hindsight is truly 20/20. Not that I would say the world shutting down was a blessing but it certainly forced me to focus on myself. Life was on airplane mode for an undetermined time so all I had was me.

The man afraid of flying was now grounded indefinitely with no choice but to walk my path I was avoiding. The road was rocky at first but since smoothed out as I kept moving forward and paving my own way. Earthbound, I stopped running and had to take root. I watered the grass where it was planted and it has begun to turn a bright shade of green. I poured into myself all the things necessary and after 3.5 years, I stand much taller than I ever knew I could. Focusing on my fears has taught me how to flip them and where grief once prevailed there now lives gratitude. I don't know what tomorrow will bring but I can't waste away in worry. The start of this widowed journey began with one single step. Now I'm able to run, jump and spread my wings again. I want to experience adventures, be in love and be a light for others. There's too much power in possibility to stay terrified in the terminal. Time to take to the skies without the weight of in-flight fears.

Year 4 A.C. – Self-Generated Joy

October 9, 2021 - The Little Boy and the Box of Crayons

As I keep walking forward along this widowed path, I'm coming across familiar terrain that I thought I left far behind in my life. No one really tells you that when you become widowed you revisit all of your old worries so I'm going to say it now for those who follow me in grief in the future. Your current bereavement will bring up your old grief days. At first I fought them rising from the space inside. I had thought I locked them well enough away but nothing lasts forever.

I have talked about fear, anger, sadness, hopelessness, anxiety and abandonment. The loss of any loved one is never a direct emotional line. When I step back and see the map of my path, it honestly looks like a 4 year old drew all over the wall with a box of crayons. The one topic I haven't focused on is my Worry.

Worry wasn't born from being widowed. Worry and I have always had a close and abusive relationship. Worry has been an underlying voice my whole life. Worried I'd get lost. Worried I'd get in trouble. Worried I'd be bullied. Worried I'd be hurt. Worried I'd be forgotten. Worried I wasn't enough. Worried I wasn't worth staying around for. Worry has always been the devil on my left shoulder. He always knew exactly what to say to cause me to crumble. He got quiet for a few years because Clayton's words of affirmation filled my heart but with Clayton gone, Worry started singing whispers and they hauntingly echoed in my empty spaces.

"You won't find anyone else and if you do they will leave you someway, somehow. They all leave you."

The Worry was fully back and louder than he had ever been. What if he was right? Safest thing is to sit still so he doesn't see you. If the room stays dark he'll stay quiet so don't open that door or the light will flood in and he'll find you. Stay quiet little one and you'll stay safe. That's exactly how I made it growing up – hiding from the bullies and hiding who I really was so I fell back into a self defense mechanism designed by that little boy with a box of broken crayons.

Year 4 A.C. – Self-Generated Joy

However, just like every child, I got restless and peaked through the door. What I saw was a bright beautiful world full of people asking if I could come out and play. For a while, Worry made me slam the door and some of those people left but many stayed and kept knocking. One day, while Worry was asleep, I heard a knock and I cracked open the door. There was that little boy, a memory of me, standing at the threshold holding out his box of crayons.

"Draw your next adventure." He said.

"What if I don't draw it right?" I replied and looked down at my feet.

"That's a silly worry. It's your adventure so it's always right. I think you should draw yourself with wings so you can see yourself soar."

That little boy with the box of crayons never gave up on his imagination and hope for better days as long as he could keep drawing.

I've been given another one of Grief's gifts – The knowledge that there is nothing more beautiful than the picture you are drawing. So keep drawing as big as you can dream…

Year 4 A.C. – Self-Generated Joy

October 16, 2021 - I'm Not Just

The past seven days has been sort of a blur. Up for work, rush around, home, dogs, dinner, some tv and then bed. You know, the usual. As I sit here and type I was struggling with what to write. What feelings of loss and grief sewed themselves in the tapestry of my week? I thought long and hard about something to share.

I started to feel a bit of guilt that I couldn't find a topic to lean into. I actual caught myself getting frustrated.

"Search Bryan. Find something."

I rewound through conversations, tv episodes, meals, both jobs, time with my boyfriend and friends but there wasn't anything that stood out to share until I realized that was exactly what I needed to share. Interesting that I write to help myself (and others) but felt guilt that I couldn't come up with a profound topic or view on life. My grief has created interesting emotions and here I am again learning something about myself. I sometimes feel obligated. Obligated towards my grief and there it quietly continues to try and control me.

"Well if you are Bryan but you're not constantly reminded about your loss than are you actual still the Bryan everyone knows? Who are you even?"

I realized this week that grief is something I carry but it has also become a part of my identity. People ask about my life and that includes being widowed.

"Are you single? Married?"

"Well actually…"

For a long time I hated being short. For a long time I was embarrassed I was losing my hair. No matter how much I'd stretch, I never got taller. I always hated seeing my height line lower on the wall. No matter how many things I tried, my genetics followed my family. After years of hyper-focusing and battling who I was, I accepted the things that seemed (at first) to be shortcomings (Pun intended because I can laugh at my height.) I couldn't change what I was given and so I made the best of it. Overtime, I forgot about my height and my hair because it didn't consume my every day.

I wouldn't be me if I were taller. I wouldn't be me if I had more hair. I wouldn't be me if my eyes were green. I wouldn't be me if I never had lost Clayton or met with any grief in my life. Although I would change it if I could, I'm not getting taller and Clayton isn't coming back. The point is that this week went by without being cloaked in grief because, just like my height, it's part of who I am not all of who I am and that is a powerful distinction. I'm not just my height. I'm not just my eye color. I'm not just a blog writer. Most importantly, this week, I've learned I'm not just my grief…

Year 4 A.C. – Self-Generated Joy

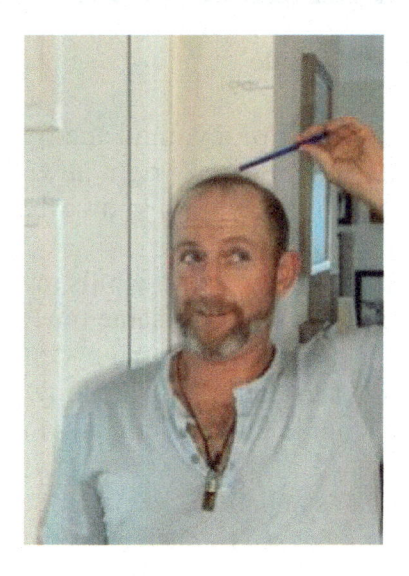

October 23, 2021 - Flash Back to Flash Forward

Today's blog is a moment of self-reflection. Once in awhile, I sit down and take stock of where I am and where I was. Right now I am on a beautiful weekend getaway with my boyfriend and his family. I want to absorb as much of our moments together as I can so sharing an old blog is a great way for me to stay on course with all of the things I like to do. This morning I looked back and 2 years ago I had just returned from a trip and I was terrified. Tomorrow I return from this trip and I'm not scared. I'm not scared of being lonely. I'm not scared of the unknowns because I have poured time and love into my own healing and the Universe is showing up just as it should. So for those who need these words today, this week's widowed blog is a flashback and a flashforward so you can see that time may not take away the grief but it sure does allow you to grow. Hang in there fellow grievers, we have healing to do together…

Love Always,

Bryan

Year 4 A.C. – Self-Generated Joy

October 30, 2021 - The Stress of the Sale

House hunting - It's been at the forefront of my mind and free time the past two weeks. We all know that the housing market is out of control right now. Some have said that it might not be the best time to buy a place but others say "you know when you know".

When Clayton passed away, I had to cover all of the bills myself. My overall security was gone. How was I going to grieve and move at the same time? I desperately needed an anchor and, for me, that was staying put. I budgeted everything, denied buying things others have daily and got a second job building a business. I worked my widowed butt off to get back on stable ground and now it's 4 years in the future. I'm ready for the next chapter in my life.

One after another they weren't up to standard. Sellers don't care about quality because they just want quantity. I get it. Selling a house is a business transaction but this is just another example where people see others as just money. I found a house yesterday that checked every box and felt "right". I put in an offer that was over asking and they came back with wanting even more. Their greed kicked in. I had to say no and I lost the house. So, to be honest, for a little while last night I was the widowed man who worked so hard to get on his feet and build himself up enough to emotionally and financially afford a home but I felt like a failure. I offered more than they asked for only to be told that all I had built wasn't actually enough.

I know my readers want to help and immediately show support by saying "that just wasn't the one" or "everything happens for a reason". I get it but the last thing a widowed person wants to hear after they finally decide to move is that they can't because there is some "Universal plan". Best thing to do is acknowledge how hard it is for me to be told "no" when my timeline and my heart screams "yes". For those of us working through grief, we need to move through it and validation of our experiences is a huge part of our growth.

So this week's lesson is two fold:

If you are selling a home, do what is best for you but don't play games because you have no idea who is on the other side making an offer. Be direct, be honest and (most of all) keep in mind that you are impacting the lives of other people. We are more than just profit. Don't price something to pray on the hope of others…

Secondly, not getting a house doesn't mean I failed. I'm proud of you for trying Bryan. That in and of itself is a huge hurdle. So you are allowed to honor the stress and struggle you have with the sale but also realize you have broken through yet another bereavement barrier. That house wasn't good enough for you…

Year 4 A.C. – Self-Generated Joy

November 6, 2021 - Change

I have a giant vase full of change. It occurred to me today that I've been collecting all the change I find along the past 4.5ish years since day 1 of widowhood. Look at all that change.

Interesting how one word can mean so much and so little to others. Some fear change and others thrive on it. Some accept change and some deny it to the end. Meanwhile, some people will walk by change on the street and others will stop to pick it up. No matter what our feelings are towards it, change happens however we value it.

When Clayton passed away, I was shattered by the change. My days changed. My nights changed. My hope changed. My fears changed. I changed - drastically. The odd thing is I underwent major change and then thought it would never change again. I would never find the change to stand up. I would never meet the change to drive me forward. I would always be trapped away from change. Those thoughts are normal at the stroke of grief but that's the most important moment to remember that nothing is forever because there will always be change.

So here is this vase that was basically empty on April 16, 2018. Only and already 55ish months later and it's quite full. I can see my reflection in this vase and I mirror the investment within myself. Either way, fast or slow, change takes place. I've build up my self value and have been able to move forward in ways I thought would never change. The most important thing to remind myself is that I didn't find all my change in one day…

Year 4 A.C. – Self-Generated Joy

November 13, 2021 - Birthdays and Beginnings

Today is my 43rd birthday. Clayton passed away just before turning 42. I've officially lived a full year longer then him. That brings up a lot of emotions and I know that's normal. Four years ago I didn't want to celebrate that I was alive another year. I felt tremendous guilt and I thought that feeling would never go away. This past year has reminded me that nothing is forever and, in time, everything has an ending, which means there is a new beginning.

I remember being in 5th grade. I was bullied. I'd hope that I'd catch a cold or have an asthma attack because that was easier than being called those names or going to the nurse's office to avoid being beat up in the boys room. I'd just keep reminding myself that nothing was forever and soon I'd have a new beginning.

"Just 7 more years and you'll graduate. None of these jerks will matter once you can leave and go wherever you want. You can be you."

Seventeen years old and I feared my 18th birthday. I had made it those 7 years and was in college. I had told myself when I was younger that those strange feelings would go away. By 18 I was sure I'd grow out of being gay but what if it doesn't go away? I told myself if I'm still feeling like this at 18 I'll begin to embrace who I'm supposed to be.

Free to be me, I started to dream about my life openly. By the time I was 40, I would have a husband, a family, a home. By that point I'd certainly be settled down and living my version of a fairytale ending. Never in my wildest dreams did I ever think at 40 I'd be widowed and beginning all over again.

This is my 4th birthday moving forward. Birthday 1 was a blur. Birthday 2 hurt. Birthday 3 was in lockdown but birthday 4 has brought the unexpected. This year has taught me so much about who I am and who I want to be. This year has shown me that I can honor my past, adore my present and have faith in the future. I've spent time on me, I've honored who I've become and that has allowed me to be better for others.

So I'm not on the fairytale timeline that I thought I'd have when I dreamt of my future. Some may feel disappointed but that's because we set our goals on a timeline we can't control. It truly isn't the destination that is the most important it is the journey. Four years ago I thought that my dreams had died forever but today I realize that my story is not done being written. Cheers to life, cheers to love and cheers to the lessons gifted by grief. Today I'm 43 and excited to step into my next new beginning…

Year 4 A.C. – Self-Generated Joy

November 20, 2021 - Moments Under A Mask

Headed into the 4th set of holidays without Clayton and the 5th set without my father I'm spending more time remembering my growth instead of my grief.

Walking into the woods of widowhood surrounded by the first Fall after losing Clayton and I had no idea how to handle things. Here came the gatherings, the get-togethers and the heaviness of the holidays. How was I going to make it through this first season of sadness? I distinctly remember Halloween gifting me the cloak I needed to hide from the holidays – a man behind the mask. What I didn't know is that Halloween mask would stay for a while to haunt me.

I learned quickly to flash the smile of the season when someone would say "Happy Holidays" and "seasons greetings". I couldn't be thankful. It was definitely not the most wonderful time of the year. Soon enough, the sadness changed to anger and wondering why everyone else got to have holidays as I widowed the winter. Bereavement was bitter cold.

Each year following that first Fall I have gone back to putting on that mask. Spreading what seasonal smiles I could to sweeten the air and appease others spirits. This year Fall has felt different. I spent more time cultivating myself through the spring, growing through the summer and this Fall brings something I never thought I'd do again – I'm harvesting the happy.

This holiday season, moments won't be under a mask…

Year 4 A.C. – Self-Generated Joy

November 27, 2021 - Grief in the Gravy

Part of moving forward is reflecting. This past Thursday was the 4th Thanksgiving without Clayton. I feel very different versus 2 years ago and I think that is important to share as I continue to grow. This has been an amazing year full of growth, self awareness, cultivating my character from grief's strangely fertile grounds and beginning to harvest the happy again. The pieces of me that fell away to decay have begun to nourish me again in new ways. It takes time but this year there wasn't grief in the gravy, there was new gratitude.

I'm stronger than I thought and in a storm of grief I've remained one who stands tall…

Thanks-Grieving: November 30, 2019

Last year I could barely walk through the grocery store during the holidays. Thanksgiving has always been my favorite and the thought of even buying ingredients was too much. This year, I told myself that it wasn't right to stop celebrating. Tin wouldn't want that at all. So I took a deep breath, swallowed what felt like a rock in my throat and grabbed a turkey. My eyes welled up and I told myself to go checkout. I had to go to the store three separate times to buy what I needed because I would hit a breaking point each time. Seasonings, cider, wine, apple pie, butter – God did Tin love butter. Those tears started in the dairy aisle and I had to go check out.

All things gathered and I could prep. I had the turkey ready for the next morning and the bread for stuffing drying out in the oven. I was making my way through it all by cooking only my favorites. I felt comfortable as I created the culinary traditions of my youth. I was floating in and out of nostalgic memories full knowing it was only because I was avoiding the reminder recipes – The Guarded Gourmet.

I woke up on Thanksgiving and fought to get out of bed. I had made it this far but putting that turkey into the oven meant I was moving forward without him. I never thought that the closing of an oven door could feel like the closing of a chapter in my life. The sound was deafening as I felt the preheat dissipating replaced by a chill reminding me his warmth was gone. I sat on the kitchen floor and cried.

Hours later, I pulled myself together and gathered up what I was bringing to a friend's. A small group, which helped reduced the anxiety. I moved through the holiday catching manageable memories like compartmentalized condiments off to the side that I could see but choose not to use – but there is always grief in the gravy.

As we wrapped up the evening, conversation lead to how many Thanksgivings it had been since I had been home with family. I couldn't remember so I started counting back and realized it was a road map though my loss. This was the second without Tin. Then the first. Then his last. Then our first in our new found beach life. Our last in Atlanta. Our first together. My last before we met.

Year 4 A.C. – Self-Generated Joy

Now I find myself Thanks-Grieving…

Photo Credit: Photos By Carlyn, LLC

December 4, 2021 - Holiday Apologies – Dusting the Grief Off the Garland

An Open Letter to the Holidays…

Dear Holidays,

As you know, the past 4 years I've been trying to figure out life without Clayton. He was always here when you arrived so after he died I couldn't handle seeing you. I knew you were coming but I couldn't hang up decorations and I refused to answer when you unselfishly sang carols outside my door.

2018 I hid. 2019 I was angry. 2020 I was lost and depressed yet you still showed up knowing I wasn't ready. You knew I needed time and I really just needed you to keep coming back around.

In 2017, Clayton, my mom and I went and got his (our) last tree. It hurt but also filled my heart to let him pick the grandest tree he could find. The next year I cried in the grocery store when the holiday songs came on. I feared the joy. 2019 brought anger. I hated to see twinkling lights and unbroken hearts. It was certainly not the most wonderful time of the year but I kept a smile because it was my holiday weight to bear.

Year 4 A.C. – Self-Generated Joy

Last year was filled with uncertainty. I was able to travel home to be with my family but the stress of the year had me exhausted and bitter. I was not in a good place and I kept handing myself coal. My heart was shattered and frozen but somehow it started to thaw in the spring. Time does not heal all wounds. Time is the quiet farmer who sows the saddened soils and slowly gathers up our grief. Time silently collects our tears and uses them to water the grief we grow from. This Fall, Time showed me something I haven't seen in years – fields of happiness ready for the harvest.

Dear Holidays,

I'm so very grateful that you kept checking in on me and you gifted me grace in my grief. You gave me time to dig out of the avalanche of sadness. So please accept my apologies dear Holidays now that I'm strong enough to dust the grief of the garland…

December 11, 2021 - Sharing My Scare

I am very open about my life, my grief journey, my faults and my growth. This week I hesitated to talk about something because I was very scared. I had to go to the doctor for something I noticed a while back that had changed. I should have gone to the doctor sooner but I just ignored it. I have had an amazing year of positivity and growth. I'll love Clayton forever but I have evolved and found love again with an amazing man and it all feels right. I haven't been able to lay Clayton's ashes to rest but I have been able to release his soul so both of us can follow our new paths. I know in my heart that we will meet again wherever and whenever the universe plans my arrival to my lost ones.

A checkup at the doctor's 4 days ago brought up the word cancer and my heart sunk. I had just found so much joy after so much pain. Why now?

"Dear Universe, I know I'm just one person on this planet and you don't need to do anything for me but haven't I been through enough? Haven't I given enough in my loss and in my sharing for others? I just found healing and happiness. Please don't take it away."

Year 4 A.C. – Self-Generated Joy

The doctor examined me and the diagnosis was a relief but surgery sooner rather than later was a better option. So yesterday I had surgery to remove something. I sat in pre-op with an IV and a blanket. I was surrounded by sterile equipment, the sounds of heart monitors and the smell of a hospital. Clayton had a sudden illness and needed to get diagnosis quickly and here I was. All of the flashbacks rushed through me. I grabbed the bars of the bed and told myself that this was very different. I knew I'd be fine after surgery. My fear wasn't the pain and healing process. My fear was not waking up and leaving others behind.

I know that someday will be my last day. Eventually this Earth will have to give me up. Regardless of how hard gravity tries to hold my soul, it has no power when I leave this body. I fought back the tears.

"Dear Universe, there are too many people on this Earth that are being held down by grief's gravity. I never want to be the giver of grief to others. My family and my partner deserve years of calm and comfort so please let them keep me longer."

I took in deep breaths from the mask and fell to sleep. Two outcomes, I'd wake up to love or move on to my lost loved ones. Either way, I wouldn't be in the one space I fear the most – alone. As soon as I closed my eyes, I opened them again. Everything done, the doctor was happy and I was still here which tells me that I have more to accomplish on this Earth.

I hesitated to tell you this story but I realize, yet again, that my widowed journey and openness about my grief is being used by something greater in order to help others. I thought yesterday was just the removal of something physical that wasn't serving me but that was just the setup for the real removal of my false belief in fear and loneliness. So for anyone who needs these words today, I openly share my scare…

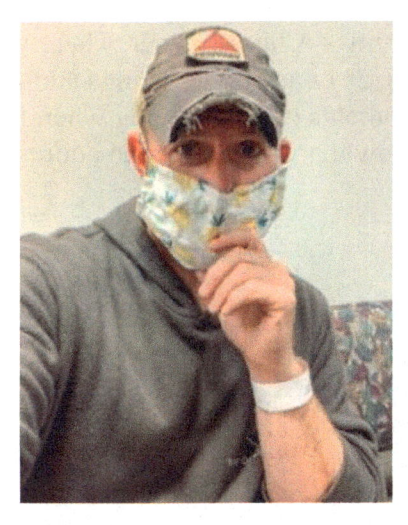

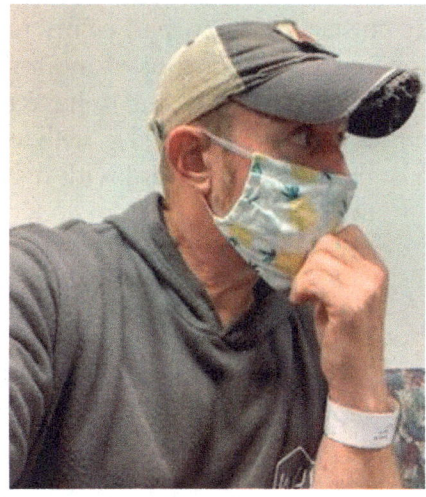

Year 4 A.C. – Self-Generated Joy

December 18, 2021 - A Change of Address

I've lived at my apartment for almost 6 years and alone in it without Clayton for almost 4 years. I am 100% full accepting that I've stayed in "our" apartment to press pause on parts of my life. I couldn't have Clayton back but I could wrap myself up in him through the photos he hung, walks he painted and the items he place. Until now, moving to me meant guilt that I was leaving him behind. I just couldn't move forward from that space for a lot of reasons. Some based in logic and others based on emotions. Regardless of the reasons, they were exactly the right ones for me.

Part of grief is grasping for grounding. For some of us, it's holding on to objects and staying put in one spot. For others it might be throwing everything out and changing your address but neither are wrong if it helps you process your new normal. Either way change is inevitable.

April 16th, 2018 brought about a 180 degree change I never expected and 2021 has done it again. I never thought id be widowed until all of a sudden I was. I never thought I'd find love again until all of a sudden I had. I never thought I'd change my address until yesterday when all of a sudden I did.

Part of me has always felt guilt that I get to live these experiences and Clayton couldn't. Yesterday at closing my realtor shared the story of how I had told him my birthday was tough from my guilt. He shared with the room that he surprised us during my birthday dinner about being under contract on the house. He shared with everyone that I deserved the good things in my life and all of a sudden my guilt was gone.

I didn't choose for Clayton to get sick. I didn't choose to be widowed at 39 years old. I did, however, chose to breathe, chose stand up and chose to take each day one step at a time. I chose to let myself smile, laugh, dance and live again.

So today I woke up starting a new part of my journey - A home owner. There will be moments of excitement and moments of mourning as I pack up the things and take the photos down that Clayton hung up. I'm going to have moments during moving when I smile and I cry at our memories and that's normal. I realize now that a change of an address isn't moving on from your past but moving forward with it…

Year 4 A.C. – Self-Generated Joy

December 25, 2021 - The Magic of the Season

I remember the magic of the holidays when I was younger. Time went by at a much slower pace waiting for that one special night followed by a day of jolly and cheer. Christmas Eve we would spend with my mom's side of the family surrounded by aunts, uncle, cousins and grandparents. Each year my grandfather would wear a Santa hat and I'd help him pass out the presents until he wasn't here for Christmas anymore.

Sneaking a peek from the stairs to see the presents left behind by Santa and waiting for my parents to give us the ok so we could rush in and create a wrapping paper tornado - A full day of new things and new memories. After cleaning up the merry mess, there'd be just a few hours with the new toys until we had to leave them behind to go see family. Of course growing up changed the holidays a bit but, for me, the magic was still there. The holidays were predictable and safe.

My job in animal care limited the places I could work and so, in my mid 20s, I ventured off to San Diego. What I didn't know was that decision would limit my holidays with my family. Time zones, travel costs and the difficulties of taking time off resulted in no family Christmas for ten years. Back than, I was ok with living my dream and having the phone passed around to all the relatives. I knew each year I'd get to say Happy Holidays until all of a sudden I couldn't. I realized that it didn't matter how much I spent and sent, I was missing the magic.

December 25, 2017 was the first without my dad and a full knowing that it was Clayton's last. There was no point in getting him all the things because we knew he wouldn't be here to enjoy them so we poured time into decorating and baking all the cookies he wanted. It was the first year that I really understood where the true magic of the season was generated.

This has been the 4th Christmas without Clayton, the 5th without my dad and there's nothing Santa can do to change that. It took a while to accept my losses but I just keep remembering that following the North Star will eventually get me closer to the next Christmas. I've been given the greatest grief gift of all and that is gratitude for the true magic of the season. It's the memories of red Santa hats, stuffed animals and acute awareness of the truly short time we have together. Happy Holidays.

Love Always, Bryan

Year 4 A.C. – Self-Generated Joy

January 1, 2022 - A Flight of Stairs

Almost six years ago and three flights of stairs up, we thought our new apartment in this little beach down was part of Heaven.

For 8 months I helped you walk up and down these stairs until up was to hard for the both of us.

Four years after you, I stayed in our apartment. I couldn't move, at first, because of finances. I couldn't move, because of safety. I couldn't move away from us. I just couldn't.

For a time I thought I would never leave. For a time I thought if I didn't leave you might come walking in that door again. For a time I thought that I wouldn't have any other reason to leave and, if I did, it was selfish.

Slowly but suddenly I found myself in similar yet unfamiliar spaces and I new it was time, time for me to move forward, time for me to move my mindset and time to move on from our apartment three flights up.

It has taken me some time to realize that moving doesn't change how important our memories are to me. Moving doesn't mean I'm forgetting about you. Moving doesn't mean that I don't still love you. Moving means that I still have life to live and our apartment wasn't supposed to hold me anymore.

So here's to our wonderful years in that apartment in the sky.

Almost six years later and this is our last walk together down these three flights…

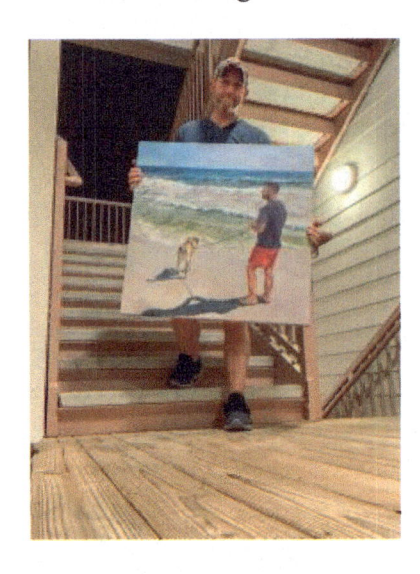

Year 4 A.C. – Self-Generated Joy

January 8, 2022 - Filtering Out the Fiction

Moving from the apartment where I became widowed has had a lot of competing emotions. Taking down the photos that Clayton hung up and seeing just my dog Roan standing in our empty apartment hit me hard. Real life becomes more real in some pretty harsh, unexpected waves and ways. Worn out carpet where Clayton passed from room to room and partially painted walls because, as he would say:

"No one will see it so why bother to paint it?"

What we didn't know was that all those little things would one day be long lost messages that would return the memories to me. Who knew an apartment could speak such volumes so loudly?

Some of the messages made me smile. Some of the messages made me cry and some of the messages hit home in ways I didn't expect. Unpacking in this new home, I found his interior design portfolio and in it I found the note I left him wishing him luck on his first day of work. I wouldn't have had to write that note had we not moved here. That's still something I struggle letting go of. I could hold back and not share that I still feel guilty we moved here. I've told myself time and time again that it was fate and not my fault. It was the infection and the poorly monitored medication increases by the doctors that his liver couldn't handle but, to be honest, part of me still thinks if we didn't move for my job then Clayton wouldn't have gotten that infection to begin with.

At the end of the day I know that it wasn't my fault but part of my growing through grief is authentically sharing the feelings as they come regardless if they are actually true. I found that having an open conversation with myself helps me validate my feelings (which I need) and allows me to weed through the thoughts that really have no basis in truths. The fact that I choose to focus on is that Clayton kept my note. He saved that message, which made its way back to me after all these years to remind me that we moved here together. Although things didn't unfold as we had hoped, I still know in my heart that we were living life together. It's those memories I need to focus on. It's those messages that hold the real truth. It has taken me time but I've learned to filter out the fiction…

Year 4 A.C. – Self-Generated Joy

January 22, 2022 - A Memory Bank

It all adds up doesn't it? I've had days where it's one bad thing again and again. I couldn't catch a break. Life seems so tough when I'm right in the middle of the storm.

I used to dwell on the harder days way more then dwelling on the good ones. You know what I mean? We do it all the time. We could have a friend say 20 positive things about us and then one thing that is off and those 20 nice things get flushed from our memory. No matter how hard we try, that one negative comment out weighs all the rest. We start walking in the worry.

Of course when Clayton passed away, and honestly his whole illness leading up to his final day, I was surrounded by fear and wounded from walking in the worry. The fog of fear wraps around and you lose your ability to see anything except the Hell your living in and your mind plays out future days full of after-death difficulties.

"I'll be alone. I'm so scared. I have to pay all the bills myself. What if I can't? What if I get sick? Who's going to take care of me? Will I be able to buy food? Will I be kicked out of my apartment? Will I survive?"

There were so many of those thoughts. There was so much extra emotion filled by worry which fueled the anxiety. I realized that meant it was me increasing the heat of my own Hell! So I started worrying about worrying.

The cycle continued until I finally admitted that I was adding to the problem - I was adding value to the hard days. That was the toughest part of my mind change but the biggest step forward. I stopped worrying about the future and I admitted to myself that I was giving all my value to my grief. I was refusing to acknowledge the good days of past and the possibility of good days in the future. I hadn't checked in on where my overall life's investments were.

A step back to look at the bank statements of my life and my good day account has a much higher value than my bad day account. Checking in on where I had recently been adding value showed me that I was investing more into the bad day account than the good day account. That's not where I want to deposit my time and I'm the only one who can invest in either those accounts.

So take a minute to stop and check your memory bank. Leave your emotions to the side and look at the data around your "feeling financials." On the hard days, help yourself to avoid adding to the financial fire and place value in the good day account. There's power in memory math…

Year 4 A.C. – Self-Generated Joy

January 29, 2022 - Year Two Times Two

Sometimes I'm not sure what to write each week. When that happens (because it's normal to not have a topic), I take it that the Universe wants me to just look back and see where I am verses where I was. So I decided to look back at the last blog I wrote two years ago. Year 2, for me and many others, is the hardest. Year 1 is a fog. Year 2 and my loss was finally real. Year 3 was acceptance and Year 4 has been moving forward. I didn't remember that two years ago I wrote about how I could not move out of the apartment Clayton and I had.

Here I sit in my new home that two years ago I never thought I'd have. Here I live with a man I have fallen in love with which I used to think would never happen to me again. The process of grieving can feel endless but when I move forward and multiply year two by two, I find myself doing things I never thought were possible again after loss. Time did not heal all wounds back to before bereavement but time toughened me enough that I could move forward...

Home is Where the Heart is - January 2019

It's taken me months and months to bring up the courage to go to dinner with a friend. Sounds crazy but she was Clayton's favorite coworker and he is all we have in common. I knew it hit her hard when he passed and I knew she would want to talk about it. I guess that is just another layer of widowhood that others don't understand – We want to see you but the memories you trigger are to strong for us to handle right now.

I finally said yes and we went to a local restaurant. It was wonderful to see her! We caught up and laughed, we talked about Tin and how much we missed him. It was scary at first but I realize hearing her remember him was a gift. It's so easy to think that, for others, out of sight is out of mind…

The evening was wonderful and we talked about many different things. My career and second job (which I need to cover my widowed bills) are both very successful. She asked if I was planning to move home near my family but, overall, things are good here so I'm staying. It wasn't the memories of Tin that crushed me. It wasn't being at a restaurant that he and I went to often. It was a question that I never thought of and certainly didn't expect the impact when asked.

"Wow! You are doing so well you should move and buy a place!"

The moths of mourning fluttered in my stomach and up in my throat. Move? Buy my own place? Leave our home? I hadn't thought of any of those ideas. I felt sick but I kept it together until we went our separate ways. I cried heading home and when I got home I looked around for any changes. It took me a bit to settle and when I did I asked myself why that idea of moving was so hard. Here is my answer…

Year 4 A.C. – Self-Generated Joy

Tin designed the layout of our apartment. Tin surprised me by painting the rooms when I was at work. Tin hung all the photos himself. If I take it down he won't be here to help me put it back up. He put so much of his heart into our home. If I move than I lose more of Tin…..

February 5, 2022 - The Grief Graduate

It's been almost 4 years since Clayton died. I was struck by that fact this week. I've been without him for as long as I was in high school. The biggest difference is that my schooling in sadness occurred much faster than K-12.

Year 1 felt like being a scared kid starting up class in emotional elementary except with no holidays or summer breaks from bereavement to look forward too. The grief grades seemed to go slow in the moment with uncomfortable classes full of life lessons yet, in the blink of and eye, I now feel like a senior in class. A look back at my complicated report card shows a rocky road that would appear I failed at times only to realize that it's normal to get an "A" in anger, a "C" in confusion and an "F" in the subjects of fear and frustration. A long list on the sensitive syllabus.
At first I only looked at how I thought I failed each semester but my transcripts show that I also got an "H" in happiness and an "L" in love. Life hasn't been pass or fail. I've actually succeeded at each task. I've survived 100% of my hardest days and I deserve the extra credit for the added homework I've done on my own self along this track.

I'm ready for the feelings finals on my emotional exams. More often than not, we hear people say they have "moved on". I'm here to authentically and honestly tell you that you will never "move on" from your grief. You can leave that little trama town behind but the bereavement goes with you because you are forever enrolled in the University of the Universe.

Year 4 A.C. – Self-Generated Joy

Years later I can look back at my yearbook yearning for simpler times. I know now that I am not done learning and I accept that I'll never fully be grief free until my time is up. I still have a lot of work to do here before that day so that means I'm not ready yet to be a grief graduate…

February 12, 2022 - Sharing a Smile

I miss his smile. It was a gift he had share with me to hold in my memories. It's been almost four years since I saw him smile in person. Sometimes I forget to remember those moments because he was so sick near the end that he didn't have the energy to smile. It wouldn't help him if I showed my sorrow so I made sure to smile for the both of us. When Clayton passed away I lost his smile and my own. My world got dimmer.

I'm spending this year looking back at my blogs in reflection, not to revel in the hurt or reinforce the pain but to remember where I was and how far I've come. I'm grateful. I'm grateful for my inner strength and grateful for my perseverance. It's become a realization that every time someone stops smiling the world gets darker. So I do my very best to keep moving forward and not let the negatives surround me. I can impact the lives of others from the lessons I've learned growing through grief. When all else has felt like it's failed I know I can just stop and smile. I can smile at my memories. I can smile at the good in my life. I can smile back at me with a sense of self-comfort that I'm doing the best I can and, if I'm having trouble, I just close my eyes and borrow Clayton's smile.

Four years ago was the first Valentine's without him. Rereading my blog from 2018 brings me right back to my lost loves of the past except the hurt from 2018 is no longer there. Losing Clayton awoke sleeping emotions from further back. Since then, I have faced the trauma with care and conviction to find that I could create my own freedom by accepting my

Year 4 A.C. – Self-Generated Joy

grief and releasing it to the universe. This year I'm gifted with a new love just 4 years later because I stopped expecting to get my expectations.

If I remember that I have the power to create light within myself by starting to smile then I can assure myself to keep going because there are smiles waiting for me in my future. If everyone just chose to smile more, we'd collectively make the world a brighter place.

"Every time someone stops smiling the world gets darker. Don't give in! We need you…Smile."

A Hallmark Heartbreak Kind of Holiday – February 9, 2018

My birthday was hard. Thanksgiving was hard. Christmas and New Years were both hard. Yet it is the "Hallmark Holiday" that seems to burn more than build the wave of sadness.

Every Valentine's Day growing up, I wrote out cards and put them in classmates construction paper mailboxes but only for the girls. Life is different now and kids can like whomever they like but I had to give Valentine's to Allison when I really wanted to give it to Andy. Either way, all I wanted growing up was to find that one Valentine.

This is the first sweetheart holiday without Tin. I'm 2 months away from the anniversary of his death. Am I the only person that wants to walk into the grocery store, dump all the Valentine cards on the floor, throw boxes of chocolates and stomp on every flower in sight? I couldn't give Andy a Valentine in high school and now I can't give Tin one now. I feel like I'm a heartbroken teenager all over again…

Year 4 A.C. – Self-Generated Joy

February 19, 2022 - Stains of the Heart

There have been moments this week where I've caught myself thinking more and more about the loss of my dad and Clayton. I had a friend from work pass away after being in the hospital. All I could think about was what his surviving wife was going through. Another coworker sadly lost his mother and it reminded me of losing my dad. I felt both the hurt of losing a parent and for my coworker's father who is now finding himself relabeled and placed on the widowed list.

I couldn't sleep well the other night. We are getting a new couch and cleaning the cushions of the old couch. The cushion covers removed revealed a long lost stain. Clayton had spilled cranberry juice saying something sassy when he was sick. Of course I laughed and cleaned it up as best I could. I got it off the cover but it remained hidden from plain sight just like my memory of him on that couch. Those memories of watching him fade day after day are forever engrained in my mind and stained on my heart.

Sometimes stains can be frustrating but other times they can bring back memories of grand adventures and moments of pure joy. That old cozy sweatshirt you love with the coffee stain on the front from where you were laughing so hard you tipped your cup. That favorite hat that is tattered and torn stained with years of wear. That hat may look like junk to others but it has been a true friend. That hat walked with you through so many days shading your eyes so you could experience the journey.

Yesterday I had a really difficult morning unable to shake what grief's imagination had conjured in my dreams. I felt heavy and wondered why today was so much. Later, a friend brought her daughter into work to see the animals. Right before my eyes I watched a little girl and her mother smile and laugh all well knowing that they both carry the grief of my friend's son, that little girl's brother, passing away almost 2 years ago. What goes unnoticed by strangers was visible to me. I will always see the stain on their hearts. However, in that moment, they didn't strengthen my grief, they gave me a gift. They reminded me that the heavy feeling of the day would undoubtedly subside. Shortly after, that little girl said she had Girl Scout Cookies to sell. My dad loved Girl Scout Cookies so I gladly returned her grief gift with gratitude by helping lighten her cookie carrying.

New grief is young and brings you back to childhood where the smallest things can seem like the end of the world. I'm constantly reminding myself that it takes time to grow. It's been almost 4 years since Clayton passed and my perspective has slowly evolved. Instead of crying over spilled milk, I'll just use what's left in that half full glass to dunk my cookies in just like my dad did and seeing a glass of cranberry juice will remind me of the beauty found in stains of the heart…

Year 4 A.C. – Self-Generated Joy

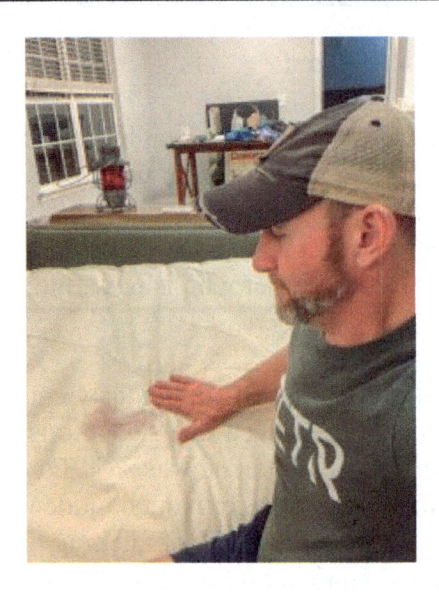

February 26, 2022 - The Grief Guard

Terrible things happen to people every single day but not everyone experiences terrible things. Some get to float through life without fear, loss or a bigger view of the world. Lucky maybe? However, true gratitude often comes from true grief. There's a mindset now that any inconvenience is a huge struggle and so many are in search of something "triggering" with no regard to who or what they try to shut down. I was a target for that on social media today because I choose to dance.

What does that have to even do with being widowed? It directly has to do with MY widowhood because MY way of handling MY grief was attacked. For those that don't know, I love to dance and I share dancing on my social media because it brings me joy. The side effect I never expected was my grief management would inspire others to smile, laugh, dance and keep moving forward verse giving up in grief. Today my dancing was attacked in a comment on a Facebook post:

"There is war in this world this is ridiculous" – Facebook Troll

While the world certainly has terrible things going on, I can't allow it to consume me or I would fall into constant despair where so many others actively choose to live and try to force others to reside. Tragedy deserves respect but do we all stop generating joy completely forever? If all of us stopped having any kind of happy because of terrible things in this world then this would forever be a globe of grief. Misery loves company and that is why those who choose to stay there want others to commiserate. It's been almost 4 years since the widowed fog descended on my world yet I must always keep watch. Based on the misery mindset, I should stay sad and you should all join me forever. That is a pandemic I never want to see plague this planet. Every time a person stops smiling the world becomes a darker place.

Year 4 A.C. – Self-Generated Joy

If my vigilance and acts of personal bravery provides safe space for others to gather, I am honored to stand guard even if it is a 30 second dance that helps just one more person smile. I bet this Typing Troll doesn't know the amount of "Thank Yous" I get in my messages and that I have had a number of people say my posts give them hope that they will have future smiles. Dear Ms. Misery, I have had messages from people that chose to not make an undoable decision because they see the hope I harvest. You may want me to stop dancing but I want those desperate people to know they are worth it!

What this Facebook foe also doesn't know is that this week held heartache for me. Clayton's family is planning to sell his mother's home here which means I'll have to go back to the place that took him from me. We never had a chance to have a funeral service and so we most likely will plan it this year on his birthday. Of course that will bring some closure for me but before I can close that door I have to walk through it. I wasn't expecting the fog to sneak in but I know there's more freedom in my future as long as I keep moving forward through it so I need to keep dancing first and foremost for me.

So to all the Social Media Satans looking to darken this world - Kiss My Light!

I will not back down and I will not be dimmed because I am the dancing widower. Regardless of whatever fog settles on this world, I will always spread whatever happiness I can and I will always be a guard against grief of both my own and any others seeking refuge. So I have an invitation to the world – LET'S DANCE!

Year 4 A.C. – Self-Generated Joy

March 5, 2022 - Grief's Gaslighting Guilt

"Why was I the one to live and not him?"

"Did I do enough when he was sick?"

"But if only I had done more then maybe, just maybe, he'd still be alive."

These are all statement I have said to myself about Clayton's death. These are all statements that I have heard other widowed people say about themselves and, for a long time, we believe them.

There is no guide to grief. There's never a class in school to warn you of the crash course you hit the minute the "after death" alarm clock starts. No matter how hard you try to hit the snooze button, you are forever a new kind of awake. All the emotions you think will come with loss of a loved one pour out of your heart all over your world. You expect sadness. You expect the depression. You expect the anger. What you don't expect is the worst of them all. This small widowed whisper that keeps saying:

"It should have been you. You didn't do enough. Why do you get to live and he didn't."

The low voice of Grief's guilt making you question everything you did. You know the truth that you loved with your whole soul but Grief turns your own argument against you.

"Did you REALLY do everything you could? What if you went to the doctor with him that first time and questioned the medication? Would he still be here Bryan? You COULD have gone but YOU didn't!"

For a while I couldn't get out of grief's sick cycle. Again and again I'd fight back with a valid reason I did the best I could and still the eerie echo would reverberate the denial from a distance. I was cornered so I just gave in to the guilt and laid down full of learned helplessness believing there was no where safe to go. The vicious voice reminded me of mean kids in school and my memories washed over me strengthening the grief. I started to replay those difficult days like a record and began to think all was lost except that grief didn't realize he had just showed his weakness. Grief's guilt was just another one of those mean kids. Grief was just a bully of bereavement and I had survived 100% of those hard days. It's time these psychological tactics were stopped. Enough was enough....

They say to take away something's power is to name it and so from now moving forward Grief's Guilt is nothing more than just a Gaslighter and your flame no longer controls my feelings. I did enough. I am enough. I loved enough and you will no longer deny me of my dignity...

Year 4 A.C. – Self-Generated Joy

"THEY SAY TO TAKE AWAY SOMETHING'S POWER IS TO NAME IT AND SO FROM NOW MOVING FORWARD GRIEF'S GUILT IS NOTHING MORE THAN JUST A GASLIGHTER..."

- SEALIONBRYAN

March 12, 2022 - Grains of Grief

"I'm too young for this loss. This isn't the way it was supposed to happen. It's all going so fast. How has so much of my life been chipped away from me so soon? We were supposed to have more of our lives together."

Those who lack loss walk through life unable to fully understand the uncomfortable burden that the bereaved must bear. They get to keep the one thing we are all born with - the privilege of innocence. Ignorance is a true form of bliss until the wind whipped gravel leaves you covered in blisters. It's not their fault that our path has lead us into the sands but I have asked many times why me and not someone else. Why am I the one who has to withstand this weather?

Erosion is often seen as a slow, natural process but the sudden impact of the widowed sandstorm sends you decades into the future buried under the dunes. We never expect to be so weathered so early. The pressure builds and some of that sand turns to sharp shards of glass. You definitely don't expect the small emotional insults that come as you continue to dig yourself out as you grow through grief.

Looking back, I thought I'd be forever buried under those dunes. In my despair, I had forgotten that nothing is forever and everything will change. Time doesn't heal all wounds but, in time, I have reached the surface.

"Stand up and dust yourself off."

Year 4 A.C. – Self-Generated Joy

Sounds familiar but shattered feelings don't drift away like dust, they stick to you like grains of sand irritating, abrasive and often times out of sight of others, the grief grit scratching beneath the surface. All of them wanting attention, each one becoming another emotional obligation after the obituary.

For a while, I thought I was just a lesser version of myself until I realized we all start off as a solid block that is carved by our experiences, eroded by our emotions and ultimately shape us into who we are meant to be. I may not have liked the erosion but I can say that I have weathered the storm. It took time but I stood up and started moving forward. I was bereavement buried but now I can breathe and start to brush off these grains of grief…

March 19, 2022 - Reflection that Resonates: PEP in My Steps Forward

This is the 169th widowed blog I've written. In 28 days, it will be the fifth anniversary of Clayton's death. I have been widowed longer than I was in high school or college. If that's the case, did I float through my Grief grades or have I been applying myself to Life's lessons? The only way to know is to do what I found to be the toughest part of the road after loss:

Self Reflection.

Day by day it's hard to see or feel positivity, energy or purpose in the start of my journey but with a library of enlightenment from my passed blogs, I can see that I have come further than Year One's fog, Year Two's anger, Year Three's fight towards acceptance. It's here, near the end of Year Four, that I stopped to look back at what I left behind that had originally left me first.

Year 4 A.C. – Self-Generated Joy

Just 2 years ago I was struggling with grief and being thrown into solitude by a world wide crisis. I was going to slip backwards and I needed to throw myself a lifeline. I had to search for gratitude in the garbage. Little did I know that anchor rope would lead me to a reflection that truly resonates in the present.

It's not hope that things will get better which lead me forward – It was gratitude. Gratitude for what I had, have and will be given. Loss is unavoidable but time and time again I realize I could stay behind lost in loss or choose to look for the gift's left behind by grief.

Finding gratitude in Grief's garbage has been the thing that has gotten me to where I am today. Sure there are days that are tougher than others but, over all, giving gratitude has, in fact, gifted me with pep (positivity, energy, purpose) in my steps…

March 26, 2022 - Another Step Upwards on this Grief Grise

The thing about a grief journey is that it's never over. Every step you take onward and upward holds an emotional echo. Some days it's constantly ringing in your ear and other times it a distant whisper at the bottom of a staircase. Either way you still keep climbing to find the next landing.

A dining table, that's what my boyfriend and I needed next for our new house. Slowly our life is beautifully coming together with all the designs and details, a room at a time together. I'm often asked why I still write a widowed blog now that I am in a relationship again. It's simple – I'll always be widowed. Just like someone who has been divorced is always divorced from someone even if they get married again. You can't erase experience and it's not healthy to ignore it either. Of course I wish I never experienced the types of loss that I have but there isn't a way to reverse it so I hold gratitude for my experiences, which have given me wisdom and perspective. I'll continue to write even after I'm married because there are many of us who walk this walk and someone should give it a voice that way others can follow the path less afraid and less lonely.

Year 4 A.C. – Self-Generated Joy

"Doesn't your current partner hate that you talk about your late partner? I'd be mad if I were him!"

Surprisingly enough I have had that said to me more often than you'd expect. My person knows I love him and he loves me for all of me, which includes being widowed. It would actually be strange if someone forces you to stop talking or remembering those you've lost. How said to think people would just replace others and forget them. I think it's a sign of self-confidence and self-assurance. His understanding is a beautiful gift to me.

Well now that I've said that, back to the dining table. We had found one we liked a month ago at a store and decided last weekend was the time to get it. Funny thing was that the store was out of the table until the Fall. As we continued on our day we drove past the furniture store that Clayton used to work at. I had never actually been. After looking through a few more stores we decided to stop in to see what Clayton's store actually had. We were greeted with an energetic woman who hadn't met Clayton but told me the staff speaks highly of him often 5 years after he couldn't work anymore. We walked around the first level. I had hopes I'd see the table we'd want but it was nowhere in sight. Perhaps we were lead hear for me to just get the message that others remembered Clayton to this day as I do?

In the middle of the store was a set of stairs to another show room. Clayton had often shared stories that strange sounds and ghostly things seemed to happen in the upstairs section. I wasn't scared, in fact I was hoping to catch a glimpse of him off in the distance arranging some chairs.

"Are you up here?" I whispered to myself. As I stepped onto the landing I saw a beautiful custom dining table with metal legs and a driftwood tabletop. Driftwood was one of Clayton's favorite things. Without a doubt, my boyfriend and I knew we found our table and the next day it was delivered.

I personally think it was all by Clayton's design and I'd like to think it was his way of blessing our new life and our new home. Call it coincidence or call it a sign, either way that soulful stairway lead me another step upwards on this grief grise…

Year 4 A.C. – Self-Generated Joy

April 2, 2022 - The Final Passing

This week has been full of up and down moments. Life always throws change at you but fast change from a high moment to a low moment and back really takes a toll on you. I certainly need to rest the next couple of days. Not just sleep but rest so I can think, feel and process what this week brought me in blessings and bereavement. You never really know all the things going on in someone's life unless they share with you and not many people share as outwardly as I do. I share so it serves as a reminder to be kind to others who are secretly struggling.

This week brought heavy news that a longtime friend was very troubled and sought some serious help. This week brought a huge jump in the business I own and built since Clayton passed away. This week I was surrounded and lifted up by hundreds of friends and supporters. This week brought fun phone calls and connections. This week time stopped while I fed a baby penguin. This week a dance video I posted online was used in an ABC – 20/20 special. This week has flown by but there is still one more major situation I've known was coming. I need it to happen but it's also bittersweet. Tomorrow I have to give Clayton's ashes away.

His family is here to start sorting and selling his mother's home. That's where he picked up the fungal infection in the backyard that got in his bloodstream leading to medication, the medication lead to terminal liver failure, which returned him to his mother's house for hospice care. His final view through a window was the scene where his passing all started. I never liked that house from the first day I saw it. Call it just a feeling but I was uneasy from the start and tomorrow I will be going back to help his family sort a life that fell apart.

When his mother was hospitalized after Tin passed, I went over to get his ashes because I wanted him out of that house. Ironically, tomorrow I'll have to bring him back there to hand his urn over to his uncle for the drive up to Illinois so Clayton can be given a service and a final resting place. It's needed closure for all of us but there is still a new finality for me. It's been almost 5 years and now I have to bring him back to the place that took him from me. I have to bring Clayton back to where he died in order to send him off. For me, placing his urn in his uncle's hands will truly be the final passing…

Year 4 A.C. – Self-Generated Joy

April 9, 2022 - Just a Pile of Ash

The conversation of letting Clayton's ashes go came up last week. His uncle was going to drive them up to where Clayton asked to be buried. So after 5 years I handed him over. I had lots of messages of support and messages suggesting ways I could keep some of Clayton's ashes to hold on to a part of him. What I love about sharing my blog is that it often inspires conversation that helps me dive more into my feelings and why I do what I do as I grow through grief.

It's interesting how people will show up in various forms depending on the situation at hand. Every time I share about my grieving process there are people who respond back (trying to help) by saying what I SHOULD do verses what I COULD do. Yet they never first ask me what I want or feel I should do. I even had people message how angry they were that his family would take his ashes away from me yet I never once said or implied such a thing was happening. I simply stated that Clayton's last wish was to be cremated and buried in the family cemetery so he would one day rest there next to his mother. Amazing how emotions and grief within others can take a last man's wish and turn it into a tornado. Grief can make a mountain out of just a pile of ash.

Yes, I reduced Clayton's whole being to just a pile of ash because, to me, it is no longer Clayton. He isn't actually in that urn. I loved him for his spirit not his physical being and the only thing that actually continues on isn't in that jar. It's his spirit in my memories.

I fully understand why some people want to keep ashes of anyone they cared about but I think it's holding on to the past in a way that I don't think serves me. Having a gift around the house or wearing my favorite old hat he gave me is one thing but to cling to carbon might as well be placing myself in chains.

The other side of this for me is very clear. When Clayton thought he would die before his mother, he told me he wanted to be cremated and scattered at the beach. On his deathbed, I watched Clayton look directly into his mother's eyes and tell her that he wanted to be cremated and laid to rest with her. His last wish was his gift to her that I will not take away. So I understand all of the sweet messages and amazing suggestions on how I can keep a bit of ash for myself but there is just one thing:

Clayton wanted to be cremated and laid to rest next to his mother. If I take any amount of those ashes to hold him close then I'm not truly and fully honoring his wishes to be fully laid to rest next to his mother. He never said that I get to withhold part of him from her and I won't choose to do that. They say if you love something let it go. I have with an open heart because I know he's exactly where he asked to be and that means he is still with me because Clayton is more than just a pile of ash.

Year 4 A.C. – Self-Generated Joy

This week his mother called and said she would love a photo of me on our paddle board in the ocean holding Clayton's urn and scattering his ashes in the sea. They both just wanted what they thought the other wanted and I was gifted yet another view of pure love from just a pile of ash…

The Care-Griever Years:

Year 5 A.C.

Harvesting The Happy

Year 5 A.C. – Harvesting the Happy

Only and already Year 5. Moment by moment, sometime my grief journey feels like it has lasted eons yet, as I growth through grief with gratitude, I see how quickly time makes everything change. Four years now fly by much quicker than four years in high school. I'd rather live in the moments than wish time to move any faster. Youth truly is wasted on the young, but I wouldn't have that perspective without both grief and gratitude. I pause to take inventory on all the amazing things that have entered my life. This year is truly about stepping fully into my future…

April 16, 2022 - These Soft and Coarse Sands of Time

The course of time is told by the passing of both soft and coarse sands. Some experiences feel gentle and powder fine while others sting and erode me in these whipping widowed winds.

Five. How is it already five years since you've been gone? How is it that I didn't know if I'd make it through day 1 but now I'm here 1,461 days later? It's interesting that my blog day lands right on your death day. It's interesting that this weekend is Easter. What if you rose from the dead tomorrow? I have wished that so many times but after 1,461 days what would I do?

It's been 5 years and, although I still love you, I'm in a new and completely different space in my life. I have so much gratitude for the gifts I have been given but it was at the expense of losing you. How do I describe these sandy grains? How does one balance both the grains of grief and gratitude?

I don't voice it much but it all makes me wonder about how things will eventually change. What I thought was the end of my world turned out to be a sudden start of a new chapter. I could have hidden away for fear of the rough times but I would have let the good times slip right through my hands. Would I even appreciate my feet in the soft sand had I not been buried first in dunes of bereavement?

I've realized now that my grief and gratitude will forever go hand in hand. My life will always consist of a balance between these soft and coarse sands of time. I don't know how much time has been planned

for me. The only thing I do know is that I deserve all the moments in soft sand and all the smiles that are waiting for me in my future. Somewhere somehow you, Tin, are guiding me forever forward…

Year 5 A.C. – Harvesting the Happy

April 23, 2022 - From My Present to My Past

Dear Bryan,

I'm imagining today that I am able to write to you in our past to give you a glimmer of hope. Where you are at the start of this widowed journey is not where you are forever trapped. I'll be honest with you and say that there will be tough days, months and seasons but you will continue to move forward. Keep being true to yourself and this journey will unfold for you in ways that you never expected.

Be ready because Year 1 will be a fog. Year 2 will bring the painful reality that Tin is not coming back. Year 3 you will be very angry. To top it all off there will be a pandemic and you'll feel more alone then you ever have felt. That will be the scariest year and you'll linger on the one question that you may never have answered – "Why?"

I know that doesn't sound very inspiring but it's necessary for what comes next. It sounds cliché, but you need to spend time understanding your losses and honoring yourself to regroup on a foundation forward. You don't know this yet but your experiences will all come together and generate an immense amount of energy. I need you to be open to it and to realize that you will be able to direct that energy in huge waves. Do the work on yourself first or you will misuse the energy. Don't use it in Year 3 because you will be too angry.

You have been writing this blog for yourself but you will start to share it on social media in hopes it helps others deal with their different versions of grief. It won't make sense to you now but it will all unfold beautifully in year 4. Hold this future faith I send as I can share we are safe moving forward through our Year 5. I still don't truly know the "why" but there are many things that will show up unexpectedly that will make so much sense in the moment.

Just know that the hurt you feel in the past will forge you into someone who has the ability and the energy to help many others. You never told anyone that back when you lost Tin you felt you had no more value. You floated through the days trapped in a real life purgatory. You had to stay there for awhile but it was not meant as a punishing consequence, it's been a calculated conditioning for your next move upward. It's going to feel easier to give in to the grief but hold on and know you have future smiles waiting for you.

I'm writing to tell you I am so very proud of how you are holding yourself together and continuing to move forward. I have just one request of you. It will seem strange. It will seem like a waste of time. You may not want to or feel like you can but I NEED you to just promise you'll do this one thing for us –

Year 5 A.C. – Harvesting the Happy

Please just start to dance again…

April 30, 2022 - The Grief Cap

"Can I buy you a new cap?"

"No thank you."

"Can you afford a new cap?"

"Yes I can. Thank you."

"Do you know people might judge you because of how your cap looks?"

"I like the worn look. It represents my well-lived life. Thank you for your concern."

"Do you know you look homeless in that hat?"

"Looks can be deceiving but I do have shelter. Thank you."

"Do you just wear that hat because you have no hair? Be proud of yourself…"

"I'm actually very proud of how I've managed to become who I am. My lack of hair doesn't reduce my value. The history behind the hat is what actually

holds value but thank you."

Year 4 A.C. – Self-Generated Joy

"Well really what's with the trash hat?"

"My partner died 5 years ago and this was one of the last gifts he gave me. We

still haven't had a funeral for him so I wear this hat each day as I grow through grief. When I look at this hat I see the widowed weathering I've endured. I wear it to remind myself that I do have the strength and I honor myself for what I have overcome. To you it may be just a sign of poverty but to me it represents self priority and an internal prosperity I can't place a value on. I'll lay it to rest when I'm ready."

"Good grief you should have just said it in the first place. Now you made me feel bad!"

"If that's the case, perhaps it best to first ask a man why he treasures something before you call it trash. You would have saved yourself the guilt. You would have gifted me the opportunity to tell you all about a wonderful man I once knew but, instead, you just wanted to put a cap on my grief…"

May 7, 2022 - Widowed Whiplash

I haven't had much downtime lately. Life is just moving at a very rapid pace and yesterday my body decided we were in desperate need of a red light and slammed on the brakes.

I was at work feeling sluggish after a night of thunderstorms and random coughing keeping me up. Not unmanageable, but on the commute in I noticed my coughing getting deeper and more regular. At work I started to feel winded and a bit confused. The coughing intensified so I put my emergency inhaler in my pocket and kept going. I noticed a tarp that had broken and needed fixing. As my coworker and I adjusted the tarp I started coughing and walked a few feet away. The coughing intensified, I couldn't catch my breath, the dizzy set in and I started to panic – asthma attack.

Year 5 A.C. – Harvesting the Happy

I slid down a pole to ground and slapped my hand on the floor to get my coworker's attention because I had very little air to cry for help. Energy fading, I got out my inhaler and took as much medicine in as I could. I held it in and kept telling myself to hang in there. Everything around got fogy, my lips started to tingle and I felt the energy leaving my arms. I was going unconscious.

"Stay Awake Bryan. Don't die young like Clayton."

Moments later my lungs released like a locked-up seatbelt and I gasped. Air reentered and my whole body relaxed. On the second breath I started to cry scared from the fear that I could have just had my last morning.

My coworkers brought me inside and I sat trying to recover with my thoughts still deep in fight or flight. All the things I wanted to do. All the people I wanted to hug. All the people and animals I still wanted to help. I thought of what it would be like if I hadn't made it. I thought of how hard it would be on my loved ones. I thought of how hard it was when Clayton died and the panic set in again. The rush of all the emotions, all the grief, all the worry and all the exhaustion hit me like a truck. I got home and I did exactly what my body has been demanding. I stopped doing all the everything and I allowed myself to just rest.

Today I feel a bit battered and bruised, my muscles are tight and my eyes are sore. Overall I guess I'm just suffering from widowed whiplash…

May 14, 2022 - A Frightening Game

I think it is important to continue to evaluate your emotions as you travel further forward into the future leaving behind that milestone marked as your new start - AL (After Loss). We categorize our lives on timelines and anniversaries of all types. My cathartic calendar holds holidays, birthdays, reunions, and all kinds of anniversaries. However my dates now hold

Year 5 A.C. – Harvesting the Happy

reminders of deaths. Some expected, some not but all peppered across the paper of my future time.

I also want to speak the words into existence and state that your grief evolves you. Grief is like a virus that enters you through your emotions and affects your DNA permanently. The adversity alters you and you become a different species of yourself. New knowledge infused in your being that brings strengths and weaknesses. As I continue my growth through my grief I have noticed subtle differences that have a larger effect on me than I realize sometime. I can't dive into all of them today but a recent event had pointed out that I carry around a strand of Grief DNA that needs slow extraction – I'm often afraid I will lose everything.

Yes it is true that nothing lasts forever but many people (and the fairytales we are taught) don't have the loss as early in their calendar as "expected". The jarring truth when you lose sooner creates deep fears that leak out in various ways. For me, I have a deep fear of losing everything. Will I be alone? Will I be jobless? Will I be homeless? Will it all be gone tomorrow? My self-preservation has been activated in a new way. Normal fears can be pushed back and controlled but the Grief DNA unleashes natural instincts, fight or flight and developmental stages we don't often think about.

When you are a baby, you lack what is called "object permanence". Babies don't know or understand that people and objects continue to exist if they can see them. For some babies, "Peek-A-Boo" can cause positive reactions like smiles and laughter but for others a fear could build at the unexpected. This past week I recovered from a difficult asthma attack. When the air returned and I opened my eyes so did a number of fears. The Grief DNA went into overdrive and sent me into self-preservation. I could lose everything at any moment. It could all go away in split second.

That episode was difficult but I've learned to seek the schooling. There's a lesson buried in those fears that I need to uncover, acknowledge and release. I fear every day that I can lose anything and everything. Is it possible? Yes. Is it probable? No. I can't hold onto the calendar and refuse the page from turning. Time holds more strength in a second than I have in stubbornness. It's time to acknowledge and begin to grow through my permanence perspective and stop being afraid the Universe will play a frightening game of "Peek-A-Boo"…

Year 5 A.C. – Harvesting the Happy

May 21, 2022 - The Department of Care-Griever Collections (DCGC)

I've brought up some of the ins and outs of being a care-griever. I can't speak to the emotions that come with sudden loss but I can speak about the experience watching someone you love slowly fade. Being a caregiver for Clayton I had the outward goal to provide him comfort for the rest of his days. The inward goal, hold on to him as long as possible in hopes we found something that could save him. Watching him go from a strong man to a shadow of himself in just 8 months and not being able to do anything to stop it made me feel completely powerless. I've talked to many care-grievers and one common denominator we all share is the after-tax. The "Department of Care-Griever collections" comes around quickly and often. The toll is different each time so you can't anticipate and set aside a rainy day feelings fund to cover the costs.

Dear Care-Griever,

The Department of Care-Griever Collections demands payment immediately on the following debts and will be paid in full by heavy bereavement burdens.

1. You did not do enough for Clayton when you took care of him.
2. You should have slept less to do more.
3. You could have gotten him his favorite foods more.
4. You didn't keep the water of the bath perfect when you had to bathe him because he couldn't do it himself.
5. You didn't save him

Total Balance to be paid in the form of fear and personal guilt:

1. Fear that everyone around you could die at any time
2. Fear that you'll have to go through it again
3. Fear that you'll be next
4. Forever wondering if you did enough for him

Sincerely,

The DCGC

It's been over 4 years of getting these notices showing up in my mind unexpectedly. The firsts were always joined with a sinking feeling and a "what am I going to do now" state of fear. How can I emotionally pay this? After awhile of paying the dues, I realized my bereavement balance wasn't going down. My payments were actually reinvesting and adding to those fear-filled finances. The DCGC had no right to continue to collect from me. I have paid my fair share in grief and loss. I decided they weren't going to get any more of me. So nowadays when the memory mailman delivers the newest Care-Griever bill I just tear it up and throw it away. It's nothing but junk mail. I know I did everything I could for him and

Year 5 A.C. – Harvesting the Happy

that's the only thing that matters so from here on out I'll continue my care-griever journey tax-free.

May 28, 2022 - Fun in Funeral?

I booked the flight for Clayton's funeral last night. It's bothering me because a funeral isn't supposed to be 4 years after someone passes. The celebration of life we had originally planned was put on pause and so has a lot of my growing through grief. Searching for flights and making travel arrangements didn't cause sadness, it caused anger and frustration. Over four years and now I'm trying to process these feelings but all I want to do is yell at Father Time for laying out such a broken schedule. I guess I can only be mad at myself for placing expectations on how someone's passing should look. It goes along with the fairytale ending – Happily ever after includes funerals that happen faster right?

Only and already over four years. Clayton I hope you understand just why we haven't gotten everyone together like you wished. I wanted every one of your last wishes to be fulfilled just as you asked. We had to put celebrating you on pause because your mother had a stroke, the world had a pandemic and I had to keep moving forward without you. So much has changed in four years and so much is just unfair. I don't even know if we will ever have the celebration you wanted at the Alamo Café in San Antonio. Time has certainly put Texas on the back burner and I'm sorry but I hope you know it's not my fault. I tried.

I thought I was past the anger phase but, to be very honest, I'm not. By now I should have had the closure I deserve from your funeral. I wouldn't be over losing you because you don't get over grief but I would have at least had this cornerstone placed in my path. I know it's all part of some journey and I'll find more lessons in your leaving but booking that flight last night really hurt. I'm at the point in life that I realize just how fast time flies. I don't take one second for granted so I'm very tired of other people directing my time and it's even harder that this demand is calling out from beyond the grave. I know that it's just part of life but I've more than earned my freedom from all this overbooked bereavement. I'm even mad that I'm

Year 5 A.C. – Harvesting the Happy

using my flyer points to make the flight affordable instead of going on a trip for myself. I feel a little selfish saying that but also don't I deserve the fun?

I know it's no one's fault. Somehow I'll see the good in this experience and share that perspective. Clayton I hope you know how many people you have helped since you moved forward but don't you think it's ironic that the word "fun" is buried in the word funeral…

June 4, 2022 - The Potential of the Infinite Empty

Each of us has a unique journey. Sometimes it can feel infinitely hard, sometimes infinitely lonely but I have found that the infinite space isn't showing us how empty our lives are, it's showing us we have the gift to fill our universe indefinitely.

I came to this understanding through a lot of self-reflection and understanding. I lost my father, lost Clayton and then the world shut down keeping me away from everyone. Widowed through a pandemic is a whole new level of delayed grief. We are finally having a funeral for Clayton this year. I kept asking why everything had to be so drawn out. Life was very empty – or so I thought.

For the past 9 months I have been in a new and amazing relationship with a man that fills my heart. I'm often asked how I could even think to find someone new and others have told me I should stop talking about my widowed grief and just move on. Those statements used to upset me. What I have begun to realize is these opinions are not meant to hurt me but to inspire me to shed more light on the world we walk through. My unique loss of my father, my partner and a pandemic pausing the timeline of healing created a unique space where I was forced to move forward in a strange way. Not having the closure of a funeral for Clayton yet falling in love with Devin was a necessary lesson to show me I had the ability to fill the empty. I didn't have to lose my love for Clayton or redirect it towards Devin - That love belongs to Clayton, Devin deserves his own and I have the ability to generate it all. The growth taught me that you don't just have a limited amount of love to shift around. I learned

Year 5 A.C. – Harvesting the Happy

that there was indefinite space for me to keep the existing love and then create more, as much as I want, because there is always more space.

Grief is just love lost. I don't mean in regards to those who have died, I mean your love for them still exists and it's lost as to where to go. Grief is focused on the loss of the physical being. I just keep reminding Grief that the love for who I lost in person still has a home with their spirit and then the Grief settles.

That feeling of empty isn't meant as punishment, it's the Universe's way of showing you the potential possibility of all the love you can place and that it's infinite. I can have love for those I've lost and those that I've found all at the same time. We have the ability to fill the emptiness with whatever we choose and I've learned that my ability to generate love is indefinite. So I will keep moving forward growing through grief and gaining understanding that the potential of the infinite empty can be forever filled with more love and light…

June 11, 2022 - The Weight of the Wait

There's a heaviness of my grief that I haven't talked much about and that grows closer to the end of watching someone die. You know it's coming. You know it's soon. For a long time you pray you get to keep them for as much time as possible but near the end my mind changed. Every day I was wondering if that day was the last day. Each day I'd see Clayton fade further and yet keep holding on.

We had a few conversations while he was sick. We talked about his wishes, his fears, his regrets of the things he'd never get to do but it was his loss of dignity that bothered him the most. Clayton was a very independent man who now couldn't make it to the restroom himself and needed me to bathe him. When he lost that independence, his eyes changed and said he was ready to go.

Year 5 A.C. – Harvesting the Happy

Every evening I asked to keep him just one more day until, that is, I saw the glimmer fade in his eyes. He was accepting of his fate and ready to die so it felt selfish to keep hoping that I keep him longer. It hurt to think about it and, at first, I felt terrible guilt when I asked the stars to stop his suffering and finally take him. Those conflicting conversations battling it out in my heart.

"Can he just stay a bit longer?" felt selfish while "He's tired. Can this just finally be over so he will be at peace?" filled me with extreme guilt. Either way we knew the end was near but the hardest part of watching someone you love slowly die is the weight of the wait…

(Sometimes the same image comes back in grief and so it does here in my blog)

June 18, 2022 - The Return of the King

Sometimes I want to look back a couple of years and reflect on where I was to help me see just how much I've grown. Day to day can sometimes feel like there's no forward momentum but looking back over months and years shows me I've traveled many miles.

I had my crown stripped and my kingdom burned down right before my eyes. I was emotionally homeless knocked from Sire to surf. I wondered the forest waiting for Robinhood to steal from the rich and give to the grieving. I waited a long time but he never showed so I began to travel again. Along the way, I've picked up courage and strength. I learned new emotional trades and begun to share what I make with others. Slowly a new

Year 5 A.C. – Harvesting the Happy

reality began to build up around me stone by stone with the help of the community my trades have grown.

As I sit and write this I look at my social surroundings and realize I've rebuilt a kingdom, a court and it has filled itself with amazing people. I am so very grateful to be back in the throne of my life and I promise to always wear a crown of kindness.

The king has returned…

June 25, 2022 - Another Layer to the Levels In Life

I'm happy to say that yesterday my boyfriend Devin and I got engaged! Yesterday I reached a new place in life that I have never been too before. Clayton and I never had the opportunity to get to this point. This weekend I am celebrating where my life has lead me, and the love that has surrounded me. This weekend is to honor the past but to enjoy and be filled with the gift of the present.

I often look back at where I was in my journey to see if I can find reasons. A year ago I wrote about finally releasing some material possessions that were no longer serving me. A year ago is when Devin found me on Tiktok and went over to my Facebook to read my blog. A year ago I didn't realize that I had started to release things not so I'd be able to forget them but for there to be space so others could come in. Reading this blog now shows me that letting go of

Year 5 A.C. – Harvesting the Happy

something that was no longer serving me was actually the catalyst for my life to propel forward and to continue to level up.

If you have followed my blog for a while, you would know that Clayton (Tin) often leaves me dimes as a sign he's near. Tin = Ten. It's been awhile since I found one. Yesterday my nerves were building up and I asked him to let me know he was there to help us celebrate our engagement. There on the ground ahead was a dime – A clear sign.

My life continues to grow and change. Some say that this new life should mean the end of my blog but my grief and gratitude journey is not over. Yesterday I got engaged. On July 15th we will finally be having Clayton's memorial service after waiting 4 long years. A huge part of my closure has been put on pause. Has there ever been someone out there that had to wait this long? Most people become widowed and have the memorial shortly after. My journey has been out of order, out of phase. Right now I feel like I'm the only person who has had to go back in time to move into my future. I feel very sure that I am on the right path and so grateful to be planning our wedding soon. I'll still need to process that I'm going to Clayton's funeral as someone else's fiancé four years later…

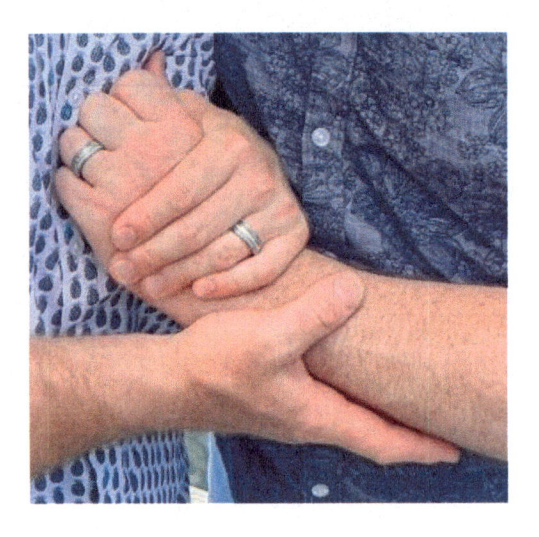

July 9, 2022 - Back in Week Number One

Clayton,

The buildup towards your funeral is tearing open wounds I thought were scared strong. I wrote about it last week and what has changed is the intensity and the heaviness. This all should have happened four years ago when the original storm hit. My grief timeline is so out of phase it's uncharted waters.

I chose a song for you. It's Adele's "Make You Feel My Love". I haven't really listened to her since you passed away. You loved her so much that it's been hard to listen and now I'm

Year 5 A.C. – Harvesting the Happy

being forced too. Her music is incredible, and I've been avoiding it so, I guess, thank you for reminding me and forcing me to allow her melodies back into my memories.

Yesterday I called to order flowers for your service. I thought it was going to be easy until the woman asked:

"What would you like the card to say?"

I couldn't control the tears and had to explain why I was so taken back. This timeline is so out of order, and it hit hardest ordering those flowers.

The rest of my day, I felt like I was outside of myself, disconnected and flooded with memories. I tried to listen to music, talk on the phone and dance around the house but memories and images kept playing on repeat. I went to sleep only to have a night of nightmares. Anything that I've ever been afraid of was showing up in my dreams. I woke up in a panic. Here I am back again in week one without you. I have to go to work because we are beyond the "normal" timeline society gives us for grief. New parents get more time off for gaining a life than we get for the loss of one.

I'm managing as best I can. I just want to get some rest but when my eyes are closed the monsters come out of the closet. So I'm wrapped up in my blanket today in hopes they can't find me and I'll stay safe. I just need to get through a few more days to finally be through week number one…

July 16, 2022 - Growing Through Grief with Gratitude

Yesterday, after waiting four years, we finally had Clayton's service and laid him to rest. Yesterday I felt like I hit the grief guardrail at 75 miles an hour. I knew it was coming and I knew I couldn't turn fast enough. It was emotionally inevitable and, as much as I wanted to avoid it, I also have been needing it. It was an intimate group of family and friends at a beautiful cemetery near where his grandparents lived, and Tin spent many summers. We had prayers, we had songs and we shared words. I dove deep into my grief to honor how much

Year 5 A.C. – Harvesting the Happy

Tin was missed but, in loss, the world gained our story, a piece of his light and a bit of hope – A true legacy.

Some say that this is a closing of a door and starting a new chapter, but I disagree. Chapter, yes. Door, no. You don't shut a door on your past and forget about it. You turn a page knowing you can revisit and reflect if or when you need. I don't know why things happen the way they do but it is very apparent that there is a reason. Had I not had to wait four years, I may not have had the experiences that lead me to my new love filled life. I might have never shared openly about my journey and introduced Clayton to so many that needed to hear their grief was normal.

I have always been one to reach down and lift others up, knock down walls and pave new ways for others to come into their light. Yes, this ends one chapter and begins a new one, but I think "closing the door" is also trying to validate ignoring grief after a set event just because society puts a timeline on "you should". Telling me what to do, tells me I should do the opposite because people try to put others in a grief gilded cage. Accepting grief is what has helped me grow through it and, in time, see the gifts that gratitude readily affords me. I found the key and I'm unlocking the cage for others so they may learn to fly again on grief's subtle ground winds.

I'll always miss Tin but yesterday had a lighter, more completed feeling I have never felt before. I know I am moving forward in a healthy way at my pace. I will look back here and there to stay humble and honor that my losses lead me towards more. I won't walk back through that door, but I refuse to close it just in case there is someone starting a grief journey of their own and needs to see there's a light ahead…

I miss you Clayton and I am so grateful for the time we had together. It's time you finally rest in peace, and I promise I will continue growing through grief with gratitude…

Love Always,

Bryan

Year 5 A.C. – Harvesting the Happy

July 23, 2022 - The Grief Hangover

My widowed journey has been unique. The timeline delt to me kept me four years from the closure of Clayton's funeral. This week has felt different, lighter but emotionally dizzy. Most of us deal with all the immediate emotional events within weeks but life decided to stretch mine out and this week I finally feel like I'm completely moving forward without holding on to the widowed wall for stability. In so many ways I felt that I had been drugged by despair. It's often a theme that I hear from many different grievers so it inspired this week's blog. I have great respect for the difficulties that drugs and alcohol can have. This comparison is not made to lighten the seriousness of those topics but to try and find some kind of similarity to help shed light on just how hard grief can be to control. If left unchecked, grief itself can become addicting. The first step is admitting it. Second step is to not shame yourself for it. The third step is to take your first step towards helping you. My first 4 years of being widowed felt like one long morning trying to get out of bed…

Year 1 you're not sure where you are when you wake up the morning after you become widowed.

Year 2 the reality that too much to handle has happened and the pain sets in. Headache, nausea from the realization that you are truly heartbroken. They aren't coming back. You have to go through this pain without them. It hurts.

Year 3 and everything dulls from sharp pain to a low throb. You try to move forward but your whole life is spinning. You try to make it stop so you put one foot on the floor. The Ferris wheel of feelings starts to wind down, you catch your breath, the double vision is fading and the ground is the first sense of solid you have felt in a long time.

Year 4 and that one firm foot on the floor is your first step in your new journey. You're beginning to move in the right direction. You gather up whatever strength is left and place your other foot on the floor. In order to move forward you are going to have to stand. You have to take care of yourself before you can do anything for anyone else.

One step then two steps then three more steps toward the bathroom. A quick glance in the mirror then down at your feet – still there under you, you're still standing. Made it this far so why not one step more? You achieve toothpaste to brush and the cool mint washes away the bad taste in your mouth left behind by bereavement. This simple act of selfcare empowers you just enough to step again so you choose the shower - a space held just for you. The warm water washes down the grimy grief and the tears you're shedding finally feeling first moments of relief.

Towel off and the new air touches your skin. You feel a bit refreshed. You feel a bit renewed. You get a cold glass of widowed water to help flush the feelings. You've taken the time you needed to start to detox some of the depression so now you start to recover from this grief hangover….

Year 5 A.C. – Harvesting the Happy

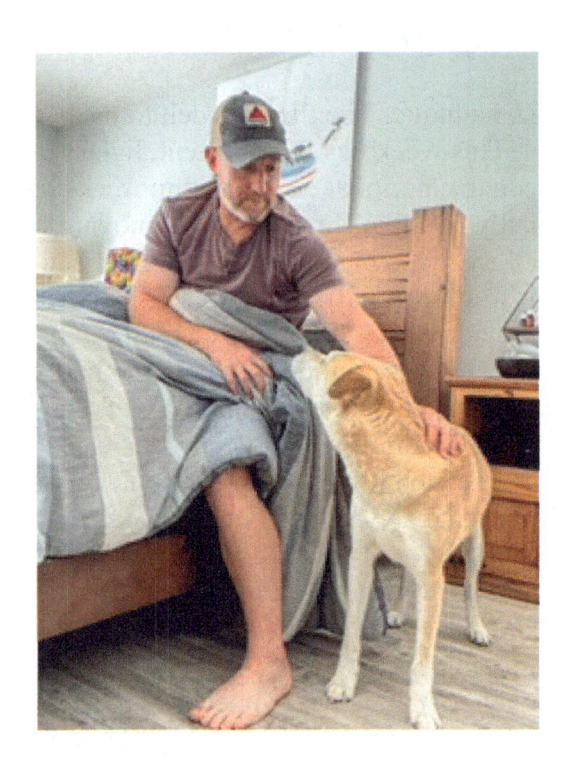

July 30, 2022 - Grief and Gratitude

It's been over two years since I wrote the following blog. We carry grief like an autoimmune issue. It's always going to be part of us and can flare up. I constantly look back at where I was to remind me of what I've grown through. Life has blessed me with a second chance and I'm not willing to take it for granted. If you are always focused on your loss then you miss the small gains. Pennies don't seem very valuable by themselves, but one million pennies can certainly add up quick. I appreciate my present more than every because of my past.

Grief unlocks many gifts when you add gratitude…

July 25, 2020 - I Have A Sometimes Invisible, Often Chronic, Incurable Condition – I Have Grief.

Hello,

For those of you new around here, Hi I'm Bryan. I'm a director of animal care at an aquarium. I'm passionately obsessed with essential oils and environmentally safe products. I'm a son, brother, uncle, cousin and a friend. I love to dance. I love to make others smile. I want to make the world a better place every day in whatever way I can.

Year 5 A.C. – Harvesting the Happy

Some days the world is better when a kid learns that recycling can save the ocean and that plastic straws can really hurt sea turtles. Some days the world is better when a new friend uses a natural product that gives them results and they toss away chemicals that are disrupting their body chemistry. Some days the world is better with a silly dance video. Some days the world is better with a nephew video chat. Some days the world is better with a smile and holding the door for a stranger. It's not hard to help make the world better but that doesn't mean life doesn't have the hidden hard moments. I find that making others smile helps keep down the inflammation.

You see, I have a chronic, incurable condition. I suffer from grief. I'm widowed. Two years ago I lost the man I thought I would spend the rest of my life with. I lost myself and I gained a whole new emotionally chronic condition. Grief is hard to explain because it affects us all differently. Sometimes it stays with just the infected individual and other times it spreads like wildfire. Grief is and isn't contagious.

Grief can be invisible and also acutely apparent. Grief can lay dormant yet appear as full triggered emotional inflammation with a simple thought, a picture, image and even just speaking one word. I live with grief every day and there is no cure. Once you have been infected with grief, you will always be a carrier. Sometimes you can move through the symptoms and put it to rest. Sometimes new grief brings up old grief and you relive what you thought you had made peace with from your past. Loss of your person reminds you of all the failed relationships you've ever had. Even down to that boy in high school you just adored but couldn't tell him because you were gay. However, someone told him and so he stopped talking to you. Lost love lasts a lifetime and grief creeps in unexpectedly.

So I move forward through the flare-ups, through the tired days, through the days with loss of appetite, through the nights of emotional eating, through the lonely days, through the memories. My grief is even triggered when I see others suffer loss. I'm reminded of those first few days after Clayton was gone. A storm of emotions and wondering if I will make it. I am reminded of that phone call. I'm reminded of the loudest sound I've ever heard – my heart breaking.

So I do my best to help make the world a better place because that keeps the chronic emotional inflammation down. You don't get over grief, you can only manage the symptoms.

Hi! My name is Bryan. I care for animals. I care for people. I'm widowed and I suffer from grief.

Year 5 A.C. – Harvesting the Happy

August 6, 2022 - Grief Gardener

I was overwhelmed with the immense inheritance of isolation that bereavement bestowed upon me. The biggest question keeping me from moving forward was:

"Where do I even begin?"

Analysis paralysis when all things seem unorganized, depression dust devils making the barren widowed wasteland look impossible. How do I even start?

This week we had the celebration of life for my Aunt Sue. We all reminisced about her love of home, family, music and her garden. When I was younger, we spent hours together and everything had to have music playing. Not a task would go by without the music beginning first. Little did I know that back then my aunt was sowing seeds I'd desperately need later to grow.

After my father and Clayton both passed, I had trouble moving forward. Hit with a pandemic and I was forced to face my grief alone. I had to start somewhere but where? I wished life was easy again like when I was younger. What else to do but start playing music. What seemed like a simple task has had a profound effect. There is a deep magic in music. The music got me moving. The music gave me life. From the music bloomed my first pure moments of joy after loss – I began to dance again.

As I continue to grow forward from my losses, I am starting to understand this landscape around isn't barren land left behind by bereavement. I've come to realize that as I learn how to grow through grief, I can cultivate its grounds. I have had to turn over much sadness into these soils. I have unintentionally irrigated the dirt with my tears and poured forth fear,

Year 5 A.C. – Harvesting the Happy

frustration and feelings which have fertilized the land. Unknowingly, I had laid forth foundations needed to continue to cultivate myself and begin to harvest the happiness. All farmers know that it takes time, work and love to reap what you sow. Gratitude shows you the lessons weaved throughout your life.

Dear Aunt Sue,

Thank you for all the music. Thank you for encouraging me to dance. Thank you for making me a successful grief gardener…

Love,

-Bryan

August 13 2022 - All in Grief Time

After 23 years of effort, I'm leaving the field of animal care. I'm turning in my whistle and taking off my watch.

A career with animals I dreamed to hold as a kid. Biology degree with minors in chemistry and behavioral psychology. I poured my heart, mind and passion into competing for minimum wage all for "the dream job" with dolphins, penguins, sea lions and hundreds of other animals.

For years, I struggled with difficult schedules, no weekends, working holidays and limited vacation time at some facilities because "the operation wouldn't allow 3 consecutive days off."

"No dad I can't be home this year. I know it's been awhile. They can't give me the days."

I missed 10 years of holidays with my dad. He died and I won't ever get any more with him but it's a "dream job" right?

Year 5 A.C. – Harvesting the Happy

"Are you coming home for dinner soon?" Clayton asked me that regularly and my response was I needed to give the animals more time. I didn't realize that the animals would be here past April 16, 2018 but Clayton wouldn't be. Now I'm widowed but it's a "dream job" right?

This year I got engaged to a wonderful man. I've been given a second chance when many don't even get a first. However, the past few months I have answered texts from him "I'll be at work longer" and when my mom asks about the holidays I've had to say "I'm not sure this year."

My losses will no longer let me accept the society forced "9 to 5" norms. I felt deep regret for my past "next times" and started feeling resentment for my future "I can'ts". Perhaps if I hadn't lost Clayton and my dad, I would be more compliant to freely give away my time but grief brings the gifts of awareness and gratitude.

So what's next? Since Clayton passed, I had to grow a second job which blossomed into something I can lean into on my timeline. I'd like to start changing societies mindset on the term "dream job". Stating someone has a "dream job" negates their actual work and the sacrifices that come along with it. We have to work to live but at what point is work actually stopping you from living?

Growing through grief I realize that happiness, joy and no regret at the end of my days is the real dream. Tomorrow isn't promised. Most of my life I have been told (and believed) that my only value was as "the cool animal trainer". This past year has proven that my life and I have much more value. I wish I had learned this when I was younger but I guess I had to learn it all in grief time…

Year 5 A.C. – Harvesting the Happy

August 20, 2022 - Taking Flight

As I pause and look at my life now, I can't help but be grateful for everything that has been gifted to me, especially the love I'm surrounded by now. This week I truly wanted to see how far I have come so I looked back to my blog post 2 years ago. As I read these lines again, I can feel the deep pain of youth and life lessons but I'm even more filled with an abundance of gratitude and understanding. I have a true understanding of love and its gifts even in grief. I've endured many beautiful failures and each one has, in turn, made me a better person. From jaded to joyful, hurt to happy, grief to gratitude - I've grown. The first step was me stopping to need validation from others. Move through life authentically and with integrity. When you embrace all your beautiful imperfections you truly begin to take flight…

August 22, 2020 - Beautiful Failures

A part of being widowed is that you are forced to remember all of the relationships that didn't work out. That sting when your first crush doesn't like you back. That feeling life is over forever when the big high school sweetheart breakup happens. College brought a whole new world. I was getting more and more responses from girls that wanted to "just be friends". Coming to terms with being gay, trying to navigate that entire new world and my first real boyfriend breaking up with me because I was "too sweet." - The usual failures.

Thicker skin and more self-preservation, a 10 year relationship that began with good intentions and ended in disaster. Faults on both sides but one half crossing the line and shattering sacred safety. I held back sharing the reasons for leaving and lost friends. I should have told them that he threw things. I should have told them that he would repeatedly tell me:

"You know all our friends only tolerate you because they like me."

I never told them what he said for fear it was the truth. Instead, I kept it to myself and they chose him. Unfortunately, validated fears. – An Unfair Failure.

At this point in the romantic film of my life, in walked Prince Charming to take my hand and help me up:

"I'll never treat you like he did. I promise."

Two years of building trust, he gave me a ring as a promise for our future. We chose to move to a new city and start fresh. We found a new landscape, new adventures, new people. He found new temptations. I found new deceit and a new failure. I wasn't good enough for my friends last time and this time I wasn't good enough to be enough for him. Shattered dreams and a broken heart – A Fairytale Failure.

A couple years of healing and the heart of a hopeless romantic, I tried again. Wholesome, secure, sweet, our families loved us. This was it. It was all fitting. It was unfolding like the

Year 5 A.C. – Harvesting the Happy

storybook dream I always wanted. Then we had a typical weekend night, typical comfortable dinner and he said an untypical statement:

"I'm sorry but I thought I'd love you more than I do by now."

I said nothing because I didn't have any air left in my lungs. The words stole my breath away. I packed up my things at his apartment and headed back out onto the road I hate traveling alone - A "better as friends" failure.

Time moves forward and after awhile I have a date or two with a nice guy but there were no sparks. Instead he gave me an invite to a pool party where I find you. I just know that it's you. It's easy. It feels right. I let down my fear of failure and you stay. I realize that us is all the good things from all of those past failures. In that moment it makes sense that had anything in my past been different, had my begging with God to just let them love me than I wouldn't be here with you. All of those relationships suddenly became beautiful failures. It was so hard in those moments to have faith that you were on your way. It's truly a gift when you are allowed to see the Universe's Why but just because you see it one moment doesn't mean things remain clear.

A new life in a sleepy little beach town, a career I have dreamt of reaching and holding you, Clayton. After all of those failures, I was finally getting my turn at what so many others have and take for granted. This part of my life was so beautifully written and then the page turned. You left me but not like all the others. An acute disease with only 8 months to do everything I could to hold on knowing you would go – A Heart-Shattering Failure.

Now I sit here and write out the storybook road my heart has had to endure. Fairytale endings are not as common as they are in books. I write to share the hard truth in hopes my lines give words to others who can't put their emotions on paper. I write my lost relationships so if all of these tragedies are part of a

bigger plan than others learn some hidden lesson that's intended for them. Then hopefully all is for not and, at least to others, my story and I become a beautiful failure…

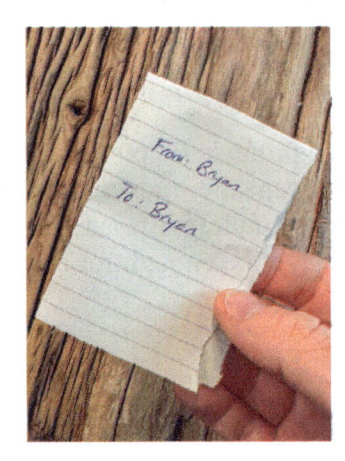

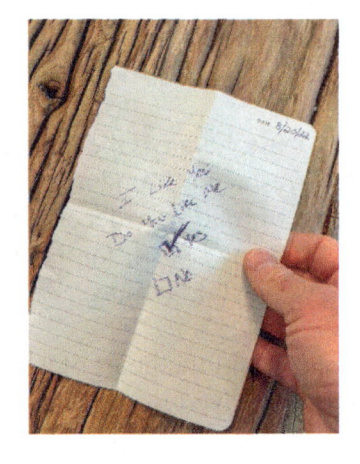

Year 5 A.C. – Harvesting the Happy

August 27, 2022 - Of God and Grief

40 days and 40 nights. Sometimes that's how grief has felt along this journey. No one quite understands the impact that first grief flood has on you until you find your floating around and all the land is gone. Nothing but a horizon. You feel helpless, alone and lost.

It has taken lots of navigating through the storms to finally find a feeling of safe harbor. The great flood recedes, and the shores return to their normal tides. Up and down and up and down enough that grief tides are predictable. Once something is predictable, it loses value and you move about your day without it effecting you. I've grown through grief ground and have firmly walked upon it's gravel. I have a new strong foundation and solid footing – or so I thought.

These past two weeks have been wrought with grief, not at my loss of my late partner Clayton but at a sudden loss of a friend. That friend is still alive but they deceived many and suddenly disappeared. No regular texts. No regular calls. All the energy put into supporting someone was absorbed and used to manipulate others under the cloak of authenticity and integrity. Today I grieve the death of someone who was never really alive. Today I grieve our false friendship.

Why does this make sense for a widowed blog? We the widowed lose the person who completes us and after the loss it takes time to rebuild. One of the biggest hurdles has been to trust that others won't just up and leave. I have a small circle of close friends that hold more value to me now than ever because I am widowed. I have appreciation and gratitude for these connections, and I thrive around the authenticity and honesty. To hear that someone in my close circle AC (After Clayton) has secretly concealed and crafted a double life hurts.

At the end of the day, I know people have to make decisions for themselves and I remind myself that it's about my "friend" and not about me. However, I have the right to feel how I feel. I have the right to hurt how I hurt. I have the right to wonder how someone could know my story and pull the wool over my widowed eyes.

I might never know the answers. Fame and fortune certainly produce fakes. At the end of the day, I know that this will be another one of grief's gifts. I see them faster and faster. Less of the "whys" and more of the clarity. Comparison is the thief of joy if you are jealous but, in this instance, comparison is Robin Hood – My truth and authenticity hold more value than ever. I don't talk much about religion so that my words help as many as possible, but I know in my heart that all things happen for a reason and actions have consequences.

I'll let the Universe continue to unfold knowing that Greed and God do not hold hands, but God and Grief do…

Year 5 A.C. – Harvesting the Happy

Greed and God don't hold hands

But God and Grief do...

September 3, 2022 - Stop Rushing Towards the Grief

I distinctly remember being in the 5th grade and saying:

"Just 7 more years until I graduate. Then it's college and dolphin training. Hang in there Bryan, it's just 7 more years."

I wanted to be free of the bullying and I wanted my dream job, so I wished for time to tick by faster. I was young and time was wasted on me worrying to get away into my future. What I wasn't aware of (or blissfully ignorant about) was that the future always brings both the better and bereaved days.

The young don't realize the Ying and Yang of joy and grief is inevitable. I never slowed down to live in the moment because I was always placing the greatest moments ahead of me. I can't wait for later, tomorrow, next week, next month, the next vacation, next holidays, when I don't have to work so hard but until then I'll just keep thinking of "the then" not "the now". That's an exhausting way to live. Here I am a few months from 44 but how did I get here so fast?

I rushed all that time to become an animal caregiver and after 23 years, tomorrow is my last day. I spent so much of my life dedicated to achieving my "dream job" that I forgot to live the other parts of life. I can honestly say that this decision is entirely driven by my losses at such an early age. I was only 38 when my father passed away. I was widowed just 10 months later and ever since those losses, I tried to understand who I am. My career in animal care has

Year 5 A.C. – Harvesting the Happy

always defined me and was the only thing that I thought made me valuable to everyone, including myself.

"You have the best job."

"This is my friend. He works with penguins."

"You're that aquarium guy."

The past year has brought me immense blessings, a chance to realize I'm more than my job. Life is not supposed to be a chase, it's supposed to be an experience. I know that there will be a grieving period not having those animals in my life daily but at the end of my life I won't be surrounded by the penguins I've raised. I'll long to have just one moment more with all the people I've loved.

My widowed wisdom is yet again showing a gift grown from my grief - a true awareness of who I am and how I want to live the rest of my life. I am more than the guy who takes care of animals. I am a fiancé, a brother, an uncle, a son, a nephew, a cousin, a friend, a shoulder to cry on, a dancer, a bad joke teller, a kind person, authentic, honest, full of hope and happiness.

Time doesn't wait for anyone, and our days are numbered but I'm done wishing for the future to show up faster because the future holds both joys and grief. I'm just grateful that I've learned what I know now – Stop Rushing Towards The Grief.

(Bottom Left and Top Right Photos Courtesty of Gulfarium Marine Adventure Park)

Year 5 A.C. – Harvesting the Happy

September 17th, 2022 - Widowed Wealth of Words

This week has been a huge transition in my life. I retired from my 23 year career to focus on my relationship and the business I own. I can work from anywhere which is giving me much more time to enjoy time. Of course, big transitions have change and responsibility. I'm organizing my own healthcare, retirement and tying up loose ends. I'm fully enjoying the time freedom but it will take a bit before I settle into a normal schedule.

Among the list of "to dos" was car insurance. They still hadn't updated my address when I moved. I wanted to talk to a human and assure I had all the discounts available to me. The representative was cheerful. As we looked over my account, one detail caught my eye. They never Removed Clayton from the policy. I had asked them after he passed and was told:

"The system can take 24 hours to update."

Well, I thought nothing else of it and forgot.

New address updated but no policy or mileage change working from home. The woman asked me if there was anything else?

"Yes. I see that Clayton is still listed on the account. He passed away over 4 years ago. I had called to have his name taken off."

"Oh, I'm so sorry about that. What day did he pass?" she responded.

"April 16th, 2018." I said clearly. That date doesn't cause me to choke anymore when I say it.

"Thank you. I'm so sorry to hear he passed but you'll be happy to know that taking him off the policy will save you one dollar!" she happily declared.

I was shocked that someone would follow up a sympathetic apology for loss with a happy declaration that I saved $1. I don't know if she was on autopilot and didn't realize, if she was heartless or if death makes her say strange things. Two years ago, that comment would have resulted in choice words back from me but my widowed growth has gifted me more patience and offering the benefit of the doubt. I'll just assume she was very uncomfortable with the discussion and her way of "looking on the bright side" was meant well.

I didn't let the comment dwell with me this week but today I spent time cleaning and organizing the office at home. Tucked in a drawer I hadn't looked through in years were

Year 5 A.C. – Harvesting the Happy

the sympathy cards sent to me after Clayton passed. In front of me was laid out way more value in words then just one dollar's worth. Opening the cards didn't upset me. They brought me the memories of all the support and love poured over me exactly when I needed it. Here I am reminded again by Grief's gratitude that I am surrounded by an incredible amount of widowed words worth more than just one dollar…

The Unconclusive Conclusion

The Unconclusive Conclusion

September 24th, 2022 – The Unconclusive Conclusion

While writing this blog, I was forced to revisit and relive more than just my widowed walk. I dove back in time through many memories I had forgotten or hidden. In reflecting back, how ironic was it that I rushed through the four years of high school and the four years of college only now to find myself fast forwarded to being widowed for over four years. I have learned that life will, undoubtedly, bring you grief. Grief is inevitable. Grief provides perspective and returns us to an ancient inner knowing - dark cannot exist without light; death cannot exist without life and grief cannot exist without joy. Powerful wisdom that can generate immense positive energy.

Like death, grief cannot be avoided but grief offers one thing that death does not, grief offers opportunity to learn and live forward. You can't find life after you die but you can find joy after you grieve, and rediscovered joy is sweeter than any other. The magic that ignites it is gratitude. Grief is, unfortunately, a renewable resource but it can be used as fuel. Through gratitude I convert grief to joy. When I learned this ability, joy became limitless, outpouring and infects others around me. Grief and joy are the two great unifiers. So, on your darkest days remember you can take that energy and use it to push you towards joy. Be your own light and you will light up the world around you. You are worth it because there are smiles waiting for you in your future.

People search for "the end" of their grief and never realize you never get over it, you never "move on" but you can "move forward". Grief has the ultimate unconclusive conclusion. To master grief, one must grow through it. Pushing up through the heavy soil into the fog, sending roots down in anger, passively waiting for a season to self-germinate and finally finding a harvest of happiness. Writing this blog has gifted me with more insight and understanding than I ever knew was possible. This blog is a true gift to me and has been an honor to write. Although I know that life still has future twists and turns, it is time I truly move forward so this will be my last blog. This blog has been an anchor in the storms, but the storm is over, and this blog is keeping me from fully appreciating the adventures ahead. So, for those who need these words today and, in the future, I openly share this man's widowed wisdom…

With great gratitude and joy,

-Bryan (Sealionbryan)

Widowed Words
of Wisdom

Widowed Words of Wisdom

"EVEN THOUGH WE DON'T KNOW FOR SURE WHAT WILL HAPPEN AFTER SOMETHING SETS IN OUR LIFE, WE CAN HOLD IN OUR HEART AND BELIEVE THAT SOMETHING WILL RISE TOMORROW."

– SEALIONBRYAN

"EVERY TIME YOU'RE FACED WITH A CHALLENGE – NO MATTER HOW BIG OR SMALL – AND YOU DECIDE YOU CAN OVERCOME IT, YOU BECOME A ROLE MODEL FOR SOMEONE SOMEWHERE WHO NEEDS YOU."

– SEALIONBRYAN

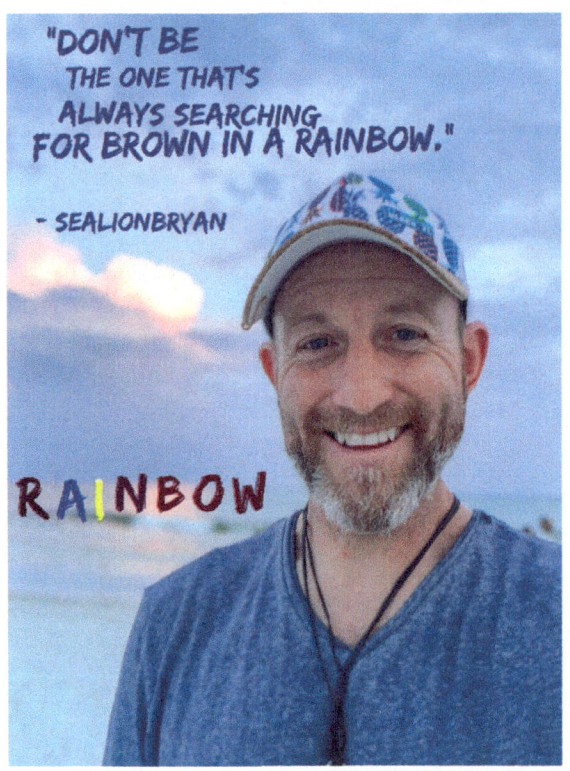

"DON'T BE THE ONE THAT'S ALWAYS SEARCHING FOR BROWN IN A RAINBOW."

– SEALIONBRYAN

"I'M SO SORRY FOR THE PERSON YOU'VE LOST AND I'M ALSO SO SORRY FOR THE GRIEF YOU'VE GAINED."

– SEALIONBRYAN

Widowed Words of Wisdom

"JUST BECAUSE PEOPLE GAIN GRIEF IN DIFFERENT WAYS DOESN'T MEAN THAT THE SAME WORDS CAN'T HELP FILL AND HEAL THEIR BROKEN SPACES TOO."

~ SEALIONBRYAN

WE SPEND A LOT OF TIME WAITING FOR SOMEONE TO SIT DOWN NEXT TO US AND GIVE US ALL THE ANSWERS. THE THING IS THAT WE ALREADY HAVE THEM INSIDE OURSELVES IF WE JUST LISTEN...

- SEALIONBRYAN

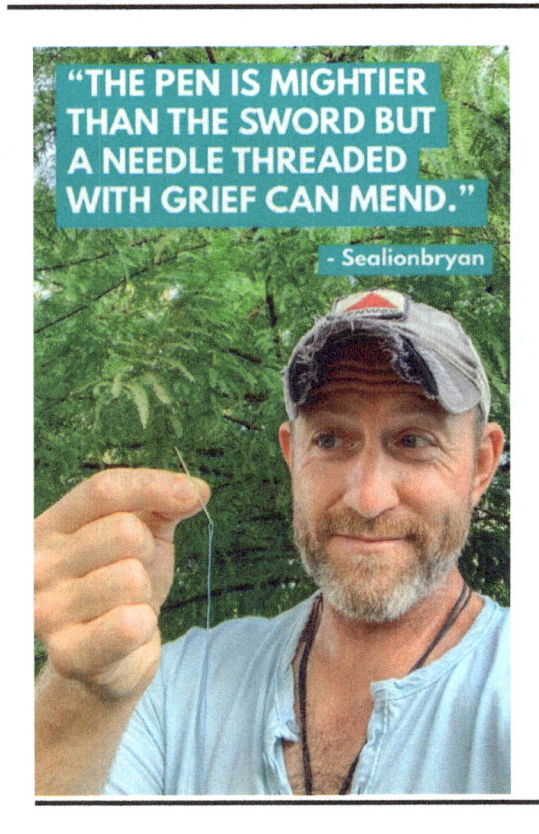

"THE PEN IS MIGHTIER THAN THE SWORD BUT A NEEDLE THREADED WITH GRIEF CAN MEND."

- Sealionbryan

"The edge of Bereavement's blade strikes blindly in battle. Don't compare your grief journey to anyone else's..."

- Sealionbryan

Widowed Words of Wisdom

"I think sometimes just asking the unanswerable questions out loud gives us some relief."
— Sealionbryan

"Happiness starts growing within ourselves. When you believe in contradicting mindsets, you create conflict within and happiness can't take root."
— Sealionbryan

"To grow through grief you need to start by planting positivity. Soon enough you'll be harvesting the happy."
— Sealionbryan

"Who's to say you've sprouted yet? Maybe the next change will be the one that pushes you to the sky."
— Sealionbryan

Widowed Words of Wisdom

"WE ALL HAVE THE ABILITY TO GENERATE OUR OWN JOY WHEN WE MAKE TIME TO DO THE THINGS WE ENJOY. WHEN YOU ARE JOYFUL YOU HAVE ENOUGH TO SHARE AND THAT'S WHEN THE MAGIC HAPPENS BECAUSE JOY IS CONTAGIOUS..."
- SEALIONBRYAN

"EVEN AT THE END OF A TOUGH DAY, YOU CAN CHANGE THE TIDE IN YOUR HEART AND GIVE YOURSELF A SMILE. IF YOU REMEMBER YOU HAVE THAT POWER WITHIN YOU, YOU WON'T GO A DAY WITHOUT A BIT OF HAPPINESS."
- SEALIONBRYAN

The best gift we can give ourselves and others along the way is grace because you never know what grief others are growing through unless you take a look through their window...
- Sealionbryan

UN-EXPECT YOUR EXPECTATIONS
-SEALIONBRYAN

Widowed Words of Wisdom

"WHEN YOU START TO OVERTHINK, YOU START TO UNDER-DO AND THAT MEANS YOU'VE STOPPED DREAMING!"
— SEALIONBRYAN

REGARDLESS OF WHATEVER FOG SETTLES ON THIS WORLD, I WILL ALWAYS SPREAD WHATEVER HAPPINESS I CAN. I WILL ALWAYS BE A GRIEF GUARD...
— SEALIONBRYAN

HOW ABOUT REVALUING YOURSELF INSTEAD OF DEVALUING YOURSELF
— SEALIONBRYAN

"There is nothing more pure than a gift given from a grieving heart. Creating comfort and safety out of thin air from grief - That is authentic magic..."
- Sealionbryan

Widowed Words of Wisdom

ARE YOU THE ONE SITTING BACK DEMANDING THAT THE WORLD CHANGES OR ARE YOU THE ONE CREATING THE CHANGE...

– SEALIONBRYAN

"MAYBE IF WE FOCUS MORE ON HOW MANY GOOD DAYS WE HAVE INSTEAD OF FOCUSING ON THE FEWER BAD DAYS THEN WE'D HAVE MORE BETTER DAYS..."

– SEALIONBRYAN

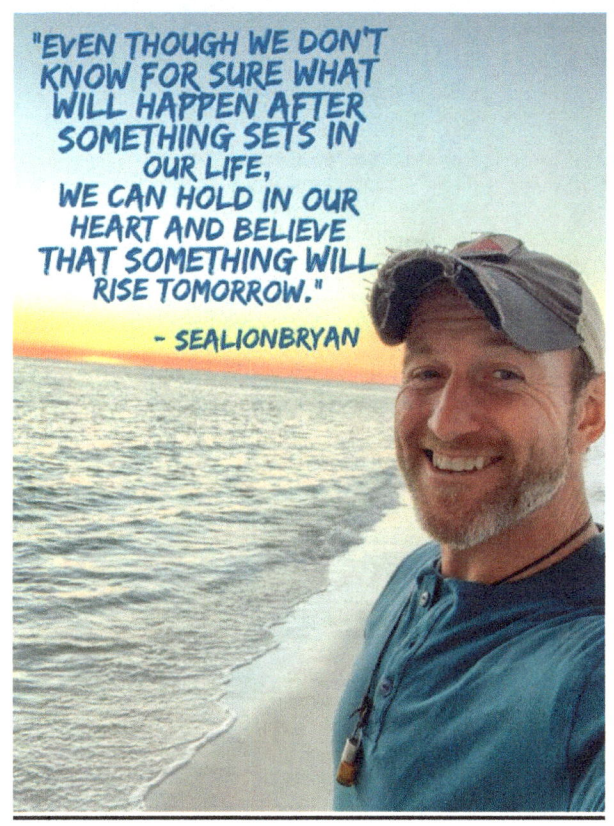

"EVEN THOUGH WE DON'T KNOW FOR SURE WHAT WILL HAPPEN AFTER SOMETHING SETS IN OUR LIFE, WE CAN HOLD IN OUR HEART AND BELIEVE THAT SOMETHING WILL RISE TOMORROW."

– SEALIONBRYAN

Widowed Words of Wisdom

"Remember on your toughest days that there are smiles waiting for you in your future!"

— Sealionbryan

You can choose
to stay in
the storm or
you can choose
to be the break
in the clouds...

— Sealionbryan